Penguin Education

Penguin Modern Management Readings

General Editor
D. S. Pugh

Advisory Board
H. C. Edey
R. L. Edgerton
T. Kempner
T. Lupton
D. G. Marquis
B. J. McCormick
P. G. Moore
R. W. Revans
F. J. Willett

Management Information Systems

Selected Readings
Edited by T. W. McRae

Penguin Books

Penguin Books Ltd, Harmondsworth,
Middlesex, England
Penguin Books Inc., 7110 Ambassador Road,
Baltimore, Md 21207, U.S.A.
Penguin Books Australia Ltd,
Ringwood, Victoria, Australia

First published 1971
Introduction and notes copyright © T. W. McRae, 1971
This selection copyright © T. W. McRae, 1971

Made and printed in Great Britain by
Richard Clay (The Chaucer Press) Ltd,
Bungay, Suffolk
Set in Monotype Times

This book is sold subject to the condition that
it shall not, by way of trade or otherwise, be lent,
re-sold, hired out, or otherwise circulated without
the publisher's prior consent in any form of
binding or cover other than that in which it is
published and without a similar condition
including this condition being imposed on the
subsequent purchaser

To Paul

Contents

Introduction 9

Part One
The Nature of Management Information Systems 15

1 G. Vickers (1955)
Communication in Economic Systems 17

2 D. Katz and R. L. Kahn (1966)
Communication: The Flow of Information 38

3 D. R. Daniel (1961)
Management Information Crisis 59

Part Two
The Design of Management Information Systems 81

4 S. A. Spencer (1962)
The Dark at the Top of the Stairs 83

5 The McKinsey Consulting Organization (1968)
The 1968 McKinsey Report on Computer Utilization 94

6 J. Dearden (1965)
How to Organize Information Systems 123

Part Three
Management Information in Real Time 141

7 G. Burck (1964)
Management Will Never Be the Same Again 143

8 A. L. Jacobs and P. Harman (1969)
The Scope of Computers in an Airline 158

9 J. Dearden (1966)
Myth of Real Time Management Information 169

Part Four
Scanning the Business Environment 187

10 F. J. Aguilar (1967)
Scanning the Business Environment: Some Practical Considerations 189

Part Five
Evaluating Management Information Systems 211

11 T. W. McRae (1970)
The Evaluation of Investment in Computers 213

12 Staff of *Business Management* (1965)
How to Make Sure Your Computer Pays Off 233

13 D. F. Boyd and H. J. Krasnow (1963)
Economic Evaluation of Management Information Systems 246

14 W. F. Bauer and R. H. Hill (1967)
Economics of Time Shared Computing Systems 277

15 K. E. Knight (1966)
Changes in Computer Performance 291

Part Six
Other Aspects of Management Information Systems 315

16 E. Mumford (1968)
Planning for Computers 317

17 T. J. Allen and S. I. Cohen (1969)
Information Flow in Research and Development Laboratories 331

18 J. J. Wasserman (1969)
Plugging the Leaks in Computer Security 347

Further Reading 367

Acknowledgements 369

Author Index 371

Subject Index 375

Introduction

The classical economists differentiated three basic inputs to the production process, land, labour and capital. From time to time one or other of these inputs has dominated production. The successful entrepreneur during a given period has been that man who is able to acquire and exploit the 'key' input for his period.

From the dawn of civilization, up till about the middle of the eighteenth century, the key inputs were labour and land. Labour to build the roads and dredge the rivers, to row the galleys and quarry the mines. Land to provide the food to maintain the vast labour force. When local labour was insufficient or the work of a character such that voluntary service was not forthcoming, the tribe or nation state went to war and acquired slaves to fill the breach.

Around the middle of the eighteenth century, the pattern of production began to change. The scientific revolution spilled over into industry and new methods in the fields, and in the factories, allowed a surplus of income to be *saved* above bare subsistence.

Capital markets evolved which channelled this saving into productive investment. The machine was substituted for muscle power and civilization took off towards the age of affluence. The key to this change of pace was capital. Capital became the dominant input to the production process, and the most influential book of the nineteenth century had this single word on its title page.

The acquisition and utilization of capital dominated industry in the nineteenth century. All of the giant entrepreneurs, such as Hudson, Carnegie, Harrington and Rockefeller, were also great financiers. The dominant industries of the period, railways, steel and shipbuilding, developed a voracious appetite for capital and that country which exported more capital than any other, Great Britain, appropriated a quarter of the globe.

Capital continued as the dominant input to production well into the first half of the twentieth century, but the pace slackened. *Skilled* labour became scarce and the new methods in metallurgy and electronics required less capital than the old. Knowledge began to be substituted for capital.

Knowledge, or as we shall call it from now on, *information*, has always been a necessary input to the process of production. But it was ignored by the classical economists and given little explicit recognition by businessmen. An information system existed in every business, but it was fragmented on functional lines; like the blind man and the elephant, no one could picture the whole structure. No one held responsibility for fitting the various pieces of the jigsaw together.

Then in a single decade, beginning around 1954, the digital computer changed our frame of reference beyond recognition. The computer is an information-processing machine, and it was suddenly appreciated that information is a *specific* input to the production process. It was found that information could be substituted for capital, just as the nineteenth-century entrepreneurs substituted capital for labour. The economies of computer processing persuaded people to centralize information systems, and the flexibility of the computer provided an infinite variety of ways of doing this. There was a change, almost overnight, from a set of poorly structured, highly inflexible information systems[1] to an *embarras de richesse*. The computer gave too many options. Should a single data bank be developed or should there be one for each functional area? What information should be fed to each line of management? How will the free flow of information affect security? What effect will a multi-access data bank have on command structure?

People tried to establish basic concepts. There were none available, or almost none. The social psychologists had done a good deal of work in analysing information flow in human groups, but which computer men read social psychology? Yet the computers were there, churning out miles of book-keeping records, and costing the earth, hopelessly uneconomic. What was to be done? Or perhaps I should say 'What are we to do?' because for many firms the last sentence represents the current situation.

1. We must be careful here. Pre-computer systems can usually handle queries about an individual datum more efficiently than computer systems.

Various groups pretended to have access to the Holy Grail which could solve our problems. First came the computer technologist, brandishing multi-channel, real time, higher language, polymorphic and other systems which would provide everything that management could possibly want. But what did management want? Management did not know and neither did the computer technologist. Then came the accountant. In 1964, 80 per cent of computer time in the USA (see Popell, 1966, p. 182) and UK (see Hooper, 1967) was spent on processing accounting information. Surely the accountant must know how to use the computer? He did – but only to process more accounting information! He had one or two interesting ideas on controlling cash flow, but his outlook was much too narrow. For a short period in the late fifties, the mathematician jumped into the ring by formalizing in mathematical language what everyone already knew in plain English. This activity was, presumably, helpful to other mathematicians. Finally two groups entered the fray who really had something to contribute. The management consultant and the social psychologist. Both these groups reduced the computer to size by emphasizing *information* systems, rather than computer systems.

The consultant's contribution is, as one might expect, institutional rather than analytical. He reviews many information systems and sets out the necessary conditions of success and failure. He is long on hypothesis and short on experimental evidence. But his contribution is valuable. These hypotheses set up the targets for later scientific investigation.

And finally, there is the social psychologist. Social groups are bound together by chains of information. Cut these chains and the group will soon disband. Social psychologists marked all this out a generation ago and a good deal has been published on the relation between command and information structure, the different effects of information flowing through formal versus informal channels and so on.

This ought to be the meat and drink of the designers of business information systems, but few seem to be aware of the existence of this literature. The systems analyst course devised by the UK National Computer Centre allocates a derisory amount of time to social psychology. However, the social psychologists themselves were not slow to see the research (and pecuniary) possibilities in business information systems and their research output is rising on an exponential curve.

However, much remains to be done, particularly in the area of evaluating information. The information field is a particularly difficult one in which to carry out *scientific* research. Investigators such as Leavitt (1963), Aguilar (Reading 10) and Allen (Reading 17) have shown that the scientific analysis of information flow is practicable. The glacial pace of advance is frustrating, though we can perhaps console ourselves with the thought that at least we have plenty of time to assimilate what is discovered.

If several of the following readings seem unscientific in spirit, the reader should compare them with what would have been available ten years ago.

This book of readings describes various aspects of management information systems. But what is a management information system? A *system* is simply any interdependent set of elements. The concept of a system is perhaps the most wide ranging concept that man has devised. It incorporates everything from cuckoo clocks to the solar system, from a scout patrol to the United Nations (see Emery, 1969).

We can classify systems into many categories, but the major dichotomy is between physical and social systems. Most physical systems, like the cuckoo clock, are *closed* systems. There is very little interplay between a closed system and its environment.

In contrast to the physical system is the social system. The elements of the social system are *people* and all social systems are *open* systems. Open systems enjoy a rich interaction with their environment. Open systems are dependent on their environment for their continuing survival.

The business system is one of the most 'open' of all social systems. A business draws materials, services, ideas and *people* from its environment and after a production phase injects products or services back into the environment.

Systems theorists (see Emery, 1969, p. 14) have differentiated three major sub-systems within the total business system. They are:

1. The *production* system which transforms the inputs to the business.

2. The *maintenance* system which maintains the fabric of the social system of the business intact. (Motivating, hiring and firing, indoctrinating, etc.)

3. The *adaptive* system which helps the business system adapt to a changing environment (research and development, long-term planning, market research, etc.).

The management system cuts a cross section through each of these three activities.

No social system can exist without a web of information channels binding the various elements together. A management information system is no exception to this rule. A management information system must first provide an efficient information system within the production, maintenance and adaptive sub-systems – and then try to link these micro-systems to top level management. This is a formidable task. The information needs of each of the sub-systems are very different. The maintenance system looks inwards, the adaptive system looks outwards, the productive system lies at some intermediate point between the two, but closer to the maintenance system.

The logical design of management information systems is not helped by the fact that the adaptive sub-system is usually fragmented between several departments far distant in organizational space, while the production and maintenance systems tend to be hopelessly tangled together. Few organizations appreciate the crucial distinction between these sub-systems.

We conclude that the design of a management information system ought to begin with the delineation of each functional sub-system within the whole. Once these are identified, the objective of each sub-system can be decided in the light of its contribution to the whole. The stage is now set for selecting the information which is needed by each sub-system.

Top management cannot absorb all of the information processed by each sub-system so a *filter* is needed to select out key information. The design of efficient filters is the most difficult job facing the system designer.

An information system consists of six component parts. The

heart of the system is the *data bank* (i.e. library) which stores information. A *scanning device* is needed to select inputs to the data bank. The scanning device might be programmed to *monitor* pre-selected variables (i.e. given stock exchange prices) or an *input filter* might be attached to it (i.e. a long range planning group) to accept or reject information. Each sub-system will use different criteria for accepting or rejecting depending on its own needs. Once the information is in the store, some type of *retrieval mechanism* is needed to find it again when required.

Various indexing methods have been devised to effect this (see Meadow, 1967, p. 14). But even if a piece of information *is* in store, *can* be retrieved and *is* relevant to a given decision, it may not be used because the decision taker does not know it is there. So an *output filter* must be designed to distribute information to those who can use it.

As several of the authors in this volume confirm (see Readings 3, 4, 5 and 10) current management information systems are adept at handling information about the production sub-system, are rather weak on the adaptive sub-system and virtually silent on the maintenance sub-system. The last is handled in a haphazard fashion by the informal information system.

Our knowledge of the anatomy and physiology of management information systems may resemble the medical expertise of the barber–surgeon of the sixteenth century. And our violent dismembering of existing information systems by the computer might suggest, in future years, that this is no bad analogy. But we must start somewhere.

I hope that the following pages might persuade the reader to start along the road, even if I cannot guarantee his eventual destination. I *can* guarantee that it will be a long road.

References

EMERY, F. E. (ed.) (1969), *Systems Thinking*, Penguin Books.
HOOPER, D. W. (1967), 'Computer survey questionnaire', *Computer Survey*, vol. 6, no. 3, p. 200.
MEADOW, C. T. (1967), *The Analysis of Information Systems*, Wiley.
POPELL, S. D. (1966), *Computer Time-Saving*, Prentice-Hall.
LEAVITT, H. J. (1963), 'Most efficient solutions to communications networks', *Sociometry*, vol. 26, no. 67, p. 260.

Part One
The Nature of Management Information Systems

Reading 1 describes the key role that information plays in binding economic systems together. Newly amalgamated organizations, such as the various UK coal mining companies nationalized in 1948, find difficulty in operating as a cohesive unit until they learn to speak a common language.

Reading 2 discusses the structure of information networks with particular emphasis on the *direction* of the information flow. Katz and Kahn describe five key characteristics of information networks and describe some recent research findings on communication nets. They also examine the behavioural characteristics of upward, downward and horizontal information flows.

All management information systems are open systems.

Reading 3 makes the important distinction between internal, competitive and environmental information. The author complains that too much attention is paid to information originating from accounting systems and too little to environmental information. He suggests that environmental-information flows should be formalized and regularized. He concludes with the interesting comment that 'better data-handling might well become a substitute for much of the laborious shuffling and reshuffling of positions and lines of authority that now goes on'.

1 G. Vickers

Communication in Economic Systems

G. Vickers, 'Communication in economic systems', in B. I. Evans (ed.), *Studies in Communication*, Secker & Warburg, 1955 pp. 69–90.

The economic process

I am going to inquire what part communication plays in the economic process by which we live.

Professor Young in his Reith lectures (1951) said that our success as a species is due to the fact that we have learned to cooperate much better than the other animals and that this is largely because we have learned to communicate in words. It is this, he said, which has enabled us to spread and multiply as we have done. He was clearly using the word 'cooperation' in a wide sense to include all the obscure processes by which we coordinate the division of our labour and which I understand by the economic process. But 'cooperation' is often used in a narrower sense, as the antithesis to conflict or as the antithesis to competition and I shall reserve its use for this narrower sense, because I believe that conflict, competition and cooperation (in this narrower sense) are three distinguishable modes of human interaction and that they all play a part in coordinating that division of labour which has paid mankind such striking dividends. All three are mediated by communication, though in different degrees.

I believe that we are becoming dependent on forms of coordination which make increasing demands on communication; and that communication is thus becoming one of the major limiting factors which determine whether we survive at anything like our present numbers and standard of living – and if this is true of the species as a whole, it is many times more true of us who live in this crowded island. If this is right, it is clearly important to us to understand what part communication does play in coordinating the activities which keep us alive. If we understood this, we should be protected against expecting too much of it, as I suspect we often do now; and we might find ways to communicate more effectively, as we urgently need to do. In doing so, we might clear our minds on what we mean by communication, a concept by no means easy to define. Language is only part – though a highly specialized part – of the stream of experience which we interpret, consciously or unconsciously, in the light of our past experience and which serves to regulate our relations with each other; so it is hard to avoid giving to 'communication' a meaning which is neither too narrow nor too wide to be useful.

To an observer from another planet, uninformed and unconfused by any subjective information about what is going on here, economic space would seem to be peopled by what he might call working societies, meaning the groups which he would see assembling in individual factories, offices, shops and mines at the beginning of each day or shift and dispersing at the end. Within each of these working societies he could see the product passing from one hand to another, up to the point at which it physically left that place of work. He could trace the division of labour further, between working societies, up to the point when the finished product is ready for consumption or use – until, for example, Antarctic whale oil and tropical ground nuts have become a packet of margarine in an English larder. But he could not easily discern how this process is coordinated, or whence comes the confidence which each human being, each working society so clearly possesses, that the stream which makes its activity possible will continue to flow.

He would, however, see communication as a physical activity. When he had plotted the channels of production, he would see that they are also channels of communication. Messages as well as goods pass along them. He could compute by volume the exchange of paper and oral noise which accompanies the production and distribution of goods and he would be surprised to observe how much is used in some cases and how little in others.

He would also notice that a lot of working societies do nothing observable except send and receive communications. Banks and brokers and remote head offices would all fall into this category. He might compare the volume of their activities but he would not easily tell the difference between them. He could not readily divine that some of his working societies were independent entities, related through the market, whilst others were parts of a single concern, related by a central programming office. Similarly, he would see that the total output of every product and the total consumption of it tended to be equated at varying levels; but he would not see whether this was due to market forces or to restrictive practices or to monopolistic control or to government action. Indeed, he might be unwilling to believe that these various controls are so different in principle as they seem to us; and he might be right.

It might be fruitful to speculate further on what could be learned about economic organization and about the part which communication plays in it from the point of view of one wholly outside the system; but I will roughly complete the picture from the point of view of what Dr Cherry calls a 'participant observer' (1955).

I suggest that by organization we mean structured human relations and that by human relations we mean mutual expectations. Both the exchange of goods and the exchange of communications take place only along channels of mutual expectation, which they in turn confirm or modify.

Business lives by mutual expectation. Ships sail across the world, confident that when they arrive, there will be berths to receive them, cargoes to fill them and hands to turn them round; and their charterers accept demurrage rates which would ruin them if these expectations were not nearly always fulfilled. Business proceeds on the assumption that a million daily expectations will materialize. The human relations to which these expectations correspond are manifold, but a threefold classification will serve my purpose.

Some are based solely on experience and habit. This man or people like him have usually behaved in such and such a way in similar circumstances; so they probably will again. I will call these experiential relations. The goodwill of a business is the expression of its experiential relations with the public.

Secondly, relations based on experience may be confirmed by express promises. I will call these contractual relations. They are the most obvious stuff of which business relations are made.

Finally, mutual expectations may grow within a continuing group relationship. My attitude to my fellow employee, to my subordinate, to my boss in any particular matter is conditioned by our joint membership of a working group and by the mutual expectations which attach to our respective positions. I will call these corporative relations – by which, of course, I do not mean that they are necessarily 'cooperative' relations.

The categories are not discrete; they are overlapping bands on a continuous scale. Yet they will serve to distinguish broad types of relationship, between which lie significant differences.

I will ask you to regard the channels of production as constituting the warp of the economic organization of mankind. They are also channels of communication; and they are made possible by organized human relationships, experiential, contractual and corporative.

Across this intricate warp runs a woof of a different sort. Trade unions, professional organizations and trade associations link their members in associations with other ends, other loyalties and other channels of communication. I will call societies of this kind 'protective societies', to distinguish them from what I have called 'working societies'. Even this two-dimensional model is too simple; for government has its relations both with the warp and with the woof, modifying their behaviour directly and indirectly, by legislation and regulation, by pressures and by promises and being influenced in turn by the opinions which they mobilize and the pressures which they exert. In each of these three planes the underlying relations are of course essentially extended in time, for they are made up of experience and expectation.

This is the complex process by which we produce all the goods and services we use; distribute those money incomes which determine our respective shares; and form some of our most significant and powerful social groups. It is what I mean by the economic process.

Economic systems

The economic process is also called an economic system and it contains many groups of factors which can usefully be regarded as systems. By a system I understand any group of interacting variables which has some power of regulating itself by its own experience. Communication engineers are teaching us to refer to this process as feedback and to regard it as expressing a principle of very wide application; and I believe that, when we have learned to understand its implications more fully, we shall be able to talk more effectively about many social processes, including business organizations, and hence to understand them better. Through language we have at least the possibility of most elaborate and responsive mutual feedback.

Unfortunately we have to apply the concept in the social field to systems which are much less perfect than the mechanical examples which occur to the engineer or the organic examples which occur to the biologist.

To use a familiar physical example, the thermostat takes account of all the factors which determine the temperature of the room in which it is placed, including the heat coming from the boiler in the basement, and feeds this information back to the boiler in such a form as to adjust the boiler's effort to keep the temperature constant. Similarly a market takes account of all the factors which determine the effective demand of buyers, including the efforts of all the sellers, and keeps the two in equilibrium. But whereas the thermostat is set by a hand wholly outside the system, the market is calculated to excite itself and takes a hand in its own setting, a difference which is more than a mere difference in the extent to which the two systems are prone to oscillate.

A single working society is also to some extent a system but the more obvious analogy here is with an organic system. We distinguish living creatures by the facts (amongst others) that in varying degrees they can produce a single coordinated response to a stimulus; that they can meet a range of situations in a variety of appropriate ways; that interference with any part upsets the behaviour of the whole; and that they can adapt internally to offset external change. These also characterize in varying though much lower degrees a flock of sheep, a football team and a business enterprise; but here again the parallel is not exact. How exact it is has been a subject of controversy for long enough and happily there is no need for me to enter into it.

Many people are interested today in comparing physical systems, such as the 'closed loop' of boiler, room temperature and thermostat with the organic systems, of which each separate creature is an example. Electronic systems parallel in some respects the working of the central nervous system. Dr Gray

Walter's synthetic tortoises behave in some ways very much like real tortoises – although they do not yet lay eggs. Dr Ross Ashby has shown theoretically that any set of interacting variables can, and indeed must seek dynamic stability to the extent to which its internal couplings give it the necessary feedback; and he has built a machine which learns by experience, just as his thesis says it should. Shall we soon, as a result of thinking such as this, be able to describe all these systems, mechanical, electronic, organic and social in common language and thus to understand better not only the similarities but also the differences between them? Shall we then have a deeper understanding of the situations which in social systems we distinguish as 'cooperation', 'competition' and 'conflict'? I hope so. In the meantime, several difficulties impede us in describing adequately as 'systems' the organizations which I have called 'working societies' or the interacting groups of them which carry on the economic process.

We lack suitable models with which to compare them. For lack of better, we use physical and organic models but neither is adequate. This is partly because feedback within and between social organizations is mediated by means different from those which operate in a mechanical or an organic system. Only part of the difference lies in the use of verbal communication, though this instrument can elicit responses sometimes so sensitive and precise, sometimes so sluggish and distorted, that we may expect systems based on it to have some distinct characteristics on that account alone.

Again, our language draws distinctions between the 'automatic' and the 'deliberate', which we may well mistrust but which we cannot reconcile, until we have a better understanding of the part which consciousness plays in human behaviour. We cannot even describe the situations which we call cooperation, competition and conflict in terms which we can apply as confidently to the economic system as to the ecology of a pond. It is unfamiliar to most and repugnant to many to regard 'stability', even 'dynamic stability', as an adequate goal for any human system, especially an economic system. In politics the idea is more familiar, but even here the concepts of cooperation, competition and conflict remain unrelated. Those who seek international stability through 'cooperation' barely share the same universe of discourse with those who seek it through the balance of power. I shall not venture further into these philosophical depths but I shall not be deterred by them from regarding all these interacting economic groups and units as systems, however different may seem the means by which their interaction is secured.

Yet we need means to distinguish between them and here again we are in difficulty. We lack a satisfactory quantitative measure of organization. In particular, we lack an adequate measure of the difference between organizations involving different degrees of 'corporative' relations. Allee, a biologist who has given much thought to the ways in which animal aggregations of various kinds are organized, has suggested a useful classification. In the simpler and more transient forms he finds the main cause of the aggregation in individual response to the environment – for example, moths round a candle. In the more complex and permanent aggregations he finds the main cause in the responses of individuals to each other – for example, bees in a hive. I find this suggestive as a means of classifying the organizations underlying the economic system.

For every increase in what I have called corporative relations increases for the individual the relative importance of his responses to stimuli from within the group and correspondingly reduces the relative importance of his responses to stimuli from outside. Thus corporative relations seem to represent closer integration, as measured by the index which Allee applies to animal aggregations. This has very important results for communication. Corporative relations, I suggest, require a much more elaborate network of mutual expectations between the communicating parties than do experiential relations and to maintain these relations is one of the main objects of communication.

Where a number of independent and competing firms are related through the market, their relations are largely at what I have called the experiential level and the system which they form is most easily paralleled by a physical model. If they are then incorporated in a single monopoly, whether by nationalization or by merger, they are required to develop to a much greater degree relations of the kind which I have called corporative; and the system which they form is more easily paralleled by an organic model. Unfortunately we have as yet no common language in which we can conveniently describe both, so it is hard to describe the differences satisfactorily.

The movement of prices on a free market establishes sensitive and continuous communication between buyers and sellers, between rival buyers and between rival sellers, through which each continually responds to the others. These are well exemplified by those international markets in London which long practice has raised to so high a pitch of technical perfection – the commodity markets, the money market, the Stock Exchange. I commend them to the attention of the Communication Research Centre.

Thus the relationships of the firms, while they are competing, are alive with communication, no less than when they are combined. Nor can we safely say that they are less 'organized', when related through the market, than when they are brought under central control; for we are not entitled to reserve the word 'organization' for those relations which we believe ourselves to have imposed and to deny it to those which we discover. We cannot even clearly distinguish between the kinds of communication which animate the two systems, so long as we regard them purely as communication.

Suppose I mark my tomatoes down because my head office tells me to, whilst you mark yours down because you notice what your rival is doing down the road. We have both received and acted upon a communication. In what respect are they different? What is it which makes a communication from a rival different from a communication from a boss?

The answer lies, I suggest, not in the communication but in the frame of mutual expectation within which it takes place. Corporative relations make possible a wider range of collective response, but they are much harder to build up. It is much easier to explain why I respond to a signal from my rival than to a signal from my boss. The preconditions required are far simpler.

Preconditions of communications

Every communication depends for its meaning on much which has previously happened to the receiving mind and itself contributes to the meaning of what will follow; so it is difficult to separate communication from its preconditions.

Two professionals talking 'shop', be they engineers or biologists or what you will, can communicate with a richness and accuracy which would be denied to them if similar training and experience had not built up in their minds elaborate and similar frames of reference. It is these which give significance to what they say and ensure that they shall understand each other or at least know when they do not.

This common frame of reference may itself be the result of communication; indeed, much communication is wholly devoted to building it up. On the other hand, it may be partly or even wholly the product of other kinds of experience.

A standing committee, for example, will usually find its discussions getting easier and more fruitful as it becomes more experienced, because its members will evolve more adequate and more similar frames of reference as a result of their mutual communications. On the other hand, two gardeners, who have never met before, can talk gardening together by virtue of frames of reference built up almost entirely of separate but similar personal experience.

These frames of reference include also attitudes – attitudes towards the subject, towards the sender, towards the group, if group action is involved, and towards communication itself.

These become far more important in communications within an organization, that is, between people in a corporative relationship. I defined an organization as a set of structured mutual expectations. These expectations are not created merely by drawing lines on an organization chart; they must be confirmed and continually reinforced by experience. This is what management means when it talks, as it so frequently does, about creating confidence. Many communications have no other effect and some no other object (greetings are a familiar example; and greetings play an important part in the functioning of every working society). Maintaining confidence plays a much larger part within working societies than elsewhere, because the web of expectation to be maintained is more elaborate and probably also because of the tensions and anxieties which tend to haunt relations within a hierarchy. I have the impression that students of communication pay much less attention than do practitioners in industry to the place of confidence in communication.

A pamphlet issued by Unilever about their organization, after defining communications as 'the relations between the centre and the periphery and of both with the advisory and service departments', goes on to say 'the quality of these communications is determined by the confidence that the key people throughout the organization have in each other'. Later on, after stressing the need for a constant flow of news from the centre to the perimeter and vice versa, it says:

As we go about we not only make sure that we ourselves tell others 'more than they need to know' but also see that they in turn tell their subordinates 'more than they need to know'. And as we go about we must encourage people to say what they think, because only by so doing can confidence be built.

You will notice that mutual confidence is held out as an end in itself. The exchange of information is only a means to this end, hence the repeated emphasis on the importance of telling people more than they need to know. The authors view confidence as an essential precondition to communication; and every modern book on management tells the same tale.

In this example, communication is deliberately used to create and maintain mutual confidence, which in turn will ensure effective communication in future; but here again the frame of reference is not built by communication alone. It may be given by other forms of experience; and here, as elsewhere, the other experience may contradict communication. A man who was once an industrial worker told me 'My father always taught me "If the manager talks civil to you, watch out, he's going to put one over you".' A well-intentioned manager, trying to communicate with a mind so set, would be at a loss to know why his signals failed to elicit the desired responses; and the situation could only be explained by uncovering, in the frame of reference of the receiver, the transmitted experience of a third party long since dead.

Another elusive constituent of the receiver's attitude, important whenever group action is involved, is attitude towards the group. This again admits of qualitative differences which I will try to classify but the primary cleavage is between acceptance and rejection. Anyone who has worked in a newly constituted organization knows that individuals tend first to accept membership of their own working group and only later and with difficulty to reconcile this with loyalty to the organization as a whole.

All new organizations are bound to face extraordinary difficulties of communication until they have had time to build up common frames of reference. For reasons which I personally think were valid, the National Coal Board was required to come into full activity at a time when its three upper levels of authority had only just been recruited. When opinions, orders and information began to fly up and down these newly improvised channels, everyone concerned found at first a curious difficulty in making himself understood. We became aware how much we are normally accustomed to rely, for the understanding of all we say, on the understanding accumulated during past intercourse with the same minds on the same subject. These accumulations are like the humus which has collected down the ages on the more favoured parts of our planet, a patchy deposit only inches thick, on which all life subsists. Where this mental humus exists, intercourse need scarcely be explicit. Where it does not exist, the earlier stages of communication are like cultivating a desert.

Happily our minds build up their humus more rapidly than does our planet. Nevertheless it is sobering to reflect that two hundred years ago it was rare for the ordinary man to receive any communication whatever from a person whom he did not know or on a subject with which he was not familiar. If this is so, the opportunities for misunderstanding have multiplied since the eighteenth century.

Consider by way of contrast how communication works in a professional football team. These eleven men coordinate their activities so well that people pay to watch, which is more than most working societies can claim; and they do so in most difficult conditions, for whatever their aim, eleven other men are continually trying to frustrate it. Yet during play no word is spoken; and words, if needed, would be useless, because they would be far too slow. Signals, indeed, are exchanged in so far as the players watch each other's actions; but even these would be too slow, if they were not constantly anticipated.

This admirable coordination was prepared before ever the game began and its constituents are the precondition of all concerted action in economic life as well as in the football field. The players learned to recognize situations and to know the appropriate responses; they learned the individual skills which they needed to play their part in each response; each learned what each situation would require of the others also and developed confidence that this would be forthcoming; and together they developed a mutually sustaining morale. Thus equipped by some teaching and much practice, they can coordinate during the game entirely through their common understanding of the developing situation.

I do not offer this example as a practicable or a desirable model for the cooperation of working societies generally. I do not want to buy good communication at the cost of stereotyping our frames of reference so completely as those of a football team, though we know from experiments elsewhere how much can be done in that direction by discipline and indoctrination. The dilemma can be escaped only if the parties to the communication realize the part played by their respective frames of reference and are able and willing to identify these differences and allow for them, even when the differences remain. This involves a specific attitude towards communication itself.

For example, there is today in Britain a wide gulf between the frame of reference which trade union teaching and experience has established in the minds of workers and that which exists in the mind of management. This may impede communication on some subjects between management and worker; consider, for example, what happens when management, believing work study to be a high road to efficiency, seek to commend it to some group of workers who have come to regard it as a short cut to exploitation. The same gulf may equally impede communication between trade union leadership and its rank and file; consider the familiar position of trade union leadership, where in some familiar situation it wishes to elicit from its members a response opposite to the one to which decades of struggle and sacrifice have accustomed them.

These differences and others like them will be less fatal to communication if they are identified and allowed for. This depends largely on whether each party to the communication is prepared to report back what he in fact receives. The feeding back of such information is essential, if any difficult communication is to be kept on the rails and I wish that our social and moral code impressed it in each one of us as a primary duty.

For the communicator cannot know. It is, I think, misleading to describe as 'transmission' the last stage of the strange process by which A communicates with B. Dr Cherry (1955) reminds us that we cannot transmit our thoughts to each other. We can only evoke in each other whatever corresponds to the symbols which we use. The effect which our words have at the receiving end depends upon all those disparate factors which I have included in the frame of reference of the receiver, personal to him, hidden from the sender, perhaps hidden from the receiver himself. The relevant parts must be made conscious and explicit, if communication is to be effective between those with different frames of reference; and this is one of the most important functions of communication itself.

Problems of communication

I have spent a long time on the preconditions of communication; I have stressed how closely communication, regarded as experience, is related to other experience; how closely, regarded as behaviour, it is linked with other behaviour. I should like to spend much longer over the specific problems of communication, which arise along all three planes of the economic process. Perhaps the most interesting would be in the growing nexus which links government with working societies on the one hand and with protective societies on the other.

Not all these techniques are new. Consider how much information is conveyed by the announcement of a change in the bank rate. It states a fact; it implies a judgement; it foreshadows a policy.

But I must limit the field. I shall keep to communications within the working society or at least within the field of corporative relations.

The communications which flow through the channels of a business organization may be classified according to the purposes which they serve and this is a convenient way of isolating certain groups of problems; but it does not mean, of course, that any one communication serves only one purpose.

One purpose is to convey information about what is happening both outside and inside the organization. In large organizations the latter is the more important and the more difficult; for the first task of any organization is to ensure that its right hand knows what its left hand is doing at least sufficiently to ensure that they do not frustrate each other; and in an organization, as in an organism, this is not achieved without constant and delicate exchanges.

A second purpose is to imprint rules about how various types of situation should be handled. Communications to this end may range from announcements of high policy by the Board to advice by a craftsman to his apprentice. It is easy to underestimate how much communication in business is devoted to this purpose.

A third purpose is to form and render acceptable collective decisions. This becomes increasingly important as the scale of organization grows.

A fourth purpose is to move to action. Some may question whether this deserves a separate category. I think it does but it is hard to be sure without a clearer understanding of how the imperative mood works.

A fifth purpose is to create, confirm or modify the attitudes of individuals within the organization to the organization itself, to each other, to the work and so far as necessary to the outside world.

Each of these purposes serves to focus a group of problems at which I can only glance.

The transmission of information is limited in the first place by logistics. The sender is absolutely limited by what the receiver can absorb in the time which he can spare from action. Volumes of paper which are circulated 'for information' are pulped without ever informing those for whom they were chiefly intended, simply because these recipients did not have or make the time to read them.

Here there is a large and relatively tractable set of problems. What information do people at various levels need to have? In what form can it be most quickly absorbed? How can more meaning be got into fewer words and figures? What training do people need to enable them most quickly to get the meaning out of information which reaches them? How much time should be allowed for the purpose?

These problems arise strikingly in presenting to executives, especially at remote levels, the information needed for control.

Much is going on in this field. Techniques for control by forecast become more refined and more widely used; standard costs provide a more informative yardstick by which to measure success and failure. Both depend on making forecasts based on assumptions and seeking explanations only for deviations from the expected. This proves empirically to be a very effective way of saving time and concentrating attention on what matters most and it might be useful to establish theoretically in what its merits consist. It also has the merit of being applicable to very varied kinds of effort and is therefore especially welcome in the increasing number of enterprises in which profit-and-loss is no longer (if it ever was) an adequate measure of success.

The coal industry, for example, has recently been given by statute new duties and hence a new concept of success and failure. It is still seeking means to measure its achievements in this new dimension, and so is Parliament and the world at large; hence the debates on public accountability. The National Health Service is an even clearer example of an enterprise in which it is hard to select indices of efficiency. There is, of course, no difficulty in either case in producing abundant facts but facts in themselves are not necessarily information. In what conditions does a fact become information? I leave this one also to the Communication Research Centre.

Compared with these accounting techniques, where real progress is being made, the art of verbal presentation seems to me to be declining. The Ten Commandments take 284 words of which 217 are of one syllable and only ten of more than two. Judged by this standard, the art of writing directives seems to be in danger of being lost. Nor is there any adequate body of formalized knowledge about the order in which ideas should be presented to a new mind in order to find acceptance there. An analysis of the best practice might disclose some body of teachable doctrine which would help us to overcome the mounting logistical difficulties of conveying ever more information to ever more numerous and dispersed minds in ever shorter time.

The imprinting of rules is the focus of another set of closely related problems. Perhaps their most interesting aspect relates to the recognition of situations. Rules apply to types of situation and if people are to be prepared in advance to take concerted action, they must learn to classify each situation as it arises in the same way. People can only carry out a policy if they can recognize the kind of situation to which it is intended to apply. This is most difficult to convey in words; hence the difficulty of writing policy directives and the fatal ease with which they degenerate into formulae; hence, in consequence, the formalism which tends to infect all large organizations.

Still more complex and thought provoking are the processes which lead to decision. As the scale of business enterprises grows, more minds participate in major decisions, more viewpoints have to be reconciled, more opinions collated, more resistances dissolved, more concurrence won, more identification achieved. Final responsibility may rest with a small group or with a single man; it is no less important that those whose views can help to frame it and whose work must help to carry it out shall be associated with the making of it and shall feel themselves to be so.

It would be possible and, I should expect, rewarding, to work out in detail how a specific policy decision was reached. Most of the facts would be found recorded in the papers of the undertaking concerned, in memoranda and minutes of meetings and so on. There should be no lack of firms willing to offer their files for analysis in the cause of this inquiry, though few, I fear, could disclose a process so urbane or a result so unanimous as that shown by those swarming bees which Lindauer observed and Professor Haldane describes to us.

It is possible that we may in time get some electronic help in the taking of large-scale decisions. It is said that the computer known as SEAC in Washington played a decisive part in at least one important political decision of the US Executive, by working out the long-term implications of various alternatives, as it might have worked out the possible repercussions of a move in a game of chess. Certain it is that, as policy decisions get more elaborate, the relevant factors may easily become so numerous and so disparate that they never all get focused at the same time – with distressing results to the course of debate, which tends to become either circular or oscillatory. I cannot help feeling that to set the computer would be nearly as difficult as to answer the question;

but it might be that a board of directors, setting out to agree how to set the computer, would find that they had at least set their own computing mechanisms more quickly and completely than they sometimes do.

Fourthly and in some ways most enigmatic of all are the problems associated with communications which move to action or which are intended to do so. A great deal of communication today takes the form of exhortation. Is it ever effective? If so, when and why?

When the conductor rings the bell the driver nearly always starts the bus. When the foreman shouts 'Come on! Get a move on!' the gang may or may not quicken its tempo. Both the bell and the shout are intended to make things move but they do not seem to be communications of the same kind. I should be inclined to say that the bell is in the indicative and the shout in the imperative mood and it is interesting that the bell has a much more reliable effect than the shout.

On the other hand, both dominance and persuasiveness are facts of experience. People will do for A what they would not do for anyone else and it is hard to explain such behaviour either as conditioned response to a signal or as calculated response to a situation, or even as the simple reflection of a 'pecking order'. Yet we must take account of this odd fact in any theories which purport to explain how communications move to action.

The issue is a lively one for several reasons. The 'kick and carrot' psychology of the nineteenth century is discredited in theory and largely inoperative in practice and the problem of making the imperative mood effective in a world of full employment is far from solved. Moreover, the authoritarian structure of industry is itself under fire; both speculation and experiment are exploring alternatives. Finally, the nature and limits of personal leadership are far from clear. We should be on much safer ground if we could fit it into place within a theory of human communication and blow away some of the mystique which surrounds it now.

Finally, and most pervasive, are the problems of communication designed to establish attitudes and in particular confidence and the sense of belonging which I have already discussed. If the right hand is to know what the left hand is doing, it must first *want to know.* It must thus be aware, if not proud, of belonging to the same body. Policies will not be accepted or implemented, opinions will not be considered or views modified, coordinated action will not take place, except within a group to which the members feel some sense of belonging. These links of loyalty form indispensable channels of communication.

Large-scale organizations today have problems arising out of conflicting and concentric loyalties. How large an association can command the effective loyalty of individual men? At what level should loyalty be focused? How many concentric loyalties can a man compass – such, for example, as in the Navy, link a man to his ship and to the service? These questions are closely linked with the practical problems of communication which beset large-scale organizations.

It is not surprising, I think, that in the literature of business management 'communications' has virtually ceased to imply the exchange of information as such. It has become a term of art to include every form of human contact which may help to get cooperation within the organization and a good press outside. But it means much more than that. How much it means is well exemplified in the story of the building of the Fawley oil refinery. Planning and progressing built the largest oil refinery in about twenty-eight months after actual building began and four months ahead of schedule. The coordination involved depended on communication of an order which we seldom attain here but which we have got to learn to attain, if we are to hold our own.

This brief survey would seem to confirm that organizations which are largely based on corporative relationships require better communication between their members and, in particular, more elaborate common frames of reference than do organizations which depend more largely on what I have called experiential relations. Failing this, they will act as if they were blind and impotent, because they will not possess the degree of internal responsiveness (of feedback, if you like) which is needed to coordinate vision and action. The difficulties of newly formed organizations arise primarily because the corporative relationship requires a refinement of communication which is impossible, until the appropriate frame of reference has had time to grow.

Relations today are becoming more and more corporative;

hence the mounting strain on communication. Working societies grow and are integrated into ever larger concerns, and even legally independent concerns are called more often and more cogently to adopt corporative attitudes. We may well pause to wonder what are the forces which are thus driving us and whither we are bound.

Communication as a regulator

Among the changes of environment with which every species must cope, are the changes which its own living creates. Forest trees, for example, may flourish so successfully that their own seedlings cannot grow in their shade. Smog provides a parallel exact in character, though not yet so extreme in degree. Other animals, I believe, seldom create lethal conditions for themselves, and when they are in danger of doing so, they can usually move on. But our present way of living alters the world we live in far more radically and far more quickly than it did in any pre-technological era; and this is equally true whether you think of the physical changes which have made Greater London or the organizational ones which have left us dependent on Canada for bread and the Argentine for meat; and unlike our fellow mammals or our nomadic ancestors, we cannot move on.

We are, it is true, far more adaptive than they. Along with our genetic inheritance we enjoy a vast heritage of socially transmitted skills and we can learn new tricks much more quickly than any other creature ever has before. Hitherto, whenever we have set ourselves a new problem, we have always found a new answer. So even if our environment is indeed becoming ever less stable, need we worry?

Stability is but balance; and wisdom lies
In masterful administration of the unforeseen.

Why should we not always master the unforeseen – assuming, of course, that we go on getting more and more clever for ever?

There are, I think, three possible reasons. We cannot tell today whether any of them will become operative.

First, we might set ourselves an insoluble technical problem – as trees do, when they throw a lethal amount of shade on their own seed bed. It is conceivable that a civilization based as completely as ours is on the use of scarce and at present irreplaceable metals might find itself in a technical impasse, through the exhaustion of these supplies. It is more easily conceivable, I imagine, that the developing use of nuclear energy might set us a technically insoluble problem in the disposal of radioactive by-products.

Sir Macfarlane Burnet in a recent address listed a formidable series of ecological traps, each of which we prepared for ourselves by our successful efforts to escape from the one before. He said:

> Urban life, a necessity for the development of civilization, inevitably led to the development of infectious disease ... the science of applied microbiology has liberated us from that ecological trap but led us into the other of over population. Birth control can save us from over population but confronts us with the new trap of genetic deterioration. Wherever we utilize knowledge for the short-term satisfaction of our desires for comfort, security or power, we are all too prone to find that on the long-term view we are creating one more ecological trap, from which sooner or later we must extricate ourselves.

If he is right, it is not clear how we escape from the one which he sees round us now.

Secondly, and more probably, we might set ourselves an insoluble organizational problem. In other words, we might find ourselves so organized that we could not respond effectively to a challenge which we could foresee. (In this country we may have reached this point already.) It is the consciousness of this danger which puts the edge on current controversy about the relative merits of competition and monopoly and the proper field of government intervention.

The whole development of land use and town planning legislation in Britain over the past generation has been an attempt to reorganize ourselves, so as to deal with challenges of a kind which our then existing organization seemed to be impotent to meet. There is no reason to suppose that such challenges will grow less. It is only within the last few years that the labours of housewives have been mitigated by those chemical detergents which today stand beside all our sinks; and already the proportion of it reaching the sewage beds is threatening that organized army of bacteria on which we rely to deal with our other waste products. It seems to me most unlikely that we shall learn to foresee all the traps which we are setting for ourselves and therefore the more important that we should be so organized that we can respond to them sufficiently quickly.

It may well be that in the long run we shall run into some technical or organizational impasse, in which case the system will break down and reconstitute itself at some more manageable level, not without much intervening chaos and distress. There is, however, a third cause which might bring us prematurely to the same fate, namely, our failure to use fully or develop fast enough the capacity for communication which we possess; and it is this which lends such interest and urgency to the aims of the Communication Research Centre.

But if we are to take a hand in developing this process of communication, we must be able to talk about it; and at present we are ill-equipped to do so. I set out to trace the part which communication plays in the economic process by which we live; but I have not succeeded. Does it offer us the means to build systems even more elaborate and even more responsive? Or are we already expecting more of it than we safely can? Our answers to questions such as these decide our attitude to some of the most urgent problems of today, political, economic and social; yet they can at present be no more than guesses. For the underlying issues are screened from us by what is itself a failure of communication. We have no language in which to discuss them with each other; and hence no concepts with which to present them to ourselves.

References

CHERRY, C. (1955), 'Communication theory and human behaviour', in B. I. Evans (ed.), *Studies in Communication*, Secker & Warburg.

YOUNG, J. Z. (1951), *Doubt and Certainty in Science*, Oxford University Press.

2 D. Katz and R. L. Kahn

Communication: The Flow of Information

Excerpts from D. Katz and R. L. Kahn, *The Social Psychology of Organizations*, Wiley, 1966, pp. 235–47, 253–7.

Direction of communication flow and characteristics of communication circuits

We shall discuss communication processes within organizations both with respect to the direction of the flow of information (who communicates to whom) and with respect to the structure of the communication network and the content of the messages carried (how and what is being communicated). The direction of the information flow can follow the authority pattern of the hierarchical positions (*downward communication*); can move among peers at the same organizational level (*horizontal communication*); or can ascend the hierarchical ladder (*upward communication*).

The major characteristics of communication networks which we shall consider are (1) the size of the loop, the amount of organizational space covered by given types of information, (2) the nature of the circuit, whether a simple repetitive pattern or a chain modification type, (3) the open or closed character of the circuit, (4) the efficiency of the circuit for its task, and (5) the fit between the circuit and the systemic function it serves.

1. *Size of loop.* Communication circuits may embrace the entire system, may be restricted to a major sub-system, or may involve only a small unit within a sub-system. Some communication loops may be confined to officer personnel or even to top-level echelons. A common organizational problem is the discrepancy between the size of given information loops as perceived by the ranking authorities and the size of the circuit which actually is found. Leaders characteristically overestimate the number of persons reached by their intended communications. Also, the larger the loop, the greater will be the problems of communication,

particularly where the penetration of sub-system boundaries is involved.

2. *Repetition versus modification in the circuit.* A large information loop may reach many members of the system through a repetitive pattern of transmitters. For example, a directive may go down the line and be echoed at each level to the one below it. A different pattern of transmission is often used whereby a chain of command will pass along messages with appropriate translation at each level in the system. The same amount of organizational space is involved in both patterns, so that the size of the loop is the same, but the second pattern calls for some modification of the message. The first pattern has the advantages of simplicity and uniformity. Everyone is exposed to identical information. What is announced publicly topside is the same as what people hear from their own superior. None the less, the simplicity of this system may be advantageous only for simple problems. For complex matters a directive repeated in uniform fashion is not necessarily uniform in its meaning across sub-systems. It may need translation in different units to be effective.

3. *Feedback or closure character.* Though the flow of a communication pattern may have a dominant organizational direction (down the line, for example) there is a circular character to communicative acts. There is a reaction to the transmission which can furnish feedback to the transmitter, though it may only be the acknowledgement of the receipt of the message.

Closure of a set of communicative acts can vary from immediate fixed response of acknowledgement and acceptance of the initial message to reports of its inadequacy and attempts to alter its character. In the latter case, though the communication cycle has been completed through feedback about the faulty character of the original communication, the communication process is immediately reactivated. In a larger sense, closure has not been achieved for the organization by the first set of communicative acts. Thus, while almost all processes of communication are cyclical, with a return to the original transmitter, we can characterize some communication circuits as having more of a closed character for systemic functioning than others.

A closed communication loop would be one in which the cycle

of transmission acts is not open to change once it has been initiated. In other words, no new information and no radical modifications in the process are provided for by the structural procedures. If the communication process is one of issuing directives and responding to the signal of mission accomplished, we have a closed circuit. The directive cannot be substantially modified. Rigid codes block out sources of information either by definition or practice. There is just no provision for admitting new information at various points in the transmission chain.

4. *The efficiency of communication nets.* A related but somewhat different aspect of communication systems is the efficiency, which can be measured in terms of the number of communication links in a given network. In the beginning of our discussion of communication we pointed out that restriction in the communication process was part of the essential nature of social organizations. Experimental work has generally supported the hypothesis that the smaller the number of communication links in a group, the greater the efficiency of the group in task performance (Dubin, 1959). There are more links, for example, in the all-channel pattern than in the circle pattern, and more links in the circle than in the wheel pattern (see Figure 1).

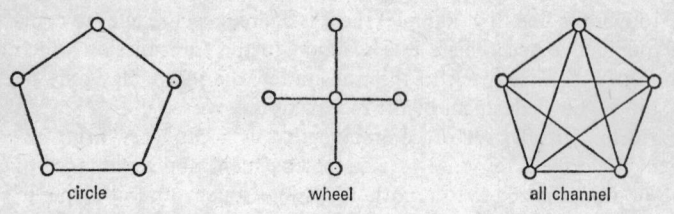

Figure 1 Types of communication networks

Using a sentence construction task, Heise and Miller (1951) found that a two-link system was more efficient than various three-link systems, as measured by the number of words spoken and the time taken to complete the task.

In an extension of Leavitt's earlier work (1951), Guetzkow and Simon (1955) used five-man groups in which the task was to discover which one of six symbols was held in common by all group members. The subjects were seated around a circular table, separated by five vertical partitions. They did not talk to one another, but communicated by passing messages through interconnecting slots. Each person was given a card with five symbols. The missing symbol was different for each subject. The experimenters employed three different networks of communication to which fifty-six groups were randomly assigned. In the circle net (see Figure 1) subjects could pass their messages to either or both of two neighbors. In the wheel net there is a key man to whom all four colleagues can communicate. In the all-channel pattern everyone can communicate with everyone else. Since messages must flow to some decision center for action and must flow back to the senders to inform them of the decision, the wheel provides a two-level hierarchy and the circle and all-channel nets a three-level hierarchy. In the circle, for example, two neighbors can send information to their opposite neighbors, who in turn relay this information with their own to the fifth member. He can then send the solution back to his group, but three levels are involved in the process.

Leavitt (1951) had found the two-level hierarchy of the wheel to be the most efficient for task accomplishment. Guetzkow and Simon, however, reasoned that this superiority might well be due to the time it took a group to discover and use the optimal organizational pattern for its specific type of net, rather than to the patterns of the networks themselves. For example, a group assigned to the circle might spend considerable time in a more complex interaction than the optimal pattern described above. Hence the experimenters provided a two-minute period between task trials for the groups to discover the best organizational pattern for their situation by allowing them to write messages to each other. The results confirmed the prediction of the experimenters. When groups in the all-channel or circle nets discovered the optimal organizational pattern, they were just as efficient as the wheel groups.

The advantages, then, for the system employing fewer links was not in the efficiency of the simpler network *per se*, but in the fact that it required little trial and error by the group to use it effectively. Moreover, since the networks with more links allow for the possibility of inefficient usage, there is some advantage to ruling out this possibility by means of more restrictive patterns.

These experiments were concerned with task-oriented communications and should not be generalized to socio-emotional or supportive types of communication. In subsequent experiments Guetzkow and Dill (1957) found that groups seemed to prefer a minimum linkage system. Seventeen out of twenty groups which had started with a pattern permitting ten links had, by the end of twenty trials, cut this to four links. Pressures were generated within the groups themselves to move toward the simpler communication networks. The groups that did not follow this pattern, moreover, were less efficient in task accomplishment.

5. *The fit between the communication circuit and systemic functioning*. A circuit may be too large, involving irrelevant people, or too small, omitting key informants. One factor in information overload is the creation of many large communication loops so that people receive frequent messages which have little if anything to do with carrying out their organizational roles. Role incumbents are called upon to decide what is functional and what is non-functional in the information they receive. Though they may make wise decisions, the time of decision-making is taken from their own basic tasks.

A common dysfunctional arrangement in organizations is to have communication loops of disproportionate sizes with respect to message-sending and message-receiving. Top echelons issue directives for the whole organization, yet achieve closure from the acquiescence of their immediate subordinates. In other words, the loop involves all levels of the organization on the sending side but only the top two echelons on the receiving side.

Another lack of fit between the communication circuit and the functional needs of the system occurs when closed circuits are used for purposes other than the carrying out of directives in an emergency setting. With complex problems, where time is not highly critical, a communication loop which permits the introduction of new information at various points in the circuit can be highly adaptive. Yet the logic of the closed circuit is carried over into the inappropriate areas of information search. The questions for which information is sought are so formulated by some executives that they predetermine the answers to be supplied. The communication process returns upon itself. For example, a department head concerned about a recent productivity decline calls in his division heads; he wants the problem explored, but it has been his experience, he informs them, that the lax practices of certain types of supervisors are the key factor in this sort of situation. His division heads report back after their exploration that he was indeed right, and they have taken the necessary steps to handle the problem. An open search for the causes of the productivity decline might have furnished a different answer.

Communication down the line

Communications from superior to subordinate are basically of five types:

1. Specific task directives: *job instructions*.
2. Information designed to produce understanding of the task and its relation to other organizational tasks: *job rationale*.
3. Information about organizational *procedures and practices*.
4. *Feedback* to the subordinate about his performance.
5. Information of an ideological character to inculcate a sense of mission: *indoctrination of goals*.

The first type of communication is generally given priority in industrial and military organizations and in hospitals. Instructions about the job are worked out with a great deal of specificity and are communicated to the role incumbent through direct orders from his superior, training sessions, training manuals and written directives. The objective is to ensure the reliable performance of every role incumbent in every position in the organization.

Less attention is given to the second type of information, designed to provide the worker with a full understanding of his job and of how it is geared to related jobs in the same sub-system. Many employees know what they are to do, but not why they are doing it, nor how the patterned activities in which they are involved accomplish a given objective. 'Their's not to reason why' is often the implicit, if not explicit, assumption of managerial philosophy. It is often assumed that an emphasis upon information about full job understanding will conflict with strict allegiance to specific task instructions. If the worker thinks he knows why he is to do a certain thing, he may attempt to do it in other than the specified fashion and the organizational leaders may not want to tolerate the variability of behavior this introduces into the system.

Information about organizational procedures completes the description of the role requirements of the organizational member. In addition to instructions about his job, he is also informed about his other obligations and privileges as a member of the system, e.g. about vacations, sick leave, rewards and sanctions.

Feedback to the individual about how well he is doing his job is often neglected or poorly handled, even in organizations in which the managerial philosophy calls for such evaluation. Where emphasis is placed upon compliance to specific task directives, it is logical to expect that such compliance will be recognized and deviation penalized. This is necessary to ensure that the system is working, and it is a matter of some motivational importance for the individual performer. The frequent complaint, however, by the individual is that he does not know where he stands with his superiors. Often an employee is identified as a major problem for an organization so late in the game that his poor performance or weak citizenship seem beyond remedy, and even transfer or discharge is difficult. There is belated recognition that there should have been an earlier review with him of his performance. Yet systematic procedures for rating and review of the work of employees by their superiors have not proved a panacea.

The reasons are not hard to find. The whole process of critical review is resented both by subordinate and superior as partaking of surveillance. The democratic values of the culture have permeated organizational members so that the superior sees himself as a leader of men, and not as a spy and disciplinarian. The subordinate, in wanting to know how well he is doing, really wants to have his merits recognized and to know how to develop his own talents more fully.

Another major reason for the unpopularity of supervisory appraisal is that many employees have little individual discretion in task accomplishment and little opportunity to excel. Both the company norms and the informal standards of the group set a uniform rate of accomplishment. The performance of workers is often so system-determined that there is little to be gained from evaluating workers as autonomous individuals. The occasional deviant does constitute a problem for the organization, particularly when his deviance is not formally recognized until it is too late. Nevertheless, such slips are probably less costly to the organization than a thorough surveillance system in which the individual does get early and systematic feedback on his performance.

The fifth type of downward-directed information has as its objective the inculcation of organizational goals, either for the total system or a major sub-system. An important function of an organizational leader is to conceptualize the mission of his enterprise in an attractive and novel form. This can be done with paticular effectiveness in organizations which are conspicuous for their contribution to societal welfare or for the hazardous character of their activities. For example, a police commissioner may describe the role of his police force as the work of professional officers engaged in a constructive program of community improvement.

Though organizational leaders are quick to recognize the importance of involving their followers in system goals, they are slow to utilize the most natural devices available to them in the form of job rationale. The second type of information in our listing, the understanding of one's role and how it relates to other roles, is a good bridge to involvement in organizational goals. If the psychiatric nurse in a hospital knows why she is to follow certain procedures with a patient and how this relates to the total therapy program for him, it is much easier for her to develop an ideological commitment to the hospital. This is one reason why some hospitals have developed the concept of the therapy team, which permits the doctor, nurse and attendant to discuss the treatment program for given patients. On the other hand, if the role incumbent receives information about job specifics without job understanding, it is difficult for him to see how his role is related to the organizational objective and hence difficult for him to identify with the organizational mission.

Withholding information on the rationale of the job not only is prejudicial to ideological commitment of the member, but it also means that the organization must bear down heavily on the first type of information – specific instructions about the job. If a man does not understand fully why he should do a thing or how his job relates to the tasks of his fellow workers, then there must be sufficient redundancy in his task instructions so that he behaves automatically and reliably in role performance. This type of problem was dramatically illustrated in the conflict about the information to be given to astronauts about their task in orbit. Some officials were in favor of reducing the astronaut's behavior to that of a robot; others wanted to utilize his intelligence by having him act on his understanding of the total situation. The result was a compromise.

The advantages of giving fuller information on job understanding are thus two fold: if a man knows the reasons for his assignment, this will often ensure his carrying out the job more effectively; and if he has an understanding of what his job is about in relation to his sub-system, he is more likely to identify with organizational goals.

Size of the loop and downward communication. The size of the communication loop is an interesting variable in processing information down the line, and has implications for organizational morale and effectiveness. In general the rank-and-file member gets his task instructions from those immediately above him. The loop covers very little of the organizational structure. Upper echelons neither know what the specific task directives are, nor would acquiring such knowledge be an appropriate way for them to spend time and energy. In industry the methods department may have worked out the standard procedures for a job, but these are transmitted to the employee by his immediate boss. On the other hand, communications about the goals of the organization in theory cover a loop as large as the organization itself. The rank-and-file member, however, may in practice be minimally touched by this loop. His degree of effective inclusion within it depends primarily upon how he is tied into the organization. If he is tied in on the basis of being paid for a routine performance, information about the goals and policies of the larger structure will be of no interest to him.

The size of the loop is also important in terms of the understanding of the message. Communications from the top addressed to all organizational members are often too general in character and too remote from the limited daily experiences of the individual to convey their intended meaning. To be effective, messages about organizational policy need to be translated at critical levels as they move down the line, i.e. translated into the specific meanings they have for given sectors of the structure. Katz and Lazarsfeld (1955) demonstrated a two-step process in the flow of communication in a community in which opinion leaders affected by the mass media in turn influenced the rank and file. Within organizations, however, not enough attention has been given to this problem of translation. Communications down the line must be converted to the coding systems of the sub-structures if they are to register and have impact.

A partial substitute for translation is the ability of some organizational leaders to develop confidence and liking for themselves as personalities among the rank and file. Their position on a policy issue will be accepted not because it is understood, but because people trust them and love them. This is more characteristic of political leadership than leadership in non-political organizations.

The translation problem is related to the fit between the communication cycle and the functional requirements of the organization. The information loop about how a job is to be done should have the immediate supervisor as the key communicant. This does not necessarily mean that a worker should get all his job directives from a single boss, but it does mean that additional bosses should be introduced only if they have an expertness about a clearly demarcated function. The research worker, in addition to listening to his project director, can also listen with profit to the sampling and statistical expert. Where the functional lines are fuzzy, the rule of a single boss has much to be said for it.

Transmitting information down the line may partake of a closed-circuit character if there is little opportunity for clarification of directives from above. Two things occur when directives remain limited and unclear because people down the line have no way of getting a fuller explanation. People will give minimal compliance so as to be apparently observing the letter of the law, or they will test out in actual behavior their own ideas of what can be done. If there is inadequate feedback up the line, this behavioral testing out can produce real deviations in organizational practice. Such deviations can run from constructive actions in support of organizational objectives to actions crippling and destructive to the organization.

Horizontal communications

Organizations face one of their most difficult problems in procedures and practices concerned with lateral communication, i.e. communication between people at the same hierarchical level. The machine model would be highly restrictive of lateral communication. A role incumbent would receive almost all his instructions from the man above him, and would deal with his associates only for task coordination specified by rules. Though such a plan neglects the need for socio-emotional support among peers, it is still true that unrestricted communication of a horizontal character can detract from maximum efficiency. What are the conditions under which lateral communication is desirable?

We shall start with the proposition that some types of lateral communication are critical for effective system functioning. Many tasks cannot be so completely specified as to rule out coordination between peers in the work process. The teamwork by which a varsity team beats an alumni group of greater prowess has many parallels in other organizations. (In fact, there is something to be said for not mechanizing coordination devices for a group task unless the whole process can be mechanized.)

Communication among peers, in addition to providing task coordination, also furnishes emotional and social support to the individual. The mutual understanding of colleagues is one reason for the power of the peer group. Experimental findings are clear and convincing about the importance of socio-emotional support for people in both unorganized and organized groups. Psychological forces always push people toward communication with peers; people in the same boat share the same problems. *Hence, if there are no problems of task coordination left to a group of peers, the content of their communication can take forms which are irrelevant to or destructive of organizational functioning.* Informal student groups sometimes devote their team efforts to pranks and stunts or even to harassing the administration and faculty.

The size of the communication circuit and its appropriateness to the function of the sub-system are important considerations for horizontal communication. By and large the nature and extent of exchanges among people at the same level should be related to the objectives of the various sub-systems in which they are involved, with primary focus on their own major task. Thus there are real disadvantages in lateral communication that cuts across functional lines and that nevertheless attempts to be highly specific. For example, if divisions with differentiated functions are part of a department, the communication between peers in different divisions should be on departmental problems and not on divisional matters. Peer communication on divisional matters can better be conducted within divisional boundaries.

Horizontal communication implies a closed circuit in that it satisfies people's needs to know from their own kind without taking into account other levels in the organization. In hierarchical structures it can mean that people overvalue peer communication with a neglect of those below them. Cabots talk only to Cabots, and vice-presidents only to vice-presidents. It is interesting to observe how often organizational leaders, when going outside their own structures for information, will seek their own status level, i.e. their counterparts in other organizations. Sometimes, however, the really critical information is at levels below them.

It is important to look at lateral communication in terms of the control function in organizations. Horizontal communication, if in operation at various levels in an organization, is a real check on the power of the top leaders. The more authoritarian and hierarchical the system, the more information is a secret property of select groups, and the more it can be utilized to control and punish people at lower levels. In such a system there is little horizontal communication across levels of equal rank. The department chief knows about his ten division heads and their respective divisions, but each one of them knows only about himself and his own division. Hence the department chief is in a powerful position to manipulate them as he will.

The simple paradigm of vertical funnelling up the line with no horizontal flow of information is a fundamental basis of social control in most social systems. As systems move toward greater authoritarian structure, they exert more and more control over any flow of horizontal information. This is done by abolishing institutional forms of free communication among equals and by instilling suspicion of informers, so that people will be restricted in their communication even to friends. Without such communication there can be a great deal of unrest without organized revolt. People cannot organize cooperative efforts when they cannot communicate with one another.

Totalitarian regimes have shown ingenuity in their use of techniques to restrict and direct the flow of information. By blocking out the channels of horizontal communication and other sources of information, they have made their people dependent solely upon communication from above. This channelling works to strengthen the hierarchical structure, but in modern society it is impossible to maintain such tight control of the communication processes over time.

Communication upward

Communication up the line takes many forms. It can be reduced, however, to what the person says (1) about himself, his performance, and his problems, (2) about others and their problems, (3) about organizational practices and policies, and (4) about what needs to be done and how it can be done. Thus the subordinate can report to his boss about what he has done, what those under him have done, what his peers have done, what he thinks needs to be done, his problems and the problems of his unit, and about matters of organizational practice and policy. He can seek clarification about general goals and specific directives. He may under certain circumstances bypass his own superior and report directly to a higher level. Or he can utilize the suggestion system of the company (an approved institutional method of bypassing). Grievance procedures represent another institutional pattern of getting problems referred to a higher level. In addition, systematic feedback and research may develop as formal processes in the system. They constitute such an important form of communication about organizational functioning that they will be considered in a separate section of this chapter.

The basic problem in upward communication is the nature of the hierarchical administrative structure. The first role requirement of people in executive and supervisory positions is to direct, coordinate and control the people below them. They themselves are less in the habit of listening to their subordinates than in telling them. The subordinates also fall into this role pattern and expect to listen to their bosses rather than be listened to. Moreover, information fed up the line is often utilized for control purposes. Hence there are great constraints on free upward communication. The boss is not likely to be given information by his subordinates which will lead to decisions affecting them adversely. It is not only that they tell the boss what he wants to hear, but what they want him to know. People do want to get certain information up the line, but generally they are afraid of presenting it to the most relevant person or in the most objective form. Full and objective reporting might be penalized by the supervisor or regarded as espionage by peers. To these difficulties must be added the fact that full and objective reporting is difficult, regardless of the organizational situation; no individual is an objective observer of his own performance and problems.

For all these reasons the upward flow of communication in organizations is not noted for spontaneous and full expression, despite attempts to institutionalize the process of feedback up the line. Suggestions for improvement of work procedures and company practices are also limited in quantity and quality in most organizations. The more top-heavy the organizational structure and the more control is exercised through pressure and sanctions, the less adequate will be the flow of information up the line. It is not a matter of changing the communication habits of individuals, but of changing the organizational conditions responsible for them.

The typical upward communication loop is small and terminates with the immediate supervisor. He may transmit some of the information to his own superior, but generally in a modified form. The open-door policy of some high-level officers extends the theoretical size of the circuit to include all levels below them. It generally contributes more to the self-image of the officer as an understanding, democratic person, however, than to adequacy of information exchange. The closed nature of the upward circuits has already been indicated and resides both in the restricted communication passed upward and in the limited codes of the recipients.

Obstacles to vertical communication occur in both industrial organizations and democratic structures. Labor unions, in which the membership possesses the formal power to elect officers and command referenda on basic issues, manifest striking gaps in understanding between top echelons and local leaders closer to the rank and file. In the fall of 1964 officials of the United Auto Workers concluded negotiations for a contract with General Motors and were ready to announce the outcome as a main accomplishment, only to have the pact rejected by their local unions. The top leaders were apparently not in effective communication with lower levels of leadership and the rank and file.

The Longshoremen's Union came to terms with shipping companies in January 1965 in a contract which the top union people regarded as favorable. It was promptly rejected by the membership. The officials responded with all sorts of measures to reach their men by way of the mass media and by a broadside of letters. In other words, the information channels between leaders and membership were closed over before and during the contract negotiations and the public demonstration of this phenomenon led to desperate efforts on the part of officials to restore communication. It is typical that the attempted solution was not only delayed, but took the form of communication *downward*.

Asymmetry of communication needs and communication flow

There are no studies of the distinctive types of communication which characteristically flow horizontally, upward or downward in organizations, although such research is much needed. The information requirements of superior and subordinate are not symmetrical. What the superior wants to know is often not what the subordinate wants to tell him; what the subordinate wants to know is not necessarily the message the superior wants to send. The greater the conflict between the communication needs of these two hierarchically situated senders and recipients of information, the more likely is an increase in lateral communication. Among peers there will be greater complementarity of information needs. Where a foreman finds little reception from his superior, he will readily turn to fellow foremen to talk about his problems. Horizontal exchange can be an escape valve for frustration in communicating upward and downward; and sometimes it can operate to accomplish some of the essential business of the organization.

Another type of communication flow, thus far not considered, is criss-crossing, in which a subordinate in one unit talks to the boss of another unit or vice-versa. Again, this process is furthered by blockages in communication up and down the line. A department head perceived as a sympathetic person may be sought out by people in other departments as an audience for their problems because they feel they cannot talk to their own department head. [...]

The organizational locus of informational sub-systems

Informational processes can have their primary locus at any level in the organization or in any one of its sub-structures. Operational feedback is received first by the appropriate operating unit and then filtered up the line as overall summaries of operations at each level to the managerial level just above. Thus the head of each production unit knows the number of pieces turned out by his unit at the end of a given time-period. The superintendent of production has summary figures for all the units reporting to him, and he again makes a summary for the echelons above him.

Since this kind of feedback is tied closely to actual operations, little distortion is possible over time, though some filtering may result in an oversimplified picture at top levels. The units with poor records may not be pinpointed in average figures covering all units. Interpretations of these figures may be supplied by the heads of units or divisions, but such interpretations tend to be coded by their transmitters as favorable to their own way of operating. If the forge shop is below expectations in productivity for any given month, the head of the forge shop will furnish reasons which do not suggest poor management on his part. He may assert that the materials were not up to par or absenteeism due to illness was great. But the major distortion is probably not the defensive explanation; it is the selective bias of each unit head, who will utilize as his basis of judgment the specific frame of reference of the operations in which he is daily involved.

Operational research is generally geared into some part of the production system. Its reports, however, can go beyond the production system to top management. Since the changes its information may suggest for organizational functioning require some degree of acceptance by the production structure, there is some advantage to tying operational research closely to the operations under investigation. A common procedure is to have the group conducting the operational research report to one level higher than the specific operation being researched. This helps to protect its results from being ignored.

Information, however, that has direct relevance for system functioning, as in all cases of systemic research, should be reported to top management. This is even true of market research, which is often placed very low in the sales structure. The locus of market research thus does not provide the organization with information about the success of its product. Rather, it supplies the sales department with ideas for promotional campaigns. What may be necessary for organizational success is an actual change in product. This cannot be achieved through a research unit serving the sales department, since the function of the sales department is to sell what is being produced, and not to tell the production people what to produce. The information of the market research unit follows the general principle of being coded by the sales department as sales information, and it fails to be coded with its proper implications for the production structure.

Another common failing is to assign to a given sub-structure whose primary function is non-informational the secondary mission of providing information about the relations of the organization with the external world. The primary task determines the types of information which will be received and its mode of processing. For example, the State Department has traditionally utilized its diplomatic personnel abroad to report on the political, economic, social and psychological conditions of the foreign country. In their primary roles as diplomats, State Department personnel move in very limited circles; they meet primarily with their counterparts in the diplomatic corps of that nation. They are not necessarily expert in the subject about which information is sought; they seldom have training or knowledge of research procedures; and their major motivation is to carry out their function in the implementation of State Department policy. It is no wonder then that we have been consistently misinformed about the structures of foreign countries and the prevailing currents within them. Reliance upon the impressions of exclusively upper-class informants, refugees from disaffected elements and émigrés from dispossessed groups has aggravated the problem. A reverse situation occurred in the Cuban fiasco in which the Central Intelligence Agency, supposedly an information structure, became absorbed in overthrowing the Castro regime rather than in obtaining accurate information about it. In both cases, however, we are dealing with closed intelligence circuits which are not open to relevant information.

Two points are involved in the above examples. One concerns the necessity of a system of information with its own staff to carry on its own function and develop its own norms, standards and expertness. The other concerns the place in the system to which intelligence should be reported.

The first problem has so far been presented as if there were only one answer. When information concerning the system as a whole and its relations to its environment is involved, there are genuine advantages in a sub-system which has this information-gathering as its major responsibility. This can mean that specialized expertness is made possible, that the coding limitations of an irrelevant function are obviated, and that standards of accurate prediction and valid assessment develop as in a scientific-research organization.

These advantages do not inevitably follow. The major values of the system still operate to affect the sub-system; directives of top management control the freedom of the sub-system and may indicate receptivity to only certain types of information. Cigarette manufacturers, for example, could set up a research agency reporting to top management with the task of investigating the relationship of cigarette smoking to lung cancer, heart disease and related health problems. They could hire competent researchers (though perhaps not top scientists) with an adequate budget to pursue a research program. It is not likely, however, that the researchers would furnish top management unambiguous reports on the injurious effects of the use of tobacco and recommendations that the company change its goals and turn to the use of nicotine as a poison against insects or some such alternative.

To avoid the corruption of information by the system of which it is a part, it is necessary to guarantee to the researcher within an organization some of the same freedoms he would enjoy in a university setting. Some of the big electric and utility companies have actually done this in the natural sciences, and the resulting discoveries have more than justified the policy. With the exception of one or two token units, no industrial concern has ever done this in the social sciences even though it is in this area that management needs information most desperately. One type of freedom absolutely essential for such research is that the directives of top management do not pose specific questions they want answered. General problem areas can be indicated, but once the lines of inquiry are restricted in particularistic fashion, we are back to a closed system of intelligence. Answers are easily predetermined by the questions asked, especially when these questions originate at the top of a power structure. This applies both to an intelligence system which is conducting basic research and to one which is gathering information at a more descriptive level. A narrow definition of the mission of an information-gathering agency means that the answers it furnishes will also be extremely limited and frequently erroneous.

Another means by which an organization can avoid corrupting or being corrupted by its own information service is the astute use of multiple channels as check procedures. Multiple channels, if based upon the same sources of information, can merely duplicate error. But they can be set up so as to utilize various sources of information and process it in similar enough fashion to produce a consistent or inconsistent picture for decision makers.

The problem of the latitude to be permitted to an intelligence operation is an extremely difficult one for top management. On the one hand, the organization needs useful information, and if it gives researchers a completely free hand, the relevance of their findings for organizational functioning is not ensured. To this rational consideration is added the irrational fear of the incomprehensible techniques and language of a suspect group of 'longhairs'. On the other hand, there is not much advantage to management in setting up an intelligence agency if it merely reflects management's coding processes.

The critical question is whether the task of the intelligence or research unit is system research or operational research. If the former is the case, then management has to be able to tolerate the differences in values, methods and approach of specialists in information-gathering. In fact, these differences are among the major reasons for hiring specialists. Some restriction on their activities can nevertheless be imposed in terms of the general objectives assigned to them. And even if no specific and immediate answers are demanded, over time the information agency must provide some useful information to the organization or forfeit its right to organizational support. An important factor working toward organizational control of information specialists (and often working too well) is the natural tendency for specialists to take on the coloration of the system and behave too much as conforming members rather than as objective outsiders.

Outside research agencies are occasionally called in to provide the types of information which organizational leaders think cannot be readily supplied by their own personnel. The more research-oriented outside agencies will seek to obtain a broader definition of the problem than management generally presents. In other words, the tendency of organizational leaders is to narrow the problem to the visible and troublesome symptoms, whereas adequate intelligence about it has to probe into the causes. The process of redefining the problem for management is often easier for the outside group than for the captive agency.

The question of the optimal place for reporting the results of systemic research becomes complicated in large organizations. Though top echelons should be the recipients of information about the functioning of the total system, it is difficult for them to find the time to take adequate note of it, let alone absorb it and give it some weight in their decisions. Hence there is generally more relevant information in an organization than its top leaders utilize. Several changes are necessary in organizational structure to achieve reform in this respect. One is the elevation of the head of the information agency in status, so that he not only reports to top levels but also can command a hearing when he and his aides believe they have some vital intelligence. The second is the perfecting of translation mechanisms, so that critical pieces of information can be transmitted up the line in the information agency itself and finally to the top echelons of the organization.

A third is the restructuring of the top jobs to reduce the component of routine administration; this will not guarantee the acquisition and use of systemic information, but it will have a powerful facilitating effect.

References

DUBIN, R. (1959), 'Stability of human organizations', in M. Haire (ed.) *Modern Organization Theory*, Wiley.

GUETZKOW, H., and DILL, W. R. (1957), 'Factors in the organizational development of task-oriented groups', *Sociometry*, vol. 20, pp. 175–204.

GUETZKOW, H., and SIMON, H. A. (1955), 'The impact of certain communication nets upon organization and performance in task-oriented groups', *Manag. Sci.*, vol. 1, no. 1, pp. 233–50.

HEISE, G. A., and MILLER, G. A. (1951), 'Problem solving by small groups using various communication nets', *J. abnorm. soc. Psychol.*, vol. 46, pp. 327–35.

KATZ, E., and LAZARSFELD, P. (1955), *Personal Influence: The Part Played by People in the Flow of Mass Communication*, Free Press.

LEAVITT, H. J. (1951), 'Some effects of certain communication patterns of group performance', *J. abnorm. soc. Psychol.*, vol. 46, pp. 38–50.

3 D. R. Daniel

Management Information Crisis

D. R. Daniel, 'Management information crisis', *Harvard Business Review*, vol. 39, 1961, pp. 111-21.

In late 1960 a large defence contractor became concerned over a major project that was slipping badly. After fifteen months costs were running far above the estimate and the job was behind schedule. A top-level executive, assigned as program manager to salvage the project, found he had no way of pinpointing what parts of the system were causing the trouble, why costs were so high, and which subcontractors were not performing.

Recently an American electronics company revamped its organization structure. To compete more aggressively in international markets, management appointed 'area managers' with operating responsibility – e.g. in Latin America, Western Europe and the Far East. After nine months it was apparent that the new plan was not coming up to expectations. On checking with three newly created area managers, the company president heard each say, in effect:

In half of the countries in my area the political situation is in flux, and I can't anticipate what's going to happen next.

I'm still trying to find out whether our operating costs in Austria are reasonable.

I don't know where in South America we're making a profit.

A small but highly successful consumer products company recently followed the lead of its larger competitors by establishing product-manager positions. Although outstanding men were placed in the new jobs, an air of general confusion soon developed, and the product managers began to show signs of frustration. After much study it became apparent that an important cause of the trouble was that no one had determined what kind of information the product managers would need in order to perform their new functions.

In retrospect it is obvious that these three companies were plagued by a common problem: inadequate management information. The data were inadequate, not in the sense of there not being enough, but in terms of relevancy for setting objectives, for shaping alternative strategies, for making decisions, and for measuring results against planned goals.

Assessing the gap

In each company the origin of the problem lay in the gap between a static information system and a changing organization structure. This difficulty is not new or uncommon. There is hardly a major company in the United States whose plan of organization has not been changed and rechanged since the Second World War. And with revised structures have come new jobs, new responsibilities, new decision-making authorities, and reshaped reporting relationships. All of these factors combine to create new demands for information – information that is usually missing in existing systems. As a result, many leading companies are suffering a major information crisis – often without fully realizing it.

Far-reaching trends

Some idea of the scope of this problem can be gained by reviewing the intensity of the three major causes of recent organization changes in American business:

Growth. Since 1945 the Gross National Product has risen 135 per cent. In specific industries the growth rate has been even greater. Plastic production, for example, tripled between 1948 and 1958; electronics sales nearly quadrupled in the decade from 1950 to 1960. Many individual companies have shown even more startling growth. This growth, in turn, has fostered organizational change:

1. Divisions have been created and decentralization has been encouraged.

2. Greater precision in defining line-staff relationships has been necessitated.

3. Organization structures that were once adequate for fifty-million-dollar businesses have proved unworkable for five hundred-million-dollar enterprises.

Diversification. Merger and acquisition have accounted for the growth of many large organizations. For these companies, the task of finding, evaluating and consummating diversification deals – and assimilating newly acquired products and businesses – has required continuous organizational adjustment. Some corporations have diversified by developing new product lines to satisfy shifting market requirements; some have used other means. But always the effect has been the same: different organization structures for parts of or perhaps for the entire enterprise.

International operations. There has been a three fold increase in the value of United States investments abroad since the Second World War. Major companies that once regarded foreign markets as minor sources of incremental profits, or as markets for surplus production, now look overseas for the bulk of their future profits and growth. They are setting up manufacturing and research as well as marketing organizations in foreign countries. Consequently, we are growing used to seeing a company's 'export department' evolve into the 'international division', and national companies grow into world-wide enterprises (see Clee and di Scipio, 1959). All this calls for extensive modifications of organization structure.

The impact of any one of the above factors alone would be sufficient to create great change in an enterprise, but consider that in many cases at least two, and sometimes all three, have been at work. It is easy to see why so many company organization structures do become unstable and how this creates a management information problem large enough to hamper some firms and nearly paralyse others.

Linking systems and needs

Organization structure and information requirements are inextricably linked. In order to translate a statement of his duties into action, an executive must receive and use information. Information in this case is not just the accounting system and the forms and reports it produces. It includes *all* the data and intelligence – financial and non-financial – that are really needed to plan, operate and control a particular enterprise. This embraces external information such as economic and political factors and data on competitive activity.

When viewed in this light, the impact of organization structure on needs for management information becomes apparent. The trouble is that in most companies it is virtually taken for granted that the information necessary for performance of a manager's duties flows naturally to the job. To a certain extent this is so. For example, internally generated information – especially accounting information – does tend to flow easily to the job or can be made to do so. Also, in companies doing business in only one industry and having a small, closely knit management group much vital interdepartmental and general information is conveyed by frequent face-to-face contact and coordination among executives. Economic and competitive information from outside is similarly transmitted, the bulk of it coming into the concern informally. Further, through trade contacts, general reading and occasional special studies, executives toss bits of information into the common pool and draw from it as well.

The point is, however, that while such an informal system can work well for small and medium-size companies in simple and relatively static industries, it becomes inadequate when companies grow larger and especially when they spread over several industries, areas and countries. At this point, most large companies have found that information has to be conveyed in a formal manner and less and less through direct observation.

Unfortunately, management often loses sight of the seemingly obvious and simple relationship between organization structure and information needs. Companies very seldom follow up on reorganizations with penetrating reappraisals of their information systems, and managers given new responsibilities and decision-making authority often do not receive all the information they require.

Causes of confusion

The cornerstone for building a compact, useful management information system is the determination of each executive's information needs. This requires a clear grasp of the individual's role in the organization – his responsibilities, his authorities, and his relationships with other executives. The task is then to:

1. Design a network of procedures that will process raw data in such a way as to generate the information required for management use.

2. Implement such procedures in actual practice.

Such action steps, while demanding and time-consuming, have proved to be far less difficult than the creative and conceptual first step of defining information requirements. Seldom is the open approach of asking an executive what information he requires successful. For one thing, he may find it difficult to be articulate because the organization structure of his company is not clearly defined.

Further, and more important, there is a widespread tendency among operating executives to think of information exclusively in terms of their companies' accounting systems and the reports thus generated. This way of thinking can be a serious deterrent because:

1. Many conventional accounting reports cause confusion in the minds of non-financially trained executives. Take, for example, the profit-and-loss statement, with its arbitrary treatment of inventories, depreciation, allocated overhead expenses and the like, or the statistical sales report, which is often a forty-page, untitled, machine-prepared tabulation of sales to individual customers. Such reports have made an indelible impression on managers' thinking, coloring their understanding and expectations of reports in general.

2. By its very nature traditional accounting fails to highlight many important aspects of business operations. Accounting systems often are designed primarily to meet SEC, Internal Revenue and other statutory requirements – requirements that, more often than not, fail to correspond to management's information needs. Accounting describes the past in dollars, usually without discriminating between the critical and non-critical elements of a business – the elements that control competitive success in a particular industry and the elements that do not.

3. Accounting reports generally describe what has happened inside a company. Just consider what this approach omits:

(a) Information about the future.

(b) Data expressed in non-financial terms – e.g. share of market, productivity, quality levels, adequacy of customer service and so on.

(c) Information dealing with external conditions as they might bear on a particular company's operations.

Yet all of these items are essential to the intelligent managing of a business.

Planning needs defined

The key to the development of a dynamic and usable system of management information is to move beyond the limits of classical accounting reports and to conceive of information as it relates to two vital elements of the management process – planning and control. In the pages to follow I shall focus largely on the planning aspect.

We hear more and more these days about new techniques for inventory, cost and other types of control, but information systems for business planning still represent a relatively unexplored horizon.

Planning, as used in this article, means: setting objectives, formulating strategy and deciding among alternative investments or courses of action. This definition can be applied to an entire company, an integrated division or a single operating department.

As Figure 1 shows, the information required to do planning of this kind is of three basic types:

1. *Environmental information.* Describes the social, political and economic aspects of the climate in which a business operates or may operate in the future.

2. *Competitive information.* Explains the past performance, programs and plans of competing companies.

3. *Internal information.* Indicates a company's own strengths and weaknesses.

Now let us consider each of these categories in some detail.

information | **management functions** | **information**

environmental data
competitive data
internal data

planning
- set objectives
- formulate strategy
- decide among alternative investments

execution

control
- measure performance
- isolate variances
- aid in replanning

financial data
- marketing
- manufacturing
- research and development
- personnel

non-financial data
- marketing
- manufacturing
- research and development
- personnel

feedback

information system characteristics

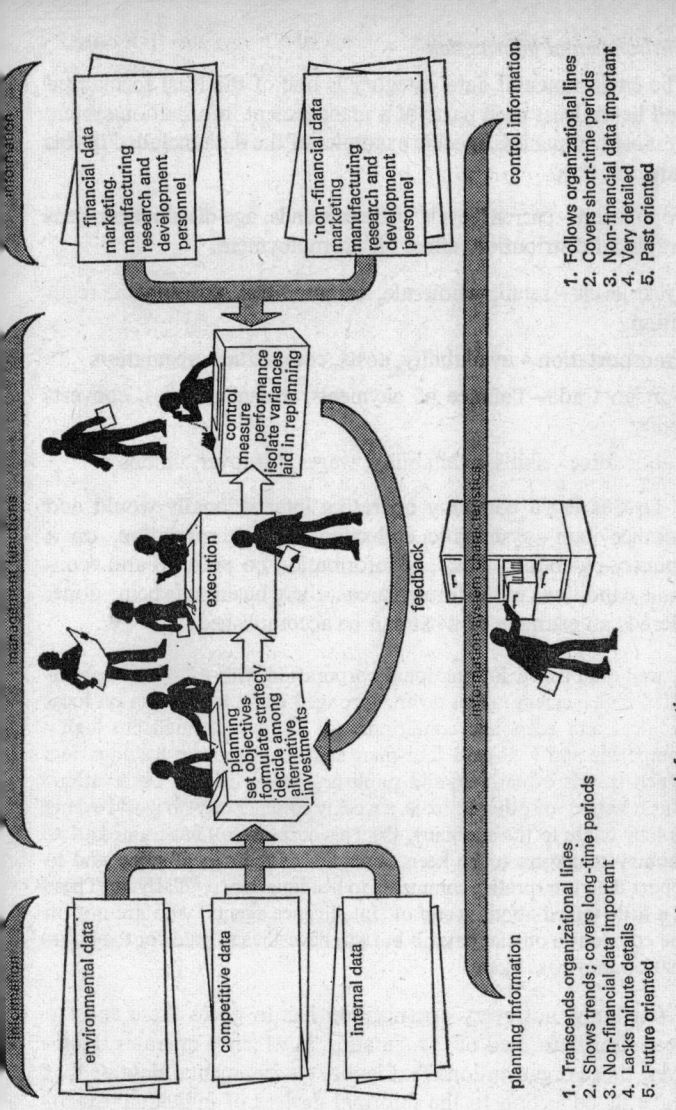

planning information
1. Transcends organizational lines
2. Shows trends; covers long-time periods
3. Non-financial data important
4. Lacks minute details
5. Future oriented

control information
1. Follows organizational lines
2. Covers short-time periods
3. Non-financial data important
4. Very detailed
5. Past oriented

Figure 1 Anatomy of management information

Environmental information

The environmental data category is one of the least formalized and hence least used parts of a management information system in most companies. Specific examples of the data included in this category are:

Population – current levels, growth trends, age distribution, geographical distribution, effect on unemployment.

Price levels – retail, wholesale, commodities, government regulation.

Transportation – availability, costs, competition, regulation.

Foreign trade – balance of payments, exchange rates, convertibility.

Labor force – skills, availability, wages, turnover, unions.

To this list a company operating internationally would add another item – systematic collection and interpretation, on a country-by-country basis, of information on political and economic conditions in the foreign areas where business is being done. Here is an example of what can be accomplished:

A well-established international corporation with a highly sophisticated management makes a three-pronged effort to get data on local political and economic conditions. (a) There is a small but highly competent and well-paid four-man staff at corporate headquarters which travels extensively and publishes, using its own observations plus a variety of other sources, a weekly commentary on world events as they relate to the company. (b) This corporation has trained all its country managers to be keen observers of their local scene and to report their interpretive comments to headquarters regularly. (c) There is a little-talked-about group of 'intelligence agents' who are not on the company's official payroll but are nevertheless paid for the information they pass along.

Certainly, not every organization has to go to these ends to keep itself informed of the situation in which it operates. However, those organizations that ignore environmental data or that leave its collection to the informal devices of individual executives are inviting trouble. Those companies that are knowledgeable concerning their environment are almost always in tune with the times and ahead of their competition. For example:

1. Good intelligence on the sociological changes taking place in the United States led several heavy manufacturing companies to enter the 'leisure-time' field with a great deal of success.

2. Insight into the possible impact of foreign labor costs on parts of the electronics industry caused some US corporations to acquire their own manufacturing facilities abroad. As a result, the firms were able not only to protect their domestic markets but also to open up profitable operations overseas.

3. Knowledge of trends in age distribution in the United States added to an awareness of the rate of change of scientific learning provides ample proof for some firms of the desirability of being in the educational publishing field for the next decade.

To be of real use, environmental data must indicate trends; population figures, balance-of-payment data or political shifts are of little significance when shown for one period because they do not help management make *analytical* interpretations.

The collection and transmission of good environmental data are often problematical. Even in the United States some kinds of information are not readily available and must be pieced together from several sources or acquired *sub rosa* from officially inaccessible sources. Transmitting environmental data, particularly political information, is so awkward that sometimes the data collector must sit down personally with those who need to know the information.

In sum, environmental data are an aspect of planning information that requires more attention and warrants formalization, especially in large geographically dispersed companies. The emergence of the corporate economics department (Teitsworth, 1959; Arthur, 1961) is one development that could lead to better results in this area, but it is my impression that so far the progress of these units has been uneven.

Competitive information

Data on competition comprise the second category of planning information. There are three important types to consider:

1. *Past performance*. This includes information on the profitability, return on investment, share of market and so forth of competing companies. Such information is primarily useful in identifying one's competitors. It also is one benchmark when setting company objectives.

2. *Present activity*. This category covers new product introductions, management changes, price strategy and so on – all current developments. Good intelligence on such matters can materially influence a company's planning; for example, it may lead to accelerating research programs, modifying advertising strategy or switching distribution channels. The implication here is not that a company's plans should always be defensive and prompted by a competitor's moves but simply that anything important a competitor does should be recognized and factored into the planning process.

3. *Future plans*. This includes information on acquisition intentions, facility plans and research and development efforts.

Competitive information, like environmental data, is an infrequently formalized part of a company's total information system. And so there seldom is a concerted effort to collect this kind of material, to process it and to report it to management regularly. But some interesting exceptions to this general lack of concern exist:

Oil companies have long employed 'scouts' in their land departments. These men report on acreage purchases, drilling results, and other competitive activity that may be pertinent to the future actions of their own company.

Business machine companies have 'competitive equipment evaluation personnel' who continually assess the technical features of competitors' hardware.

Retail organizations employ 'comparison shoppers' who appraise the prices and quality of merchandise in competitive stores.

Commercial intelligence departments are appearing more and more on corporate organization charts. An excerpt from the charter of one such group states its basic responsibility thus:

To seek out, collect, evaluate, and report information covering the past performance and future plans of competitors in such a manner that the information will have potential utility in strategic and operational planning of the corporation. This means that in addition to reporting factual information, emphasis should be on determining the implications of such information for the corporation.

Internal information

The third and final basic category of planning information is made up of internal data. As it relates to the total planning process, internal data are aimed at identifying a company's strengths and weaknesses – the characteristics that, when viewed in the perspective of the general business environment and in the light of competitive activity, should help management to shape its future plans. It is useful to think of internal data as being of three types:

1. *Quantitative-financial* – e.g. sales, costs and cost behavior relative to volume changes.

2. *Quantitative-physical* – e.g. share of market, productivity, delivery performance and manpower resources.

3. *Non-quantitative* – e.g. community standing and labor reations.

In reporting internal data, a company's information system must be discriminating and selective. It should focus on 'success factors'. In most industries there are usually three to six factors that determine success; these key jobs must be done exceedingly well for a company to be successful. Here are some examples from several major industries:

1. In the automobile industry, styling, an efficient dealer organization and tight control of manufacturing costs are paramount.

2. In food processing, new product development, good distribution and effective advertising are the major success factors.

3. In life insurance, the development of agency management personnel, effective control of clerical personnel and innovation in creating new types of policies spell the difference.

The companies which have achieved the greatest advances in information analysis have consistently been those which have developed systems that have been selective and focused on the company's strengths and weaknesses with respect to its acknowledged success factors. By doing this, the managements have generated the kind of information that is most useful in capitalizing on strengths and correcting weaknesses. For example; an oil company devised a system of regularly reporting its 'finding' costs – those costs incurred in exploring for new reserves of oil divided by the number of barrels of oil found. When this ratio trended upward beyond an established point, it was a signal to the company's management to consider the acquisition of other oil companies (together with their proved reserves) as a less expensive alternative to finding oil through its own exploratory efforts.

In the minds of most executives the accounting system exists primarily to meet the company's internal data needs; yet this is often an unreasonable and unfulfilled expectation. Accounting reports rarely focus on success factors that are non-financial in nature. Moreover, accounting practices with respect to allocation of expenses, transfer prices and the like, often tend to obscure rather than clarify the underlying strengths and weaknesses of a company. This inadequacy should not be surprising since the *raison d'être* of many accounting systems is not to facilitate planning but rather to ensure the fulfilment of management's responsibility to the stockholders, the government and other groups.

Tailoring the requirements

If a company is to have a comprehensive, integrated system of information to support its planning process, it will need a set of management reports that regularly covers the three basic categories of planning data – i.e. environmental, competitive and internal. The amount of data required in each area will naturally vary from company to company and will depend on such factors as the nature of the industry, the size and operating territory of the company, and the acceptance by management of planning as an essential function. However, it is important in every case for management to *formalize* and *regularize* the collection, transmission, processing and presentation of planning information; the data are too vital to be ignored or taken care of by occasional 'special studies'. It is no accident that many of the most successful companies in this country are characterized by well-developed planning information systems.

What is gained if such an approach is taken? What difference does it make in operations? We do not need to conjecture to answer these questions; we can turn to concrete company experience. For instance, Figure 2 illustrates how the information used by the marketing department of an oil company changed as a result of a thorough study of the information needed to formulate effective plans. In this instance, the study indicated an increase in the data required by the vice-president and his staff. (However, this result is not inevitable; it holds only for this particular situation. In other circumstances reviews of this kind have led to significant *cutbacks* in information.)

Several points should be noted in examining Figure 2:

1. The information shown is not all for the *personal* use of the vice-president, although much of it is generated and used in his field.

2. For simplicity, most of the information listed in the exhibit was presented to company executives in graphic form.

3. The exhibit highlights only the reports used for retail gasoline marketing; omitted are fuel oil marketing, commercial and industrial marketing, and other topics which the new reporting system also covered.

Many companies have found that the most effective approach to determining requirements for planning information, whether it be for one executive or an entire company, is to relate the three types of planning data described earlier to the steps in the planning process – i.e. setting objectives, developing strategy and deciding among alternative investments. Thus, one asks himself questions like these:

What political data are needed to set reasonable objectives for this company?

reports formerly used for planning

defects

- division and district expenses
- sales volume by product for divisions and districts
- marketing department profit and loss
- capital budgets by division for five years

- no information on the total market for gasoline and other automotive products — its size, its location, its rate of growth, etc.
- no information on competitors — what they are doing, where, and how well
- marketing 'profit and loss' concept encouraged faulty planning because of arbitrary transfer prices
- no information that discloses the company's marketing strengths and weaknesses by class of trade, e.g. company-owned stations, independent dealers, distributors, etc.
- marketing expense information misleading because of allocations of headquarters' overhead
- inadequate data on size 'mix' of stations, e.g. number and percentage of stations selling different volumes of gasoline
- inadequate data on the sales performance of newly built or acquired stations

environment

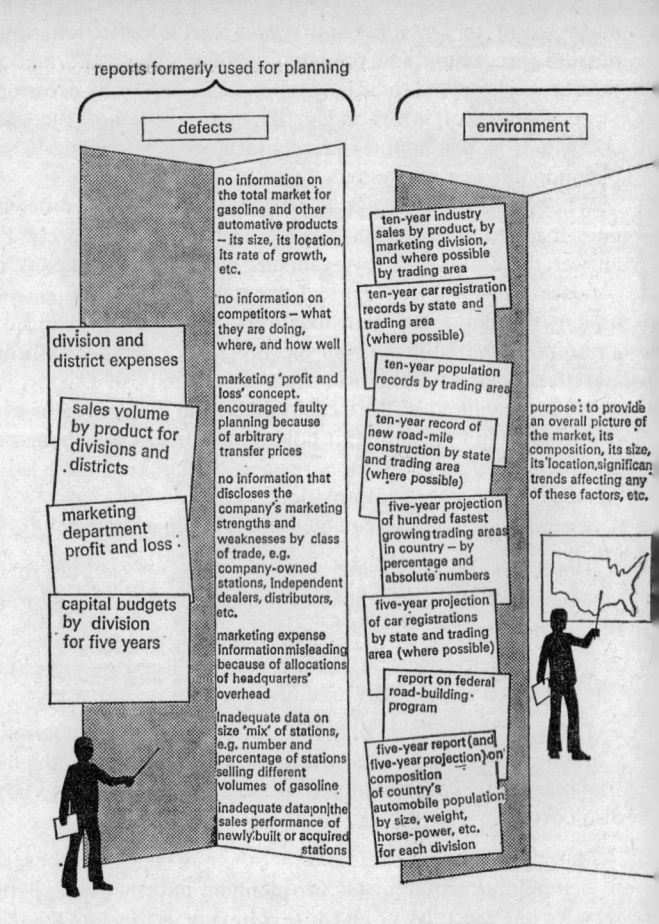

- ten-year industry sales by product, by marketing division, and where possible by trading area
- ten-year car registration records by state and trading area (where possible)
- ten-year population records by trading area
- ten-year record of new road-mile construction by state and trading area (where possible)
- five-year projection of hundred fastest growing trading areas in country — by percentage and absolute numbers
- five-year projection of car registrations by state and trading area (where possible)
- report on federal road-building program
- five-year report (and five-year projection) on composition of country's automobile population by size, weight, horse-power, etc. for each division

purpose: to provide an overall picture of the market, its composition, its size, its location, significant trends affecting any of these factors, etc.

Figure 2 Comparative analysis of marketing planning information

reports used after the management information study

competition

- ten-year share-of-market reports by product, by division, and where possible, by trading area
- special price reports intended to show (a) competitor's price strategy and (b) areas of the country classified by the nature of price conditions — stable, volatile, strong, weak, etc.
- five-year record of new station construction by competition, by division and trading area
- five-year summary of new refinery, terminal, and bulk plant construction by competition
- analysis of hundred largest and hundred fastest growing markets (trading areas) showing leading competitors in terms of volume, market share, laid-down costs, facilities, construction or acquisition activity, etc.
- special reports on key market developments, e.g. re-brander activity, additional qualities of gasoline, multiple octane pumps, etc.

purpose: to identify who competitors are, how well they have been doing, and the likely direction of their future efforts

internal

- five-year sales and realizations by product, by division, by class of trade
- division and district expenses per gallon (without allocation of headquarters' expenses)
- marketing 'net back' statements by product, by division, by district and by bulk plant (realizations less expenses)
- 'laid down' costs by product, by terminal and bulk plant
- frequency distribution studies of gasoline sales by size of retail station, by division and district
- share of company's total sales by product for each state
- five-year report of number of stations by type (owned, leased, etc.) by division and district
- five-year report of capital budgets by division and district (amounts authorized and spent)

purpose: to assess the company strengths and weaknesses, thus permitting a correlation between the company's capabilities and the opportunities of the market place

What sociological and economic data about the areas in which this company operates are needed to formulate new product strategy?

What competitive intelligence is necessary to develop share-of-market objectives?

What internal cost information is needed to choose between alternative facility locations?

Contrast with control

In Figure 1 I have listed the five principal characteristics of planning data compared with the characteristics of control data. Note that in all but one case (non-financial information) they are different. It is most important to keep these differences in mind, lest the 'fuel' for the planning system be confused with the 'fuel' for the control system, and vice versa. Hence, I should like to emphasize the contrasts here:

1. *Coverage.* Good planning information is not compartmentalized by functions. Indeed, it seeks to transcend the divisions that exist in a company and to provide the basis on which *integrated* plans can be made. In contrast, control information hews closely to organizational lines so that it can be used to measure performance and help in holding specific managers more accountable.

2. *Length of time.* Planning information covers fairly long periods of time – months and years rather than days and weeks – and deals with trends. Thus, although it should be regularly prepared, it is not developed as frequently as control information.

3. *Degree of detail.* Excessive detail is the quicksand of intelligent planning. Unlike control, where precision and minute care do have a place, planning (and particularly long-range planning) focuses on the major outlines of the situation ahead. In the words of two authorities, Root and Steiner:

The further out in time the planning, the less certain one can be about the precision of numbers. As a basic principle in planning it is understood that, in the longer range, details merge into trends and patterns (1958).

4. *Orientation.* Planning information should provide insights into the future. Control information shows past results and the reasons for them.

Future developments

The heightened interest of management in its information crisis is already unmistakable. Dean Stanley F. Teele of the Harvard Business School, writing on the process of change in the years ahead, states:

> I think the capacity to manage knowledge will be still more important to the manager.... The manager will need to increase his skill in deciding what knowledge he needs (1960).

Ralph Cordiner of General Electric Company in his book, *New Frontiers for Professional Managers*, writes:

> It is an immense problem to organize and communicate the information required to operate a large, decentralized organization....
>
> What is required ... is a ... penetrating and orderly study of the business in its entirety to discover what specific information is needed at each particular position in view of the decisions to be made there ... (1956, p. 102).

Invariably, increasing attention of leaders in education and industry precedes and prepares the way for frontal attacks on business problems. In many organizations the initial reaction to the management information problem is first evidenced by a concern over 'the flood of paper work'. Eventually, the problem itself is recognized – i.e. the need to define concisely the information required for intelligent planning and control of a business.

Following this awakening interest in business information problems, we are likely to see the acceleration of two developments already in view: improved techniques relating to the creation and operation of total information systems, and new organizational approaches to resolving information problems.

Improved techniques

While the crisis in management information has been growing, tools that may be useful in its solution have been under development. For example, the evolution of electronic data-processing systems, the development of supporting communications networks, and the formulation of rigorous mathematical solutions to business problems have provided potentially valuable tools to help management attack its information problems. Specifically, progress on three fronts is an encouraging indication that this kind of approach will prove increasingly fruitful:

1. Managements of most companies are far more conversant with both the capabilities and the limitations of computer systems than they were five years ago. This growing understanding has done much to separate fact from fancy. One key result should be the increasing application of electronic data-processing concepts to the more critical, less routine problems of business.

2. Computer manufacturers and communications companies are learning the worth of their products. They show signs of recognizing that it is not hardware but an information system which is extremely valuable in helping to solve management's problems.

3. Significant improvements have been made in the techniques of harnessing computers. Advances in automatic programming and developments in creating a common business language are gratifying evidence that the gap is being narrowed between the technical potential of the hardware and management's ability to exploit it.

Organizational moves

The development of new organizational approaches is less obvious. Earlier in this article I noted that progress in the systematic collection and reporting of information dealing with a company's environment or with its competitive situation has been slow, and traditional accounting reports are often inadequate in providing the data needed for business planning. These conditions may result from a very basic cause; namely, that most organization structures do not pin down the responsibility for management information systems and tie it to specific executive positions. Controllers and other financial officers usually have been assigned responsibility for *accounting* information – but this, of course, does not meet the total need.

Nowhere has the absence of one person having specific and *total* responsibility for management information systems had a more telling effect than in defence contractor companies. In such organizations the usual information problems have been compounded by the rapid rate of technological advance and its attendant effect upon product obsolescence, and also by the requirement for 'concurrency', which means that a single product or product complex is developed, tested, produced and installed simultaneously. Under these conditions, some companies have been nearly paralysed by too much of the wrong information.

Having recognized this problem, several corporations have attacked it by creating full-time management information departments. These groups are responsible for:

1. Identifying the information needs for all levels of management for both planning and control purposes. As prerequisites to this responsibility it is necessary to define the authority and duties of each manager, and determine the factors that really contribute to competitive success in the particular business in question.

2. Developing the necessary systems to fulfill these information needs.

3. Operating the data-processing equipment necessary to generate the information which is required.

To some extent these departments, reporting high in the corporate structure, have impinged on responsibilities traditionally assigned to the accounting organization since they are concerned with financial as well as non-financial information. But to me this overlapping is inevitable, particularly in companies where the financial function operates under a narrow perspective and a preoccupation with accountancy. The age of the information specialist is nearing, and its arrival is inextricably tied in with the emergence of some of the newer tools of our management sciences. This notion is not far removed from the concept of Leavitt and Whisler, who foresee the evolution of information technology and the creation of a 'programming elite' (1958).

Conclusion

The day when management information departments are as common as controller's departments is still years away. But this should not rule out concerted efforts to improve a company's information system. In fact, I would expect many broad-gauged controller's organizations to assume the initiative in their companies for such programs.

To this end, the nine questions listed below are for the executive to ask himself as a guide to assessing the improvement potential in his organization's planning information. If the answers to these questions tend to be negative, the chances are strong that changes are in order.

1. Does your company regularly collect and analyse information about population, price level and other important trends affecting the general picture of business?

2. If it does, are such analyses reported to operating management in a manner that permits their utilization in the planning process?

3. Does your company regularly collect and analyse significant information about competititors?

4. Is this information effectively 'factored into' the planning process?

5. How good are your internal data for planning purposes?

6. Do you know in what products and in what geographic areas you are making profits?

7. Do you know how your costs behave in response to volume changes?

8. Are the factors that condition success in your business explicitly stated and widely communicated in the management group?

9. Has your company's organization structure remained unchanged during the past fifteen years?

The impact of the information crisis on the executive will be significant. To an increasing extent, a manager's effectiveness will hinge on the quality and completeness of the facts that flow to him and on his skill in using them. With technology changing at a rapid rate, with the time dimension becoming increasingly critical, and with organizations becoming larger, more diversified in product lines, and more dispersed geographically, it is inevitable that executives will rely more and more on formally presented information in managing their businesses.

What is more, some organizations are concluding that the easiest and most effective way to influence executive action is to control the flow of information into managerial positions. This notion holds that the discipline of information can be a potent factor in determining just what an executive can and cannot do – what decisions he can make, what plans he can draw up, what corrective steps he can take.

To the extent that this is true, information systems may be increasingly used to mold and shape executive behavior. Better data handling might well become a substitute for much of the laborious shuffling and reshuffling of positions and lines of authority that now goes on. Most reorganizations seek to alter the way certain managers or groups of managers operate. But simply drawing new organization charts and rewriting job descriptions seldom ensure the implementation of new concepts and relationships. The timing, content and format of the information provided to management, however, *can* be a strong influence in bringing about such purposeful change.

Thus, developments in management information systems will affect the executive in two ways. Not only will the new concepts influence what he is able to do, but they will to a great extent control how well he is able to do it.

References

ARTHUR, H. B. (1961), 'Help from the company economist', *Harvard Bus. Rev.*, vol. 39, no. 5, pp. 80–86.

CLEE, G. H., and DI SCIPIO, A. (1959), 'Creating a *world* enterprise', *Harvard Bus. Rev.*, vol. 37, no. 6, pp. 77–89.

CORDINER, R. (1956), *New Frontiers for Professional Managers*, McGraw-Hill.

LEAVITT, H. J., and WHISLER, T. L. (1958), 'Management in the 1980s', *Harvard Bus. Rev.*, vol. 36, no. 6, pp. 41–8.

ROOT, L. E., and STEINER, G. A. (1958), 'The Lockheed Aircraft Corporation master plan', in D. W. Ewing (ed.), *Planning for Management*, Harper & Row.

TEELE, S. F. (1960), 'Your job and mine', *Harvard Bus. School Bull.*, vol. 36, no. 4, p. 8.

TEITSWORTH, C. S. (1959), 'Growing role of the company economist', *Harvard Bus. Rev.*, vol. 37, no. 1, pp. 97–104.

Part Two
The Design of Management Information Systems

Reading 4 presents a brief, but pungent critique of many primitive management information systems by an experienced management consultant.

Reading 5 consists of the much-discussed (but seldom read) McKinsey Report of 1968. The report confirms the unprofitable nature of many computer systems and provides a lucid summary of what has gone wrong. Lack of top-management involvement, economic feasibility ignored, system designers lacking business background and so on. The report debunks *total* information systems – whatever that much-abused term may mean.

Reading 6 presents an interesting attempt at classifying systems activities into *vertical* and *horizontal* categories. The horizontal category classifies systems activities by type of systems work performed – systems specification, data processing, programming. The vertical category classifies systems work by kind of information handled – financial, personnel, logistic, etc. The author uses this classification to suggest a logical organization of the information handling activity in business.

4 S. A. Spencer

The Dark at the Top of the Stairs

S. A. Spencer, 'The dark at the top of the stairs', *Management Review* vol. 51, 1962, pp. 4–12.

Top managers who are in the dark about things they need to know in order to make intelligent decisions obviously cannot expect to guide the fortunes of their company with any degree of assurance. The fact remains, however, that the information systems on which many companies rely to provide top management with vital facts and figures are inadequate to the task – and, ironically, many executives who fondly believe that they have established a 'total information system' may be no better off than those who realize that their systems are antiquated or inadequate but do not quite know how to go about improving them.

Where systems go wrong

What makes present information systems ineffective? Analysis of a wide range of companies in various industries indicates that the following are some of the most common failings of present information systems. They serve as a useful check list in diagnosing the reasons for the failure of information systems to serve top management as well as they should.

Information systems are not designed for the three levels of management planning and control. Most company information-design efforts are concerned with information systems that flow from time-tickets to payroll checks to labor-variance reports, from orders to production schedules to invoices to sales reports. They report deviations in daily operations from previously established standards, and they truly blanket the whole business with information. Thus, they are called 'total' or 'fully integrated' management information systems.

But top management's job is not just in the area of daily

operations; it also involves planning the company's long-term destiny and introducing short-term change to improve operations. And the information needed for these two processes includes a great deal more than daily operational reports. Needs for long-range planning include long-term strategic, economic, political, social, competitive and global intelligence. Short-term profit-improvement needs include intelligence on opportunities in the markets currently served and in the plants currently operated; they also encompass information on the status of programs for achieving changes in current operations.

Any information system in any one of these categories, viewed by itself, may be excellent, as some of the new computer-based systems are. But they cannot be described as *total* information systems, because they do not serve all management's information needs, whether the company recognizes the deficiency or not.

The information system does not match the organization. The planning and control processes just described must be correlated with specifically named individuals or positions. As background for overhauling an information system, it helps to slot into boxes on the company's organization chart the related 'cost-center' numbers and show the amount of money spent 'in that box' last year. In many cases this proves difficult, because reports from accounting and other departments simply do not match people and responsibilities in the organization.

Such a situation reflects a shortcoming not only in the information system, but also in the company's management philosophy. Managers make assignments to individuals and then hold them accountable. When the information system bears no relation to these individuals, it is nearly impossible to tell whether they are performing satisfactorily. Thus, the manager cannot help his subordinates to correct and improve their performance – and any improvement that is achieved might not even be reflected in the system.

In short, not enough management information systems answer clearly these three simple questions about each unit in the organization:

1. What is this unit supposed to accomplish?

2. What does it spend to produce this result?
3. When is it delivering outstanding performance?

The system covers dollars – not information. Most information systems consist primarily of dollar reports. Certainly, such reports are important and must be in the system. But dollars are only the final results – the reflection of things that happened earlier.

Such factors as the number of salesmen trained, the number of calls made, the speed of service, the on-time delivery performance record, the level of quality, the frequency and nature of complaints, share of market position, productivity, absenteeism, waste, remakes, parts turnover and the like – these are all *causes* of dollars. They are as important to the manager as are the final dollar effects.

The system produces encyclopedias instead of brief, pointed reports. Many companies deliver to their executives encyclopedias about all the details of the company's operation. Such masses of information convert the executive into a high-priced clerk forced to sift through to find the bits of information that are important to him. On the other hand, he may not bother, and this costs even more.

In one company, a monthly operating report delivered to thirty-two key executives contained twelve thousand separate figures. Obviously, this report did more to impede action than to stimulate and channel it.

A great deal of respect is sometimes voiced for a man who can assimilate massive reports like these. Perhaps more respect is due the executive who gets only eight to twelve key figures on the main elements of performance within his area. This executive will know immediately if one of those key figures goes wrong, and he will know where to go to correct matters. Then he uses his time profitably. Encyclopedic systems make the profitable use of executive time difficult.

Internal operations are covered extensively, but external factors are disregarded. Many companies have elaborate procedural networks for gathering internal information, but they ignore the environment surrounding the company. This is symptomatic of the 'blind side' that many companies have toward effective long-range planning and annual improvement planning. It is a costly lack, because events outside a company can affect it as much as or more than its internal activities, particularly in today's world.

For example, a Midwestern dairy company relied exclusively on internal reports showing solid profits over several years. Meanwhile, competing dairies had followed the larger-size, larger-income families to the suburbs. This left a greater share of the urban delivery market to this company, but when the price spread between store milk and delivered milk increased, sales and profits all but disappeared. All its internal reports did not warn the company against this development.

Two-thirds of the top blue-chip companies of the 1900s are no longer in leading positions today. Most of the casualties on this list did not founder from lack of internal reports, but from failure to meet change *from without*. Thus, an information system is clearly deficient if it does not give 'distant early warning' of major opportunities and threats outside the company.

Causes of the problems

Understanding of these weaknesses in management information systems can be increased by an appreciation of their causes.

Cause number 1. Most management information systems are really only accounting systems. History accounts for this: banks, investors, the Securities Exchange Commission, stock exchanges, regulatory agencies and other government agencies and institutions have virtually legislated major accounting departments into being. Now, accounting departments are older and larger, while market-research, economic, long-range planning and operations-analysis departments are relatively new. The advance has been lopsided, designed more for government requirements than for management of the business.

Cause number 2. Most management information systems are old. In many American companies, the report structure dates back ten to twenty years. In today's fulminating world, a company without sharp, sensitive management information tools is as out-of-date as an airliner without radar.

Cause number 3. Information systems were developed for people and organizations no longer around today. When a new man moves into a top spot in management, companies will paint the office and change the sign on the door, the organization charts and the telephone directory. But they will almost never re-examine the information with which the man is supposed to run his operation, and most of the time the new man will accept the existing information and use it, riding on the momentum that was established in the past.

Cause number 4. The management information system has rarely been looked at as one overall company problem. Hence, most reports are totally unrelated to any other report, and efforts to initiate changes or improvements have been local and sporadic rather than company-wide and continuous. Moreover, effective techniques for overhauling the information system have not been widely applied.

Cause number 5. Most information systems were developed before EDP. Admittedly, companies have not always had a very clear idea of just how EDP could best serve their purposes, and when they have not been able to justify the acquisition of a computer by pointing to clerical savings, they have said: 'But look how much better we will be able to control the company.' Such vague concepts of future benefits have seldom been realized after the computers have been put in. Nevertheless, one simple proposition is valid: Every company is sitting on thousands of figures that are not being used.

In a recent study, a chemical company found that over three-hundred-thousand numbers were being generated in its business each day. Obviously, no amount of sheer human effort could bring such masses of data into effective use. Here is where computers *can* help – by digesting such mountains of data, summarizing them, computing averages and preparing reports that point out exceptions.

One company in the transportation business, for example, converted freight and revenue accounting to a computer application. Through this means, the company is keeping track of shipments by shipper and consignee for the sales department.

Each time business falls off, the computer produces an exception report that says, in effect: 'Here is a customer who needs separate attention, and here is why.' This is the kind of application in which a computer can boil down voluminous data and out of it produce the key facts on which action should be taken. This sort of an approach, however, is still the exception in computer usage.

Overhauling the system

Obviously, the solution to a problem so deeply rooted and so broadly based requires a careful and fundamental approach. In most cases, unfortunately, the scope of the attack is much too narrow. Often, someone calls for a report inventory – a list showing who prepares the reports, who gets them, and when. Usually, a redundancy chart is made to spot duplications, and survey forms are sent out to ask people: 'Can you get along without this report?' After that, some reports are eliminated and others are redesigned. This approach does some good, but it cannot accomplish major change.

In contrast, some companies have mounted a thorough and effective frontal attack on the information problem. The exact approach has varied from one company to the next, but here are the key steps.

Recognizing the problem

First, top management becomes aware of the problem and decides to do something about it in a fundamental way. This decision may come about when top management has already lived through several report-improvement efforts that did not appreciably change the situation; when some top executive becomes disturbed by the overhead costs of the current system; when a computer is being installed largely to provide better management information; or when managers feel that the company reacts to change too slowly.

Forming the team

However the initial decision is reached, the second step is appointing a team to carry out the program. Probably no step influences the outcome as much as this one.

A really effective information overhaul cannot be carried out by people who are busy with daily operations. Such part-time committee efforts usually stretch out interminably, then dwindle away. Companies that have achieved the best results (and a good climate for change) have used a small, full-time team to carry the entire program through to the finish on a company-wide basis. As it moves through the company from department to department, this core team works with an interim – but full-time – task force from the given department.

The controller is often selected to lead this team, since he is considered the chief information-executive in the company (in line with the thought that management information equals accounting reports). If the controller is of the old school, with a compulsion to produce completely detailed reports balanced to the penny, his approach to the problem is not likely to be sufficiently broad. If, on the other hand, the controller is a broad-gauged executive interested in the physical operations behind the figures and in economic, marketing and general information of a less precise nature than accounting numbers, he is well equipped to provide leadership for the project.

More than anything else, the caliber of the leadership and membership of the team determines the success of this kind of effort.

Critical factors

Once the core team is assembled, its first order of business is to analyse the company as a whole, examining it to achieve a real understanding of the basic nature of the company's industry, what it takes to succeed in that industry, the long-term goals of the company, its organization structure, and its distribution of resources to achieve its goals.

A key part of this basic analysis is identification of the critical elements of performance that most influence the company's profit results. Usually, just four to six major factors are critical; that is, if the company did those four to six things extremely well, it would gain a competitive advantage or significantly increase earnings.

It is important to distinguish between critical and non-critical factors. If a company had the best accounts-payable operation in the country, that might save a few dollars, but it would not represent a significant advantage; it would not make earnings-per-share go up. On the other hand, the most effective cost-control system in the country, or a continuously productive research and development program or a top-flight dealer or distributor organization would clearly make money for the company.

Down to bedrock

The factors that exert the greatest leverage on profits will differ among industries, and even among companies within the same industry. Finding out what these factors are in that particular situation is the team's job in this step. This is not easy; it requires interviews with top executives, analysis of competitors' operations, and similar steps aimed at acquiring a sophisticated understanding of the economics of the business. But painstaking and difficult though this analysis may be, it should produce a truly valuable result: a clear statement of the factors on which the company – and, therefore, the management information system – should concentrate.

Designing the system

With these elements as background, the team is now ready to design an information system for planning and control. To facilitate this step, some basic concepts need to be re-emphasized.

First, an information system should not simply report what happened; it should help make things happen. This means that information is for planning as well as control, and it must be fitted to the steps in the planning and control processes.

Second, it is usually not enough to specify only the information needed. In addition, the team often has to evaluate and strengthen the company's planning and control processes themselves. This means specifying who in the company is to do what in using formal information for planning and control.

When this evaluation of the underlying processes is required, it is no small job. It means that the team members must learn how to do long-range planning and annual planning – both subjects in themselves – then design or modify these processes for their company.

Many of the design criteria for the information structure

have already been mentioned and need only to be summarized here:

1. Information should highlight the critical factors controlling the company's success.

2. Information should be keyed to the individuals responsible.

3. Information should include non-dollar or causal factors, as well as dollar results.

4. Information should cover the external environment as searchingly as it deals with internal factors.

5. Information should be presented in brief, to-the-point, easy-to-use form. This means using computers, where appropriate, to distill the points requiring action out of masses of data.

As a final guideline, this whole approach should not be tied too closely to the company's existing information or report structure, which is probably rooted in factors that should no longer be of concern and may actually confuse the team. For this reason, it is a good technique to ignore the existing structure – at least initially. After learning basic functions and critical factors in the company's business, the team withdraws to design an ideal planning and control system to meet today's needs, just as though the business were starting from scratch. This is a difficult task, but out of it come the really fresh guides on how it *should* be done. This, in turn, produces the fundamental challenges to the old ways that are needed to achieve major improvements.

At this point, the team is then ready to turn to the existing structure, use or modify what fits in, and arrange for the creation of data not available at all. Finally, as the last step, the remainder of the old information and report structure can be reviewed to eliminate what is no longer needed.

The whole process is essentially one of creating a tailor-made system for the present business in its present environment – building a new system, then gradually dismantling the old. It is more a process of substitution than modification.

Some cautions

Some cautions are needed if this approach is to be fruitful.

First, the approach outlined here is heavily dependent on the *will to plan.* Top management and down-the-line managers must be insistent on the organization's taking the time, before a period begins, to plan what is going to be accomplished during the period. By the same token, they must be willing to do something about the control reports that reflect execution of the plan. This takes time and new discipline; it is a long step forward for a company that has not engaged in tough planning and control in the past.

Second, the approach outlined is a major undertaking under any circumstances. Hence, teams sometimes do well to limit the initial effort to a major department, or to the major businesses, without attempting to cover all parts of the company in the beginning. This, incidentally, is a 'plus' feature of the critical-factor concept, which, through its identification of key areas to be planned and controlled, helps the team to avoid getting into too much detail on too many fronts.

Third, because of the real need for management leadership and performance of the planning and control process, teams should usually work closely with the managers concerned. Managers should feel that they have helped develop the system and are, thus, committed to executing it. This point is particularly valid when the team has to design or upgrade the planning and control process; in these cases, it must work out with management assignments for the individuals who are going to do the planning work.

Finally, these efforts take time. Depending on the size and nature of the business and the state of its planning and control system, such an information-overhaul effort could take three months to a year – and even then it should not be viewed as a permanent system. Rather, managers should continuously be encouraged to make further improvements under some kind of central control to keep the entire system up to date and in balance.

Refocusing effort

Management information systems designed in accordance with this approach produce many benefits beyond improved information.

The very process itself causes a refocusing, throughout the company, on what is important to profitability and competitive strength. In this way, the improvement effort blows a breath of fresh air through the company. It induces people to draw away from day-to-day details and to start looking at the fundamentals of their operation.

No-man's land

Sometimes this focus on critical factors discloses that important areas have been management no-man's lands, with nobody really responsible for them. When this fact is faced and corrected, the company closes gaps in its organization and upgrades the present level of performance, even before getting a better information system.

Companies with large fixed investments usually gain a better long-range planning system from these efforts. This is particularly important to all heavy industries, since their investments remain in operation for ten, fifteen or twenty years and influence earnings all that time.

Finally, one of the greatest benefits lies in the training gained by members of the team that conducts this project. The people on such teams develop an almost unequalled appreciation of the basic economics and problems of the whole company – the sort of understanding that produces a pool of high-potential executive talent for the future.

5 The McKinsey Consulting Organization

The 1968 McKinsey Report on Computer Utilization

McKinsey and Company Inc., 1968, pp. 1–38.

About the study

In the course of this study, we interviewed staff and line executives, up to and frequently including the chief executive officer, in thirty-six large US and European companies representing thirteen industries. Some but not all of these companies were clients of McKinsey and Company. Their distribution by industry, sales volume, and relative level of computer expenditure is shown in Figure 1.

The companies represent all levels of achievement and experience with computers. One of them, a major European manufacturer, installed its first computer as recently as 1963. Several others have more than a dozen years' experience, and some of these have computer applications in almost every major department.

The computer practices and achievements of these companies are so diverse that quantitative performance measures are both difficult to formulate and easy to misinterpret. In this report, therefore, we have relied mainly on anecdotal evidence to exemplify the problems that can beset computer development efforts and the means that have proved most effective for solving or avoiding them.

Our findings strongly indicate that 'keys to success' in the use of computers can be expressed only in very general terms. Even for a particular industry, it is seldom possible to pinpoint inventory management, or financial planning, or sales performance measurement as the application holding most immediate promise of profit in 1968 and beyond. And, as Figure 1 indicates, success with the computer shows no consistent correlation with level of computer expenditures. Some companies are spending heavily for a very dubious payoff; others with less ambitious programs are reaping major rewards.

The distinction between 'more successful' and 'less successful' computer users, which is explicit in several figures and implicit in much of the text, requires a word of explanation.

In view of the many variables involved, any absolute standard of computer success must necessarily be arbitrary. Instead of attempting to legislate such a standard, therefore, we decided to let 'success' be defined by the range of performance observed in the survey sample itself.

For this purpose, we ranked the thirty-six companies judgementally on their overall achievement with the computer, taking into account such factors as measurable return on the computer investment over time, range of meaningful functional applications, and chief executive satisfaction with the computer effort to date. The companies identified in Figure 1 and elsewhere as 'more successful computer users' are simply those falling in the upper half of this order-of-performance ranking. The 'less successful', again by definition, are those in the lower half.

As any executive experienced in the management of large-scale computer efforts will recognize, an element of subjectivity inevitably enters into judgements of this kind, and there is almost always room for legitimate difference of opinion on the rankings assigned to individual companies. However, we believe that any experienced analyst having access to the same data would arrive at essentially the same results.

Introduction

In terms of technical achievement, the computer revolution in US business is outrunning expectations. In terms of economic payoff on new applications, it is rapidly losing momentum. Such is the evidence of a new study by McKinsey and Company of computer-systems management in thirty-six major companies.

From a profit standpoint, our findings indicate computer efforts in all but a few exceptional companies are in real, if often unacknowledged, trouble. Faster, costlier, more sophisticated hardware; larger and increasingly costly computer staffs; increasingly complex and ingenious applications: these are in evidence everywhere. Less and less in evidence, as these new applications proliferate, are profitable results. This is the familiar phenomenon of diminishing returns. But there is one crucial difference: as yet, the real profit potential of the computer has barely begun to be tapped.

Almost twenty years ago the first computers for business use made their debut. Five years ago, when we published our first research report on the computer (1963), business was well on the way to exploiting the awesome clerical and arithmetical talents of its new tool. Today the early goals have for all practical purposes been attained. Most large companies have successfully mechanized the bulk of their routine clerical and accounting procedures, and many have moved out into operating applications.

by size of company
- foreign companies
- US companies

number of companies

annual sales in millions of dollars	under $200	$200-499	$500-999	$1000-1999	over $2000
	6	5	10	9	6

classified by industry, the distribution of the thirty-six companies is as follows:

airlines	2
apparel	1
chemicals	8
food	3
forest products	1
insurance	3
machinery	6
paper	1
petroleum	3
primary metals	2
railroads	1
textiles	1
transportation equipment	4

by computer outlay
- more successful computer users
- less successful computers users

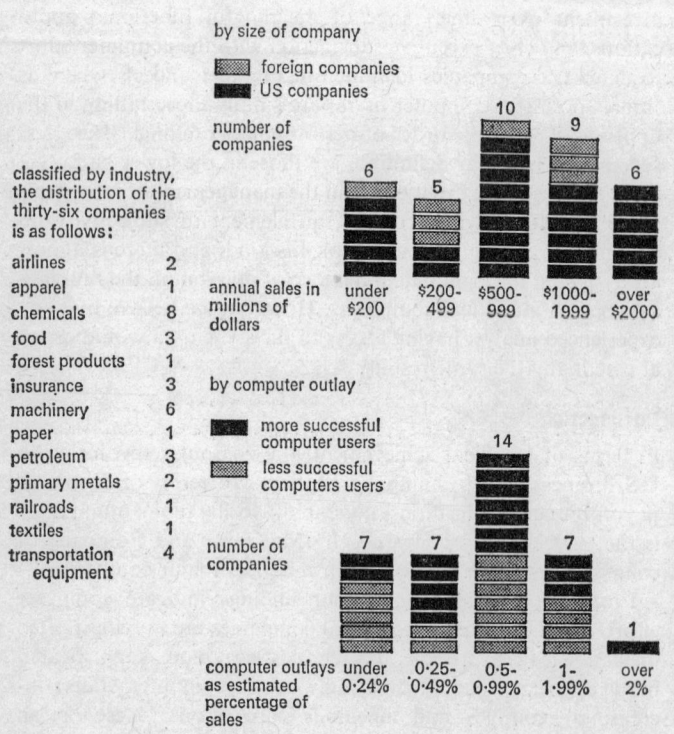

number of companies

computer outlays as estimated percentage of sales	under 0·24%	0·25-0·49%	0·5-0·99%	1-1·99%	over 2%
	7	7	14	7	1

Figure 1 Profile of the study sample

96 The Design of Management Information Systems

As a super-clerk, the computer has more than paid its way. For most large organizations, going back to punch cards and keyboard machines would be as unthinkable as giving up the typewriter for the quill pen. Yet in these same companies – including many that pioneered in the mechanization of paperwork operations – mounting computer expenditures are no longer matched by rising economic returns.

What has gone wrong? The answer, our findings suggest, lies in a failure to adapt to new conditions. The rules of the game have been changing, but management's strategies have not.

There was a time, less than a decade ago, when management could afford to leave the direction of the corporate computer effort largely in the hands of technical staff people. That time is past. Yet the identification and selection of new computer applications are still predominantly in the hands of computer specialists, who – despite their professional expertise – are poorly qualified to set the course of the corporate computer effort.

It is not hard to understand how this situation has come about. Historically, profit-oriented companies have undertaken computer development work for the sake of a single ultimate objective: improved financial results. There are just three ways such results can be reflected in the income statement, and three general categories of computer applications by which this can be accomplished directly:

Purpose	*Application*
1. To reduce general and administrative expenses	Administrative and accounting uses
2. To reduce cost of goods sold	Operations control systems
3. To increase revenues	Product innovation and improved customer service

Improved financial results, of course, can also be achieved indirectly, through better management information and control. This gives rise to a final purpose and application category:

4. To improve staff work and management decisions	Information systems and simulation models

The McKinsey Consulting Organization 97

Mainly because of rising clerical costs and the desire to cut clerical staffs, the practical history of computers in US business to date has been dominated by the first of these four purposes. A look at current computer development projects shows that the prime objective in many computer departments is still the refinement of administrative systems and the reduction of G & A expenses. But this, our study indicates, is an area where the cream (and some of the milk) has already been skimmed. It is high time for a change in emphasis, if not a change of course, in the computer development effort. And the next move is up to management.

Many senior executives are already beginning to recognize their dilemma. 'How can I keep on justifying major computer expenditures when I can't show a dollar saved to date from our last three applications?' asks the president of a large consumer goods company. 'Maybe I'm a fool to let it worry me – after all, who tries to find a dollar justification for telephones and typewriters? But I do worry. After all, we know that what we're doing with telephones and typewriters makes sense. But that's more than I can say for some of the things we're doing with the computer, at many times the cost.'

The ill-justified expenditures, however, are insignificant compared to the opportunity costs. Though it has transformed the administrative and accounting operations of US business, the computer has had little impact on most companies' key operating and management problems. Yet, as Figure 2 suggests, this is where its greatest potential lies.

In our 1963 report, we noted that no company had yet come anywhere near exhausting the computer's potential. Today the gap between technical capability and practical achievement is still wider, and the stakes have risen sharply. Until the computer is put to work where the leverage on profits is high, the penalty of lost opportunities and lost profits will continue to mount.

Subsequent sections of this report will set forth the dimensions and implications of the issue. We shall outline the developments that have shaped it, explore the current problems to which it has given rise, and indicate some of the future opportunities open to companies that take timely action to resolve it. Finally, we shall offer a few practical guidelines for the chief executive who recognizes his own vital personal responsibility for the success and profitability of his company's computer effort.

The stakes and the problem

In 1963, computer manufacturers shipped hardware worth $1·3 billion to their US customers. By 1967, the value of computer shipments had risen to $3·9 billion, an increase of no less than

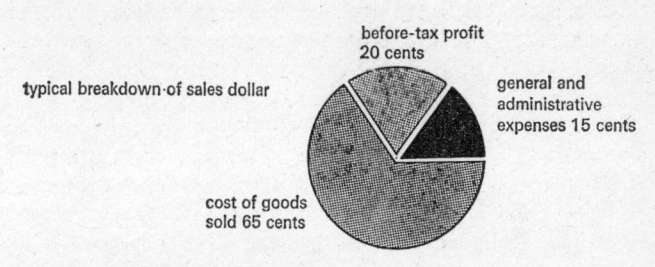

typical breakdown of sales dollar

before-tax profit 20 cents

general and administrative expenses 15 cents

cost of goods sold 65 cents

potential profit impact of 10 per cent reduction ...

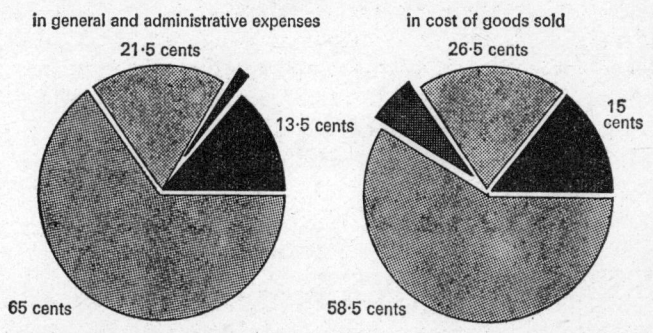

in general and administrative expenses
21·5 cents
13·5 cents
65 cents

in cost of goods sold
26·5 cents
15 cents
58·5 cents

Figure 2 Where the opportunity lies

200 per cent in four years. Of every $1 million that business laid out on new plant and equipment in 1963, $33,000 went for computers and computer-associated hardware. By 1967, the computer's share had risen to $63,000, and each dollar was buying at least half as much again in capacity. Computer spending, both absolutely and as a proportion of all plant and equipment outlays, is still rising.

Another index to the growth of computers as a factor in the national economy from 1963 to 1966 can be found in the published accounts of the largest computer manufacturer, the International Business Machines Corporation. IBM's gross investment in 'factory and office equipment, rental machines and parts' grew from just under $2 billion in 1963 (double the 1957 figure) to just over $5 billion in 1966. In its annual report for 1966, IBM chose for the first time to report separately the value of its investment in machines on rental. Valued at cost, that investment had grown from $3·3 billion to $4·4 billion during the previous twelve months, a one-year growth of 33 per cent.

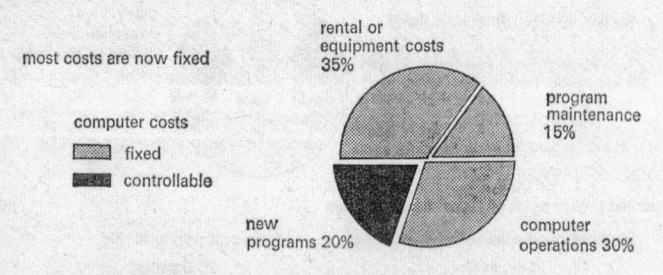

most costs are now fixed

rental or equipment costs 35%

program maintenance 15%

computer costs
- fixed
- controllable

new programs 20%

computer operations 30%

for every $100 spent on hardware, companies spend $187 on staff

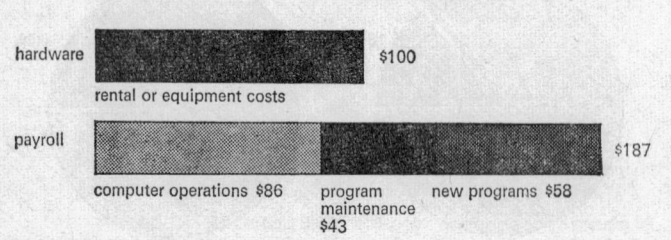

hardware $100
rental or equipment costs

payroll $187
computer operations $86   program maintenance $43   new programs $58

Figure 3 How computer costs are distributed

Massive as it looks and rapidly as it is growing, the investment in computer hardware is far from an adequate measure of business's stake in the computer. For every dollar spent on equipment, the typical company in our current study spent close to $2 on people and supplies in 1967, as Figure 3 indicates; and the payroll component of the total outlay is clearly rising more rapidly than the rental bills. Thus, a company that is paying as little as $125,000 a year to rent equipment of very modest capacity is probably spending upwards of a third of a million dollars on its total effort. It is a fair estimate that well over a hundred industrial companies have rental bills running into seven figures, and there are a handful whose total computer outlays approach $100 million a year.

Because so much of the total cost is payroll, and because staffs are dispersed and personnel classifications and accounting conventions differ from company to company, attempts to formulate 'yardsticks' for corporate computer outlays (e.g. as a percentage of assets, capital expenditures, administrative expenses or sales volume) are likely to end in confusion. Even if precision in such figures were possible, what a particular company 'ought' to be spending on computers will not be discovered by studying industry averages or the outlays of individual competitors. At best, such yardsticks will provide a bench mark from which to start; but the final answer can only be determined in the light of the company's own situation, strategy and resources (including the depth and sophistication of its computer experience).

The distribution of costs which go to make up total computer expenditures is, however, fairly consistent among the companies participating in our study. Figure 3 indicates this distribution. Of every $100,000 of total computer expenditures about $35,000 goes for hardware; $30,000 for computer operations staff payroll; $15,000 for maintenance programming (i.e. keeping current systems updated); and the remaining $20,000 for development programming and other staff time devoted to new applications.

These development dollars, the only computer outlays subject to significant short-term management control, are typically a smaller fraction of the total than the company's annual bill for hardware rentals. Yet their leverage on future costs and benefits is enormous; in fact, they hold the key to the company's long-range success or failure with its computer effort. For unless management segregates these costs and understands the nature of the resources they buy, the direction of future computer developments will be in doubt, and the whole activity will be vulnerable to precipitate, perhaps emotional, review.

The computer-management problem as it confronts corporate executives today, then, is a matter of future direction rather than current effectiveness. The key question is not 'How are we doing?' but 'Where are we heading and why?'

Five years ago this was a less critical issue at the top-management level. As long as computer developments were largely confined to accounting departments there was less reason for corporate executives to concern themselves with direction setting. If the controller carried out his function and kept his costs in line, no one outside his department worried very much about *how* he did it. The situation is very different today. Now that the conversion of accounting work to computer processing is virtually complete – as it is in thirty of the thirty-six companies in our study – the question: 'What next?' comes into urgent focus. Many of the alternatives currently being proposed are complex and costly enough to require executive approval, but their justification is obscure at best. When top management, reviewing a proposal, looks in vain for the promise of profit, it is right to hesitate.

For example, the following three proposals, submitted for approval during 1967 in one company we studied, would have consumed 80 per cent of the computer staff time available for development:

1. *Design a computer-based 'strategic management information system'*. This was candidly described by its sponsor, the manager of the systems and procedures department, as 'a basic research project', as indeed it would have been. Management's information needs had not been determined; the cost of making information available was uncertain; and the proposed techniques for putting the manager (assuming he was interested) in a position to manipulate the information (if it could be provided) had never really been tried out.

2. *Design a model of the corporate distribution system, to be used in both long-range planning and daily management of operations.* Cost data on the present distribution system were scanty and out of date. Moreover, responsibility for distribution lay with the marketing vice-president, a man who had made no major changes in distribution policy or practice for fifteen years, and had a well-earned reputation for being hostile to innovation. Perhaps understandably, he had not been consulted on the proposal. Yet his support would obviously be indispensable to its success.

3. *Design a revised system of sales-call reporting.* As this project was envisioned, the computer would analyse salesmen's routes and product and customer profitability; it would then print out detailed instructions to salesmen each week, specifying customers to be called on, sequence of calls, target sales by product, and weekly sales quotas. This project looked promising, but it had not been evaluated by the very sales people for whom it was intended. And its assumptions were based on present account volume, not future potential.

All these proposals were listed, without specific cost or benefit estimates, in the annual request for budget approval submitted by the systems and procedures department. The president, when they were presented to him for review, reacted with irritation. Were they the best opportunities available for the application of the computer resources? What economic results could realistically be expected? No good answers were available.

Essentially the same questions are raised by any computer development proposal. They are basically questions of *feasibility* – a concept often misunderstood and even more misapplied where computer projects are concerned. It is this concept, crucial to soundly based computer-development efforts, that we will now briefly consider.

The three tests of feasibility

Recently the president of a German chemical company was asked to examine and approve a proposal for an exciting new management information system. Featuring a desk-side cathode-ray tube inquiry terminal that would display on demand any data in the computer files, the system would enable the president to compare current production figures, by product and/or by plant, against plan; it would break down current sales figures in half a dozen different ways; it would display inventory levels, current labor costs and trends, material costs – in short, just about any kind of operating data he might care to request. A few years earlier such a project would have looked like science fiction; in 1967, its technical feasibility was assured.

Nevertheless, the president turned the proposal down. As he

explained his decision to a McKinsey interviewer, 'I care more about what will happen five years from now than what happened yesterday. Anyway, I already get all the routine data I can handle. What would I do with more?'

The incident is significant because it typifies a trend. Computer technology has made great strides in just the past few years. Fewer and fewer applications are excluded from consideration because of limits on computer file capacity, internal speed, or input/output ability; more and more technically exciting projects are being proposed for management approval.

Particularly when corporate management is unaccustomed to dealing with the computer department, it takes a certain amount of hard-boiled scepticism to insist on proof of a payoff. Yet the fact is that technical virtuosity is no guarantee of problem-solving potential. The most ingenious new proposal may be merely a fancy new wrapping for an outmoded product. Instant access to data generated by an outmoded cost accounting system, for example, is at best a dubious blessing.

Back in the days when the computer's full potential, and hence its full impact on operating systems, was not foreseen, the overall feasibility of a proposed computer application was generally equated with its technical feasibility. That being the case, it made sense to let the computer professionals decide how to use the computer. Today, judging from the findings of our study, this same policy of delegation is being followed in most companies. But it no longer makes the same kind of sense. Technical feasibility is only one aspect of overall feasibility. For the great majority of business applications, it is no longer an important stumbling block.

The concept of 'feasibility' really takes in three separate questions. There is the test of *technical feasibility*: 'Is this application possible within the limits of available technology and our own resources?' There is the test of *economic feasibility*: 'Will this application return more dollar value in benefits than it will cost to develop?' And there is the test of *operational feasibility*: 'If the system is successfully developed, will it be successfully used? Will managers adapt to the system, or will they resist or ignore it?'

Particularly on complex and ambitious computer development

projects, these key questions of feasibility can seldom be answered once and for all at the time the project is proposed. Continuous reassessment of the technical and economic risks and payoff probabilities may be vital to keeping such a project on the right track. But a careful initial assessment can go far to avert costly misapplication of scarce computer resources.

It is dangerously easy, however, to avoid confronting the full implications of feasibility until a project is well under way. Technical feasibility, though less often a question mark today, is still the test most commonly considered at the start. The issue of operational feasibility is far too often neglected until the new application is actually tried out in practice and perhaps found wanting – the costliest kind of feasibility test. And economic feasibility – the measure of how much expected dollar returns will exceed expected costs – is frequently given only superficial examination.

Since a company's computer resources are seldom equal to its computer opportunities, economic feasibility should almost always be a key criterion in weighing the merits of technically feasible projects. Yet it is frequently assessed rather casually, on the grounds that the important benefits are intangible, and intangible benefits cannot really be evaluated. Actually, of course, the very difficulty of measuring intangible payoffs is the best argument for imposing on managers the discipline of explicit evaluation.

In assessing the cost-benefit balance of a proposed application, computer personnel can, of course, provide the needed input on costs. The assessment of benefits, however, requires a full understanding of the operations affected and the policies that govern them – an understanding that only operating executives can really bring to bear.

To achieve its economic potential, a computer project may also require substantial operational changes – changes in corporate policies, staff reorganizations, the construction of new facilities and the phasing out of the old. It will certainly require the support of operating managers and their staffs, and it may also depend on the cooperation of dealers, suppliers and even customers. Consider the case of a hardware distributor who requires his customers to submit orders on coded forms designed for the computer. All his customers may want the faster service promised by the system, but some may balk if it entails a messy problem of staff retraining.

Corporate computer staffs cannot really judge the necessity of such changes, much less implement them. At most, they can advise the operating managers who must make the final assessment of operational feasibility.

Against this background, let us look more closely at the problems and opportunities confronting the companies in our study.

Past successes and present problems

Ironically, the basic problems currently besetting the management of the computer effort in most of the companies we studied have their origin in the successes of the past. In thirty of the thirty-six companies, conversions of routine administrative and accounting operations to computer systems are already complete, or so close to completion that only minor incremental savings are expected from the mechanization of remaining manual procedures. Typically, most of the people who accomplished these conversions are still operating and maintaining the systems they helped to install. But others who participated in the early installations now enjoy a different organizational status. They constitute the nucleus of a corporate computer staff. Instead of reporting to the controller, in some cases they now report directly to top management.

For obvious reasons, these computer department staffs are under pressure to show results in the form of new computer systems. Technically speaking, they may be superbly equipped to respond to management's expectations. Typically, they are highly skilled in computer systems design, and their status as professionals is unchallengeable. But they are seldom strategically placed (or managerially trained) to assess the economics of operations fully or to judge operational feasibility. These limitations, although they reflect no discredit on the corporate computer staff, are raising ever more serious obstacles to the success of new corporate computer efforts, our findings indicate.

Another obstacle to future success, also stemming from past experience, is management's lack of exposure to the feasibility problem. Back in the days when corporate computer efforts centered on the conversion of accounting and administrative systems, management seldom had to concern itself with the issue of feasibility. With a relatively orderly manual system, the feasibility question centered on the technical problems of programming the computer. Economic benefits could be determined with relative ease in terms of clerical payroll reductions. Once a company had learned how to estimate conversion costs realistically, assessing economic feasibility was relatively simple. Operational feasibility was assured when a single executive, such as the controller, had charge of both the development and operating phases of the new system.

Today the situation is very different. Applications are not only more complex, but also more far-reaching in their impact on different operating departments. Feasibility is no longer an issue that operating managers can ignore, for it is affected by complex economic and operational questions that the staff specialists are unequipped to answer. Yet many managers – far too many – are still leaving the whole question of feasibility to the computer professionals. At the same time, they are neglecting their own responsibility for setting the direction of the company development efforts.

The background sketched above, then, typically affects the computer effort today in two ways.

First, today's management practices and attitudes, inherited from a time when the full scope of the computer's potential was not foreseen in most companies, are falling short of the demands of today's task. Over the past five years, computer staffs have typically doubled. The department that had forty people in 1962 has eighty or eighty-five now, and expects to double again by 1975. Yet no overhaul of the management practices of earlier years has taken place. In fourteen of the thirty-six companies we studied, as Figure 4 indicates, nothing deserving the name of an overall plan for a full range of computer applications is yet in evidence, and the economic and operational feasibility of individual projects is seldom fully explored. Ten companies, including a number that do have a computer plan, are providing few if any short-term objectives against which the progress of individual computer projects can be measured.

Second, the range of computer projects now open to the company is circumscribed by the limited background of its computer personnel and the limited initiative of its managers. Consider a list of four proposed applications recently submitted to the president of a midwestern electric machinery manufacturer:

1. Put labor records on random-access files, so that production department or machine group efficiency (now the subject of a weekly report) can be measured daily.

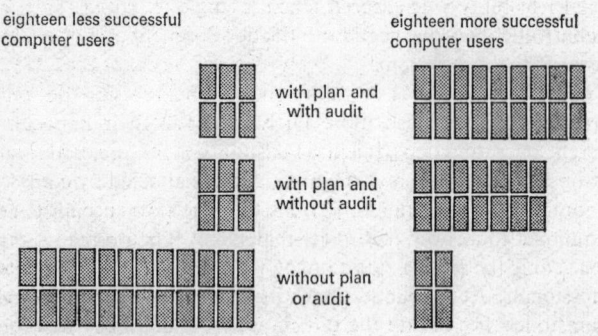

Figure 4 The payoff from planning

2. Mechanize the follow-up of delinquent accounts receivable. (At present the computer lists delinquent accounts and shows the age of outstanding debits, but clerks review the list and handle the follow-up.)

3. Install a data-transmission terminal at the warehouse receiving dock so that receipts can be recorded immediately on the computer file when shipments are unloaded. (At present good pieces are counted and the count punched into cards only after a quality control inspection.)

4. Double the core memory of the computer to permit multi-processing of data processing jobs instead of running them one at a time as at present. (The computer is currently loaded less than two shifts, five days a week.)

None of these proposals had much relevance to the well-being of the corporation. Individual machine shop efficiencies, for example, had long been appallingly low, and the vice-president for production was convinced that efficient production runs would be impossible until the design department learned to reduce the catalog of parts used in assemblies. But no attempt had ever been made to put bills of material on computer files, and an overall analysis of the catalog of parts would have to be done manually, an excessively time-consuming job. Accordingly, the president decided to postpone proposal number one, making his reasons quite clear to both the computer department manager and the production head. Later, these two men came up jointly with a project, which was promptly approved, to transfer bill-of-material descriptions from a manual file to computer files. With this application 'on stream', production managers are beginning to show real interest in making more extensive use of the computer, and the computer staff is gaining a valuable understanding of the practical problems of production. At least in this area of the business, the prospects for profitable future computer applications look good.

Operational feasibility was the Achilles heel of proposal number two. The sales vice-president firmly opposes automatic dunning of delinquent accounts. The clerks who now analyse the delinquent listing are pensioned salesmen who make collections by phone and call personally on seriously delinquent customers. This system of debt collection will not be changed until there is a change at the top – and that is unlikely to happen until 1971 at the earliest.

As for proposal number three, the quality control inspection is essential since high-value components make up 40 per cent of all receipts at the dock, and typically between 3 and 5 per cent of all items received are returned to the manufacturer or held pending billing adjustments. Thus, although a data-transmission terminal would put data on the computer file two to three days earlier and might avoid some of the interruptions in work flow that now result from reported stock-outs, the data would be faulty and would require detailed subsequent correction and audit.

Such examples, symptomatic of the unbridged gap between computer staff and operating management, could probably be duplicated in most corporations. They are as discouraging to computer professionals as they are to operating management, and they doubtless account for the tendency, observable in many of the companies we studied, for computer staffs to take refuge in refining the internal operating efficiency of the computer department itself (as in proposal number four).

If computer systems design must be so closely linked to operating procedures even in apparently simple applications, it should not be surprising that the more ambitious projects conceived by computer staffs so seldom meet the tests of economic and operational feasibility. To make better use of computers in the future will require expanding the scope and capabilities of computer professionals and bringing managers to a fuller awareness of the computer's vast potential. The history of computer developments to date has limited both.

The opportunites: near and far-out

The computer's credentials as a cutter of clerical payrolls are now beyond dispute. On the evidence of its achievements in a few exceptional corporations, we believe that the computer can make an equal or greater contribution to corporate profits by reducing the cost of goods sold.

The more successful companies in our study have recognized this potential and are already beginning to exploit it. The dominant lesson of their experience so far is that this second stage of the computer revolution, unlike the first, entails real operational changes – new, and at first uncomfortable, ways of doing business that will quite possibly encounter resistance within the company.

For the companies moving into operating system applications, moreover, the issue of feasibility has emerged on a new level of importance. They have found that technical feasibility is often a problem because marketing, production, and distribution systems are subject to outside influence and therefore less orderly than accounting systems. Since the benefits do not derive from reductions in payroll dollars, they have often found it harder to determine economic feasibility. Most significantly, they have found that the operational feasibility of a project is vitally dependent on the attitude of operating managers.

Teamwork, then, is the key. Where top management provides leadership, and operating managers actively and enthusiastically cooperate with professional computer staffs, major economic achievements can result. Even a fairly commonplace computer application such as inventory control requires such cooperation. Design engineers must give adequate notice of design changes; sales planners must furnish detailed product sales forecasts; and management must give guidance on spares requirements and desired customer-service levels. But once developed on the early projects, cooperation between managers and professional computer staffs becomes an important stimulus to the development of profitable further applications.

Consider the case of one manufacturer of heavy construction equipment. In this company, whose first computer-based inventory control system went into operation well over a decade ago, computers now play such an integral role in production planning and control that it is difficult to picture the company without them. These are some of the jobs now being done by computer:

Consolidating sales forecasts from thirty-one countries. Forecast data are first consolidated by region, product and model; then they are correlated with figures for seven previous years. Trends are established for each product group, and forecasts that seem not to 'fit' are pulled out for further staff review. The president and the vice-president for sales use these staff analyses in their annual budgeting discussions with division heads at corporate headquarters.

Establishing a quarterly manufacturing plan for each of thirteen plants. These plans are up-dated monthly by reconciling revised sales forecasts with records of finished goods inventory and work in process in final assembly. The revised manufacturing program is then exploded into component requirements, and a 'net component requirement' analysis is prepared. Extensive manual analysis by production planners is still required to supplement these computer analyses, but lead time between customer order and delivery has been reduced, and the cost of shipping finished goods from depots in surplus to those with shortages has been cut drastically.

Maintaining cost schedules in all plants showing the economies of make-or-buy decisions. In conjunction with the 'net component requirement' report, these cost schedules make possible intelligent work-load levelling and allocation among plants. Where there is an option to contract work out, managers can make their decisions with full knowledge of both the costs and the effect on specific work centers within each plant where bottlenecks are predicted.

Central recording of all engineering changes. Before an engineering change is put into effect, components in stock are exhausted first wherever possible. With changes occurring at a rate of about two thousand a month, the costs of writing off obsolete stock used to run as high as $1·5 million annually before the advent of the computer. In the past three years, these costs have been reduced to approximately $500,000 a year.

Maintaining cumulative records on labor efficiency. In addition to detailed information on direct labor costs and trends, this system provides production planners with data on the work content of each component by work center. These data have been invaluable for scheduling manpower requirements to meet a varying production schedule, and particularly in planning the start-up of two new plants, which required the transfer of hundreds of skilled manufacturing workers.

The complex network of systems which produces such results has been evolving for twelve years now, and its net benefits to date have been outstanding. Overall, management credits computers with reducing lead time between order receipt and delivery by three to five months for US customers, and with cutting direct labor requirements by 2 per cent through improved materials availability and better control of work flow. Since direct labor costs are approximately $100 million per year, this fractional saving is significant both in absolute terms ($2 million) and as a percentage of before-tax profits (5 per cent).

Another example of evolutionary development is offered by a major consumer goods corporation. This company gives its product managers and marketing staffs access to a comprehensive, detailed sales-history file, in which total US sales over three years are cross-referenced to show product sales data by geographic region, type of outlet, timing with relation to promotions and packaging. This system evolved from an order entry and billing system that recorded sales solely by customer number.

The direction of this company's development effort was set early in 1959 by a product manager who foresaw the potential value of a comprehensive marketing information system. Today, in addition to recording orders centrally, the system he envisioned is used to schedule production at nine plants and to coordinate shipments from thirteen warehouses. One gauge of its usefulness is the willingness of marketing men to pay the salaries of the programmers who prepare on demand whatever analyses may be needed by marketing managers.

Evolutionary development is typical of systems requiring audited data bases, since these cannot be built up overnight. But other systems, equally ambitious, can sometimes be developed quite rapidly where management recognizes that the data-base approach is not the only, nor necessarily the best, way to develop advanced computer applications.

A manufacturer of high-style clothing, with national outlets and multiple plants, decided two years ago that computers, hitherto used only for accounting purposes, could furnish major help in forecasting sales and establishing preliminary cutting schedules at the beginning of each season. The resulting computer forecasting model has already proved so successful in matching production to demand that a project is now under way to put computer forecasting methods to work in planning purchasing decisions.

Similarly, a number of oil companies have moved quickly into new fields unrelated to previous computer development work. Several have successfully undertaken crash programs to develop computer-based seismic analysis techniques to assist in the planning of exploratory drilling, and more than one has developed a computer model of the crude oil distribution system in order to improve the scheduling of its tanker fleet, at potentially vast savings.

In a matter of months, one oil company moved to transfer the production and maintenance records of thousands of domestic oil wells to computer files where they can be correlated and analysed. This system enables production decline curves of wells and fields to be plotted and future production forecast under various alternative secondary recovery programs. It also calls management's attention to wells that are no longer producing enough to cover marginal costs. The principal task in developing this computer system was one of data reduction and file design, and here there was ideal matching of the talents of the computer systems men and petroleum engineers. With the engineers' enthusiastic support, the computer staff is now exploring the feasibility of making the same data accessible to engineers in the field through graphic display units. The obstacles are great, but the potential payoff from improving the effectiveness of operating engineers, who control expenditures in the hundreds of millions of dollars per year, is greater still.

Finally, in industry after industry where such data are critical, the science of communications is being wedded to the science of computing to centralize record keeping, planning and control in an ever more complex economic environment. Railroads have 'control centers' where up-to-the-minute central records are maintained on the movement of freight and rolling stock. Retail chains are using teleprinters and central computer-based dispatch systems to reduce branch-store inventories by cutting the stock-replenishment cycle. A wood-products company is coordinating production at its nine mills to match sales orders transmitted by branch offices throughout the United States directly to a central computer. Banks are handling branch accounting centrally; it is interesting to note that one of the main reasons cited for the recent merger of three large British banks was the opportunity to consolidate the banks' computers and computer knowhow. And virtually all the major airlines now have their own versions of the seat reservation system that first proved computers able to control large communications networks on a commercially feasible basis.

It is often extremely difficult to assess the overall economic effects of these advanced computer applications, for the simple reason that where the corporation would be now *without* its computers is well-nigh impossible to determine. But many of these companies are convinced that they have the computer to thank for the fact that they are beginning to outdistance their competitors.

The resources – computers, professional computer-systems men and programmers, management scientists and communications experts – are available to all. But the team needs leadership. Advanced computer application concepts, with potential impact on the central activities of a corporation, must have sponsors high in the management pyramid to plead their case. The leadership of enthusiastic managers will gain the commitment of operating men – and teamwork between operating men and computer professionals will turn concepts into practical reality.

If the situation prevailing in the companies we studied is typical of US industry as a whole, it is a fair guess that more than half of the proposed computer applications currently awaiting man-

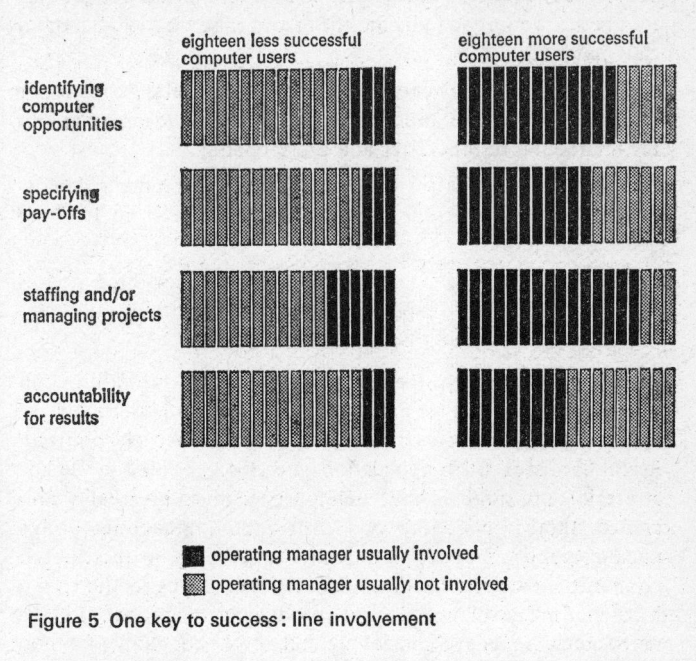

	eighteen less successful computer users	eighteen more successful computer users
identifying computer opportunities		
specifying pay-offs		
staffing and/or managing projects		
accountability for results		

■ operating manager usually involved
▨ operating manager usually not involved

Figure 5 One key to success: line involvement

agement approval were not originated by operating managers in consultation with computer staffs but proposed independently by systems and programming professionals. Yet as Figure 5 indicates, the experience of the more successful computer users leaves little doubt that operating managers, well motivated and equipped with some knowledge of computer capabilities, are likely to be a better source of ideas for profitable changes in operations than are computer professionals. The most profitable applications uncovered in our study had originated with operating executives pondering such ideas as these:

If only we had a way to test the reliability of the sales forecasts made by these regional managers of ours, we might not find ourselves out of manufacturing capacity in Italy at the same time that we're laying off valuable skilled labor in Brazil.

If only we had a way of recording and analysing all our customer orders in one place, we ought to be able to allocate our production better – improve mill efficiencies and raise the yield from our raw materials.

If only we could easily check out our historical sales performance by product, package and so on, maybe we could interpret our test-marketing results faster and more reliably.

If only we could play with alternatives on our tanker deployment, we might use our capacity better – charter in less and charter out more.

If only we could project our needs for skilled labor three months out, we could save the expense of these crash recruiting and training programs.

Two lessons emerge from all the varieties of successful computer experience that we have studied. First, there is a unique set of *feasible and profitable* computer applications for each company. Second, most of these applications are closely related to the key strategic opportunities that the top executives are really concerned about: marketing and distribution operations in the package-goods company; production operations in the capital-equipment concern; facilities-planning operations in the chemicals maker; exploration and producing operations in the petroleum company; financial planning in the conglomerate; and so on. Such applications may be designed to reduce costs of goods sold, or to increase revenues by changing operating methods directly. Or, as already noted, they may seek to improve the staff work and analyses available to decision-makers.

These lessons, in turn, have important implications for the top manager. Since each corporation has its own unique pattern of problems and opportunities, there is danger in trying to duplicate the successes of others. The computer development strategy that has worked well for one company may not work at all for its competitor. For the same reason, a company would be unwise to pin all its hopes on vendor-produced 'applications packages' where major-development projects are at stake. Nor can the answers be left to the professionals. No top executive is going to turn over the operation of his key departments to specialists with little or no operational experience.

In almost every industry, at least one company can now be found that is pioneering in profitable new uses of computers. In such companies, our findings suggest, the key to success has been a strong thrust of constructive interest from corporate operating executives who have put their own staffs to work on computer-development projects. (See Figure 5 for evidence on this point.)

We believe that other companies will follow their lead. Indeed, it may soon be a nearly universal practice to transfer operating staff to computer-development projects, either by making them members of a project team or by attaching them for a year or two to the corporate computer staff.

Another much-discussed area of computer use is management information and control. A few companies have already succeeded, by means of computer systems that sort out and speed routine data to the user, in notably improving the quality and quantity of specific information available to operating managers. Others, as noted earlier, have made profitable use of the computer in decision-making through simulation models designed to improve decision-making by predicting the impact of alternative actions on economic and operating realities. Skills in the construction of such models are widespread and growing, and their results have frequently been noteworthy.

A fertilizer manufacturer has used computer-based simulation to help top management answer such questions as these:

How much should we plan to manufacture, ship and store at the plant location in order to minimize total accumulated costs of production, distribution and storage over a one-year period?

How much, if at all, could we reduce total costs by renting additional storage in outlying locations? What would be the effect on our present production, shipping and storage program?

How large a market area should be served from each of our warehouse locations?

Where should new plants be located with respect to warehousing locations and market areas?

A well-known food products company has constructed and used a computer-based simulation model enabling it to assess, under various possible 1970 and 1975 environments: (1) the relative profitability of different product markets; (2) the desirability of investing in new-market development; (3) the impact of investment in added plant capacity; and (4) detailed income statements based on these projections.

Again, computer-based risk analysis techniques have demonstrated their value in a wide range of capital-investment situations. The industrial chemicals industry is known for the magnitude of both its investment and its risks. Since industry capacity directly affects market price, these risks are aggravated by the uncertainty of industry intelligence regarding competitors' plans for adding new capacity. Risk analysis, made practical by computers, has proven invaluable for evaluating alternative strategic plans with the help of simulation models, sometimes even including simulation of alternative competitive responses by the application of game theory. To exploit the potential of these and related techniques, an increasing number of corporations are finding it necessary to supplement the professional skills of computer men by recruiting specialists in the management sciences.

What is true of simulation models, however, is hardly true of the so-called total management information systems that have beguiled some computer theorists in recent years. Much effort and ingenuity have been devoted to the design and promotion of such systems, and many businessmen are understandably intrigued by their possibilities. Yet in terms of economic payoff and operational feasibility they are as yet ill-defined, and certainly they are a long way from practical realization in business.

Doubtless the computer's information-processing capabilities will one day eliminate the need for large staffs occupied with collecting and interpreting information from various sources for the use of decision-makers. But whether the computer will ever be able to evaluate strategic opportunities or indicate the proper timing for corporate actions is by no means assured. Nor are man-machine dialogs via desk-side consoles likely to become a feature of life in the executive suite any time in the foreseeable future; top management's 'interface' with the computer is unlikely to be anything more exotic than a telephone, with a human information-specialist at the other end of the line. What counts, of course, is not the sophistication of the interface but the responsiveness of computer-based systems to management's information needs, and the quality and timeliness of the information they can provide. Here, without doubt, the potential of the computer is only beginning to be realized. But 'integrated total management information systems' drawing on a single-data base, which have so often been touted as the wave of the future, are another matter. They have not yet come to pass – and it is far from clear that they ever will.

In short, the potential of comprehensive computer-based information systems and the role of the computer in decision-making are still surrounded by question marks. Research in these areas may be a sound investment for some companies, even though the costs of experimentation are high. But no company should embark on a program to develop a major management information system except to meet a specific, well-defined need. Even then it should carefully weigh its options – including the option of applying its scarce computer resources to areas where operating success and economic payoff can be predicted with greater confidence.

Keys to the future

In embarking on the present study, McKinsey and Company analysts were not seeking fresh evidence of a gap between potential and performance with respect to the management of the computer effort. The existence of such a gap has been obvious for some time to most informed observers. We were concerned, rather, with determining the present dimensions of the gap, analysing its background and causes, and synthesizing from the practices of the top performers a few succinct management guidelines for maximizing the computer's effectiveness and unlocking its profit potential.

Evidence on the first two points – the performance gap and its underlying causes – has been reviewed in the earlier pages, and the general nature of the remedies has been indicated. Against this background, certain lessons emerge for the senior executive who is dissatisfied with the performance gap he sees in his own company and is determined to do what he can to close it.

In the computer field, as in other areas of management, the usefulness of generalizations from successful experience is rather sharply limited. It is possible to state *some* of the principles a company must follow to have a reasonable chance of success with the computer. But there will always be other factors – constraints, needs or opportunities – which are peculiar to each company and can only be determined in the light of the individual situation. Hence it is useful to state general precepts only if their neglect is rather widespread and the consequences of that neglect are costly. This is the case in the management of the computer effort today.

The common denominators of successful computer practice, as seen in the companies we have examined, may be expressed in terms of three principles: the rule of high expectations, the rule of diversified staffing and the rule of top-management involvement.

The rule of high expectations. In all of the companies that are realizing outstanding *economic* results from computer applications, top management is simply unwilling to settle for anything less. In the less successful companies, many managers exhibit a tendency to keep the computer at arm's length for fear of exposing their technical inadequacies. This tendency is conspicuously absent among the top computer users. Departmental and divisional managers in these companies know that top management will insist on economic results – and that they will be held personally responsible for achieving those results.

The new president of a capital equipment manufacturer, who has succeeded in getting a badly stalled computer program in his company moving again, typifies the prevailing tone of management expectations in the better-performing companies. Said he: 'I ask my department heads to give me regular formal reports on their current successes and failures with computers and their future objectives. Right now they're a bunch of sheep with computers. I aim to convert them into enthusiasts, so that later I can be jockey, not herdsman.'

The rule of diversified staffing. A computer staff whose experience is limited to successful conversion of accounting and administrative operations is seldom really qualified to design and install new systems in major operating functions such as manufacturing and marketing. Computer professionals alone seldom constitute an adequate corporate support staff.

To make the most of their opportunities for profitable corporation-wide use of the computer, therefore, the top-performing companies take one of two organizational approaches. Some assign to the corporate computer staff – along with the usual operations-research specialists and other professionals – at least one talented individual with experience in each of the major functions of the business. Others, relying on the project approach to computer development, use project teams staffed by temporary transfers from operating departments. This arrangement, too, encourages good support from all levels of management.

To head up the computer staff and assume responsibility for the implementation of development plans, the outstanding companies have in all cases been careful to pick a manager who commands, or can quickly learn to command, respect and confidence through the organization. The appointment of the right man to this position is seen as a key contribution that top management can make to the success of the computer effort. It is also recognized that this individual's effectiveness depends more on his personal stature and professional skills than on the precise location of his unit in the corporate hierarchy. We found no evidence, statistical or otherwise, to suggest that high organizational status assures effective performance on the part of the corporate computer staff.

The rule of top-management involvement. If any one man can be said to hold the key to the computer's profit potential, it is probably the chief executive. He has a very definite responsibility for the success of the computer development effort, and it is not a responsibility that he can safely delegate.

At a minimum, the chief executive who wants maximum results from his company's computer effort must do five things. *First*, he must approve objectives, criteria and priorities for the corporate-computer effort, with special attention to the development program. *Second*, he must decide on the organizational arrangements to carry out these policies and achieve these objectives. *Third*, he must assign responsibility for results to the line and functional executives served by the computer systems – and see to it that they exercise this responsibility. *Fourth*, he must insist that detailed and thorough computer systems plans are made an integral part of operating plans and budgets. *Fifth*, he must follow through to see that planned results are achieved.

There is nothing novel in any of these recommendations; they are standard operating practice for most chief executives in most of their traditional areas of responsibility. Many otherwise effective top managements, however, are in trouble with their computer efforts because they have abdicated control to staff specialists – good technicians who have neither the operational experience to know the jobs that need doing nor the authority to get them done right.

Only managers can manage the computer in the best interests of the business. The companies that take this lesson to heart today will be the computer profit-leaders of tomorrow.

Reference

MCKINSEY & COMPANY INC. (1963), 'Getting the most out of your computer', private publication.

6 J. Dearden

How to Organize Information Systems

J. Dearden, 'How to organize information systems',
Harvard Business Review, vol. 43, 1965, pp. 65–73.

Many companies today are faced with serious problems in utilizing the capabilities of computers. Computers are not being used effectively in providing management with the best information available for decision-making; they are not being used efficiently in terms of properly integrating the various information systems. Moreover, the situation appears to be getting worse rather than better. From observing this situation in business, I have come to the following conclusions:

The problem of organizing for effective management information systems will become progressively more severe in most companies as computer applications are extended.

Present concepts for organizing the systems and data-processing activities have fallen far short of providing a real solution. In fact, the favorite current approach – total systems – is leading us in precisely the wrong direction.

A new and different approach to the organization of systems responsibility is necessary if business is to begin to tap the potential of the modern digital computer and the related data-processing and transmission equipment.

The purpose of this article is to suggest an approach to systems organization which will help business to take advantage of future developments in modern data-processing equipment and techniques.

The wrong direction

About ten years ago, when computers first began to be acquired by business, the computer was used to automate a few independent systems. Typically, the first system to be automated was the payroll, followed by such applications as customer billing and stockholder records. When these applications were safely digested, the company might next consider automating the general accounting system and perhaps the inventory records.

At this point, redundancy of input, processing and output began to appear. It became evident that developing and maintaining a series of independent, automated information systems was not an efficient way to utilize the computer. With many companies reaching this stage at about the same time (five to seven years ago), a new term came into wide use – 'integrated data processing' (IDP). IDP was used to indicate the need to integrate the various automated information systems. The term soon was replaced by another phrase – 'total systems'.

Ambiguity and illusion

For at least four years, the term 'total systems' has appeared with monotonous regularity in the literature about computers and systems. The term has been used so much by so many people to mean so many different things that, as far as I can see, it has become completely meaningless. For example, take two recent definitions:

The total systems concept came about several years ago in view of the complexity of business systems. Simply interpreted, it calls for an overall study of all systems in a company before making major revisions in any one system (Field, 1969).

The goal of this management effort and investment of funds is often called the 'total systems concept'. This is nothing less than the complete monitoring of the business enterprise by a computer, or group of interconnected computers; the automatic control by machine of inventories, production scheduling, shipping, accounting and all other operations that can be reduced to mathematical representation; and the limiting of human control to such functions as setting over all objectives and reacting to such totally unexpected situations as earthquakes or wars (Klein, 1964).

In other words, total systems can mean anything from our old friend 'integrated data processing' to the ultimate automated business. The problem with the term, however, is not only its lack of precise meaning but also the implications it has for most systems people. The term implies to them that there is a single information system for a company and that this information system should be considered in total.

If the total systems concept assumes a single information system for a company, I have two objections to it. First, the entire information system of a company is just too large and all-encompassing to be a meaningful and useful classification. Second, the development of an information system requires such different kinds of skills that the term has little use in helping management approach the problem of organizing for the development of effective management information systems. In fact, the concept of a single information system implies a central control of the systems effort, and this is where I believe that the total systems concept (regardless of how it is defined) is leading us in the wrong direction.

More useful approach

I believe that a more useful way to approach the organization of the systems effort is to break down the systems and data-processing activities both horizontally and vertically. Horizontally, the systems activities can be classified by the type of work performed; vertically, the systems activities can be classified by the kind of information handled. Let us examine these classifications and see how management can use them in organizing a company's systems and data-processing activities.

Horizontal classification

The development of an information system is a more or less continuous process from the time that it is first conceived until it is in operation. Each phase tends to blend into the following phase so that there is rarely a clear cut-off point where one phase ends and another phase starts. Consequently, the development of an information system is frequently considered to be a relatively homogeneous operation. The result of this is a tendency to classify certain people as 'information-systems specialists' and certain organization components as 'systems departments', and then to consider these people and departments as specialists in the entire continuum of the development of an information system.

Stages of development

I believe it is incorrect to treat systems development as a homogeneous operation. It appears to me that there are three stages in the development of an automated information system which are distinctly different and which, consequently, should be treated differently – even though the points where one stage stops and another starts will always overlap, since the exact divisions are somewhat arbitrary. These stages are as follows:

Stage 1: Systems specification. Systems specification includes the design of all of the aspects of a management information system that are important *to the users*. It includes principally the basic decisions as to what information should be provided by the system. In many systems the timing of the information, the output format, and the input format will be defined in this stage. For example, in a budgetary-control system, the format of the budget proposals, the procedure for approval, and the format and timing of the budget performance reports would all be specified because they are important to the users. On the other hand, the specifications for an automated inventory control system might not include the format of the replenishment order to the supplier; as long as the order is intelligible, it makes no difference to the warehouse manager what the order format looks like.

Stage 2: Data-processing implementation. Data-processing implementation is concerned with those things that are important *to the processing of the data*. The purpose in this stage is to design a data-processing system that will most efficiently implement the systems specified in stage 1.

Stage 3: Programming. Programming generally starts with the systems flow charts and ends when the program is running on the computer.

The foregoing stages of systems development are, of course, interrelated. The systems specification must take into account the restraints inherent in the data-processing function; the data-processing stage must take into account the capability of the equipment available and, to some extent, the abilities of the programmers. The important point is that the person responsible for data processing can restrict the systems requirements only as a result of the data-processing capabilities; *he is in no way responsible for deciding what kind of information should be generated by the system.* The same is true of the programmer. He develops as efficient a program as possible to provide the specified data-processing system. This system would be modified only because of equipment requirements.

Distinguishing characteristics

One of the principal reasons why these three stages are often confused in business is that different systems go through different stages. Some systems will go through only the specification stage. For example, a system for accumulating personnel information on top executives might be handled exclusively at that stage, for the data-processing, being relatively trivial in nature, could be managed as part of the design of the system.

Other systems go through only stages 2 or 3. There are two major reasons for this:

1. Many systems are well established. Their specifications are already defined when they come up for management decision; the only problem is to automate them. This is often true, for example, when accounting systems are automated.

2. Many systems require no system design at all of the stage 1 type. The requirements are prescribed by the nature of the task, as, for example, in payroll or customer billing.

What are the distinguishing characteristics of the stages? Let us look at each in turn.

Systems specification. From an organization point of view, the most important characteristic of systems specification is that, as a general rule, it should be *decentralized to operating management*; that is, it should be controlled by the people who are to use the system. I conclude this for the following reasons:

1. The operating manager is responsible for the effectiveness of his information system. He cannot delegate this responsibility to a staff group outside his control. In many areas, developments in

new information techniques make it vital that a continuing program of keeping up to date be maintained. It is likely that this process will become more important in these areas. Already here the seat-of-the-pants operating manager is a thing of the past. The operating manager must now accept the responsibility for adopting new, improved information techniques or be replaced by someone who will. But he cannot be held properly responsible for the adequacy of his information system if the function is performed by an independent staff group.

2. In general, systems responsibility has proved to be less successful in actual business situations when it has been centralized than when it has been decentralized. In a study he made of the systems activities of several companies, Philip H. Thurston observes:

It seems to me that the specialist should *not* dominate, and that companies would do well to give more responsibility to operating managers (1962).

A somewhat similar opinion was reached by John T. Garrity in his study of computer effectiveness in twenty-seven companies (1963). He concludes that the factors which marked the difference between those companies that used computers effectively and those that did not were the involvement of operating management in the selection of computer projects, the manning of these projects and the responsibility for the progress of these projects.

My own experience completely supports these findings.

1. The design of different types of systems requires different types of skills and knowledge – and frequently there is little overlap. For example, the skills required to design a manufacturing expense-budget system are quite different from the skills required to design a production-scheduling system. In other words, the task of specifying those things that are important to the user varies from function to function and company to company, a fact which argues for decentralization.

2. In designing an information system for management, an intimate knowledge of the problems in the particular field is necessary. Often this requires spending a not inconsiderable amount of time working directly with users and in installations. For example, it would usually be necessary for a man to work in budget-

ary control for some time before he would be qualified to design a budgetary control system. On the other hand, it would be quite easy for a budget man to gain a knowledge of computers sufficient to enable him to understand how they could improve the budgetary control system.

3. Many information systems use new communication devices other than the computer. For example, James Bright listed twenty such devices used in production scheduling and control (e.g. closed-circuit television and two-way radios) in a paper presented at the international conference of the American Institute of Industrial Engineers in September 1963. These devices tend to be different for different kinds of information systems. The staff-systems specialist will, therefore, usually be less well informed about them than about machines like the computer which are standardized.

In summary, the systems specification function should be decentralized because management cannot delegate this responsibility to a staff group, because the work does not usually progress well when done by a staff group, and because the knowledge and capabilities required to perform these jobs are not usually found in staff-systems specialists.

Data-processing implementation. As contrasted to systems specification, the data-processing activity *can and should be centralized*. I conclude this for the following reasons:

1. Integration of the information systems of a company is desirable from an economic point of view. Information once captured and recorded on punched cards, magnetic tape or a disc file may be used in several different systems. Also, the storing, updating and processing of the data can usually be accomplished more efficiently with one integrated system. Finally, integration of the data-processing *requirements* of a company can be accomplished best where the responsibility for data processing is centralized.

2. Many companies are moving toward developing a company-wide (or, in large, decentralized companies, division-wide) data base. This consists of storing in one place all the data that will

be used in the various automated systems. This not only helps to achieve the economies of integration just mentioned, but frequently makes it possible to provide management with information that otherwise would not be practicable to obtain.

3. The development of data-processing systems can be handled best by staff specialists because knowledge of equipment and data-processing techniques is the primary requirement. When automated information-systems development reaches the data-processing stage, there is a great deal of similarity among systems. Consequently, data-processing development tends to be a homogeneous type of activity, not significantly different for different kinds of business-information systems.

4. There is no reason why operating management should not delegate to a staff group the responsibility for implementing the information system *once this system has been specified.*

In summary, therefore, I believe that the work of implementing a new data-processing system should be centralized because it provides economies through the integration of information systems, because it can best be handled by staff specialists, and because it is the type of activity that operating management can delegate to a staff function.

Programming. As might be expected, of all of the three stages programming lends itself best to centralization. The reasons are:

1. Programming is more economically accomplished on a centralized basis.

2. Writing business programs requires a special knowledge of equipment and programming languages, and there is practically no difference in the skills required to program the different systems.

3. Management must delegate the task of programming to someone, and it makes little difference whether it is a staff unit or a department reporting directly to the manager.

Vertical classification

I believe that there are three major information systems in a typical company, and a varying and indefinite number of minor systems. A major system is one that affects the entire structure of an organization. A minor system is one that is confined to a limited part of the organization. Let us look at the major systems first.

Financial information

Every company has a financial information system of some kind. The basis of this system is the flow of dollars through the organization (see Culliton, 1960). The financial system is largely concerned with internal and historical information, although in budgeting or capital investment analysis the system does provide future projections.

The financial information system frequently involves handling huge amounts of data. To this extent, therefore, computers and related data-processing equipment can be very useful. The computer's main purpose, however, is to reduce the cost of data handling. In most instances the quality of the data will not be significantly changed.

The financial system is used principally for management control; hence speed of data in terms of minutes (or even days) is not generally important. It is important that deadlines be met, once established; but deadlines are not likely to be such that information must be transmitted as soon as it is known. For example, it is important to meet a payroll date, but you have considerable flexibility in setting this date. It is not imperative that you pay your people as soon as possible after they complete their work.

The financial system is perhaps the most important single management information system in any company. It is also, probably, the oldest and best developed. The custom has been for management to give the controller the responsibility for administering this system, but management cannot delegate the responsibility for the *adequacy* of the system. Top executives have the continuing responsibility for evaluating how well the controller is performing his functions and for replacing him when this performance is not adequate.

Personnel data

The personnel information system is concerned with the flow of information about people working in an organization. Almost every company maintains records of its personnel. In the smaller companies these records may be quite sketchy. In the larger companies they can be very elaborate and, in some instances, maintained on random-access equipment.

A personnel information system has many uses to management. It provides a systematic way for accumulating data that can be used to make promotional decisions by every level of management. It is a means of knowing what talents are available to fill specific jobs. A good personnel information system will ensure that a company is not firing people in one plant while hiring people with the same skills in another plant.

The data in a personnel information system are exclusively concerned with people. The information is largely internal and historical, although some information is obtained from outside sources. As in the financial information system, timing in terms of minutes or hours is usually not critical.

Computers and related equipment may be used in a personnel information system. The main use of such equipment is information storage and retrieval. Consequently, the size of a company and the amount of data maintained for each employee will determine whether computers, or even punched-card equipment, are economically feasible. Computers can increase the efficiency of storing and retrieving data, but I do not see that they can make any substantial improvement in the *quality* of the data available to management.

The responsibility for the personnel information system is usually assigned to the industrial relations officer. Here, also, management is responsible for evaluating the adequacy of the system.

Logistics information

The logistics system is concerned with information about the physical flow of goods through an organization. It covers procurement, production and distribution. As with the other two systems, it uses mostly internal and historical data; but, unlike them, it is largely concerned with operating control, not management control. Thus it includes such activities as inventory control, production planning and control, scheduling and transportation.

In this type of system, timing is very important. Moreover,

huge amounts of data must be handled and manipulated. Consequently, the logistics system offers the greatest potential for using the new communication equipment – in particular, the computer and related information-processing and transmission devices.

There can be several separate logistics systems in any one company. Where separate product lines are manufactured in separate facilities, each product line could have a more or less independent information system.

The assignment of the responsibility for the logistics information system is not nearly so well developed and thought out in the typical company as the other two systems are. For one thing, being an operating control system, it has not required the degree of top-management involvement which is characteristic of the other two systems. The main concern of top management is that production schedules are being met. (If they are not, this condition is reflected in the financial information.) A second factor is that the responsibility for coordinating a logistics system is frequently not assigned to a particular executive. As a result, the system in many companies is relatively uncoordinated and far from optimum in development. In fact, much of the total systems activity has been started because of the problems in the logistics field. If you examine carefully the description of a typical total system, you will find that it is concerned almost exclusively with the logistics system.

Other systems

The financial, personnel and logistics information systems have several characteristics in common: they exist in nearly all companies; they affect almost all parts of the business; they usually involve handling large amounts of data; and they are principally concerned with internal and historical data.

But what about other information systems? Some of them can be integrated to some extent with the three main ones just mentioned; others may be completely separate. I shall describe a few of them briefly:

Marketing information. One of the most important information systems to many businesses is marketing information. The characteristics of this kind of system will differ widely among companies. For example, some systems maintain a great deal of data about such things as competitive actions, customer profiles and advertising effectiveness; other systems maintain only information about sales records. A marketing information system tends to be handled completely within the marketing function and usually presents no problem of coordination with the other systems.

Research and development. Many companies have systems for exchanging information on the results of research findings. Other companies set up systems to examine and store the literature on relevant research.

Strategic planning. The three main information systems in my classification are largely concerned with historical, *internal* data. The two minor ones just described are largely concerned with historical, *external* data. A strategic planning system deals with still another aspect: future projections. Many companies have formal systems for long-range planning. Although a strategic planning system will use information developed for other systems, it will tend to use it in a different manner, i.e. as a basis for projecting the future. Also, because of the confidential nature of much strategic planning, this group tends to be separated organizationally, and the information developed is carefully guarded.

Executive observation. Much important management information comes from the personal observations of company executives or discussions with outside people at clubs and meetings. These sources comprise a system (if it can be called a system) which is concerned with *non*-documentary information; yet it can be of primary importance to top management. In fact, some companies would miss this information more than they would miss the monthly financial statements!

Proposed organization

I would now like to propose an organization structure based on the vertical and horizontal classifications just described. This structure is represented diagrammatically in Figure 1.

The principal features of this proposed organization are as follows:

1. The systems-specification function (the first stage) is organized by type of system.

2. The responsibility for systems specification is decentralized to the managers who are responsible for using the data.

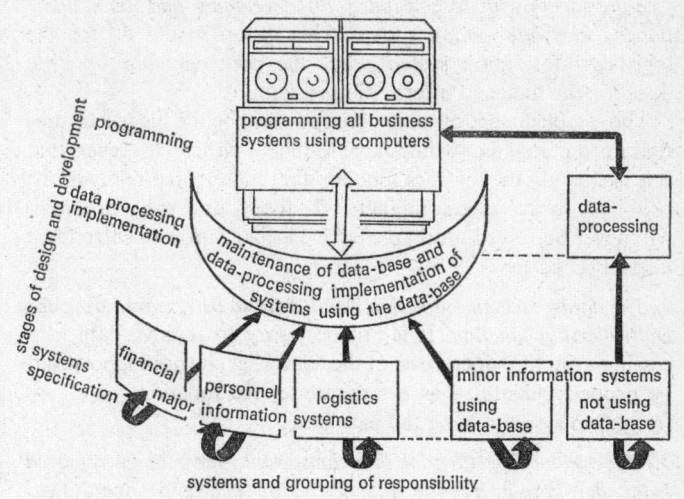

Figure 1 Generalized organization chart for systems and data processing

3. The data-processing function (second stage) is centralized to the extent that it encompasses the responsibility for implementing the data-processing of all systems using the same base of facts, figures and other data.

4. Information systems not using the data base generally control their own data-processing implementation (see the right side of Figure 1).

5. The programming (third stage) is centralized for reasons stated earlier in the article.

Changes in management

The effect on the typical company of changing to an organization similar to that proposed in the preceding section may not be so great as might be supposed at first glance. For one thing, most companies have organized their financial information system and their personnel information system in a manner very similar to that proposed. To the extent that this is true, only four major changes are necessary.

1. *A group must be established (probably under the manufacturing vice-president) with responsibility for developing and maintaining the logistics information system.* This group would do for the logistics information system what the controllership function does for the financial information system.

The establishment of such a group would be the biggest change that most companies would have to make. Notice, however, that it is frequently the logistics function that has created many of the problems in utilizing computers effectively, and these problems will never be solved until an effective organization to solve them is established.

2. *The data-processing function would have to be removed from the controllership function.* It is not necessary to remove data processing from the supervision of the controller; it should, however, be properly identified as a separate-service function for all information systems using the data base.

3. *The systems-specification functions would have to be removed from the data-processing function.* For example, operations-research personnel working in the data-processing group would properly be assigned to logistics information specification.

4. *Management must assign the responsibility for developing and maintaining a data base to a central data-processing group.* The extent of this group's responsibilities and authority should be precisely and explicitly stated.

Conclusion

At the present time, many companies tend to mix data-processing functions with the task of designing logistics information systems. A symptom of this condition is the development of an inventory control system by a data-processing group which reports, say, to the corporate controller. I believe that this condition has led to severe problems in the effective utilization of the computer.

Coordination is necessary among the people responsible for the various stages in the development of an information system and among the various types of information systems. The need to coordinate, however, is no reason to combine unlike activities and differing levels of responsibility into a single group responsible for all information systems.

If the data-processing function is to be reasonably effective in integrating the data requirements of the various systems using the same main reservoir of data, it will be necessary for it to coordinate carefully with the people responsible for systems specification concerning future plans. This, also, is no reason for combining two types of different activities.

As for the proposed organization plan, it does not preclude the 'team' approach to systems development. In fact, this will always be a useful approach, particularly when a company is undertaking a considerable amount of new systems work. The important point is that the responsibility for a team that is developing systems specifications should be with the operating management.

Nor does the proposed organization preclude the use of staff specialists. These specialists, however, should perform as an advisory function and, when working directly on a systems-specification project, report to the operating manager who is to use the system.

In the new scheme of things the data base does not constitute a 'total system' by any means. It includes only the information common to the participating systems that can be stored economically and maintained centrally. It will be largely historical, internal information. There is a great deal more information than this that management will need. In fact, the higher up in the managerial hierarchy we go, the more important becomes external and projected information that may be no part of the data base.

There appears to be a fad developing for storing as much data as possible on random-access equipment. This is all right if it is more economical to do so or if the availability of the information is sufficiently vital to warrant the extra cost. It appears to me, however, that much management information is not meaningful, nor is it necessary to obtain it on an instantaneous basis. Management should, in my opinion, question the unbridled use of random-access equipment and be sure that the added expense is offset by added benefits.

Perspective on progress

It will never be possible to have a perfectly integrated data-processing system. Nevertheless, it is vital to have adequate management information. Consequently, care should be taken not to delay the installation of an information system merely because it does not fit conveniently into an integrated plan. Executives may be losing some important advantages of developing an information system earlier in order to save a few dollars in data-processing costs. Sometimes, too, delay is a cover-up for inadequate performance on the part of data-processing personnel. They argue that they are giving up benefits now for the large future benefits of having a total system when, in fact, the delays are the result of poor implementation.

The important thing is to have effective management information systems. Any organization that will accomplish this objective is satisfactory. If, for example, the controller is the only one in an organization who is able and willing to develop logistics information systems, he must be the one to do it. (But in such a case it should be recognized that the step is taken for purposes of expediency, not because it is the best way to operate.)

At some time in the future, the dream may materialize of having *all* of the information relevant to the management of a particular company stored on random-access equipment in one place; of having this information continuously updated; of having any information management wants immediately available on request; of having all information systems controlled by a group of high-level experts. At the present time, however, I believe that this dream is not possible, practicable, or even desirable. We do not have the equipment or the techniques. Indeed, at present the typical company does not have people with anywhere near the ability to develop such systems even if they were practicable. In fact, most companies have trouble obtaining people who can perform the much less demanding tasks that are required by the organization scheme described in this article.

We should not be sacrificing today the real gains from practical computer applications for the sake of this will-o'-the-wisp concept of 'total systems'. We can realize these gains only by organizing in a realistic manner, using the resources we have and meeting the needs we can understand.

References

CULLITON, J. W. (1960), 'Diagram of management control', *Harvard Bus. Rev.*, vol. 38, no. 2, p. 144.
FIELD, J. W. (1964), 'A new brand of data-processing manager – Part 2', *Computers and Data Processing*.
GARRITY, J. T. (1963), 'Top management and computer profits', *Harvard Bus. Rev.*, vol. 41, no. 4, pp. 6–12, 172–4.
KLEIN, H. E. (1964), 'The office: management's billion dollar system', *Dun's Rev. Mod. Indust.*
THURSTON, P. H. (1962), 'Who should control information systems', *Harvard Bus. Rev.*, vol. 40, no. 6, pp. 135–9.

Part Three
Management Information in Real Time

Reading 7 discusses the likely effects on management of powerful real-time management information systems based on comprehensively indexed data-banks. The author predicts centralization of decision-taking and the elimination of middle management. He suggests that the style of top level management might be dramatically altered.

Reading 8 describes the operation of a large-scale real-time system used to control airline seat reservations.

Reading 9 has become a minor classic in the literature of management information systems. The author debunks a good deal of the literature on real-time management information and suggests that real time information becomes more valuable the *lower* down the management ladder one goes. Top-level management are interested in what will happen in two years time, not in what happened two minutes ago.

7 G. Burck

Management Will Never Be the Same Again

G. Burck, 'Management will never be the same again', *Fortune*, vol. 70, 1964, pp. 197–200, 202–4. G. Burck is a member of the Board of Editors of *Fortune* Magazine.

One horror story making the rounds in the data-processing world tells of a new centralized computer system that delivered divisional operating results to the executive suite before the division managers themselves received the tidings. The company's sadistic president, to show these poor middle managers how superfluous the computer had made them, called them in and harassed them about the data they had not yet seen. The story is probably apocryphal, and certainly should be; but it suggests tolerably well the momentous change that is overtaking the art and science of management as computers become more widely used.

The change is most visible in middle management. Because the computer replaces manpower directly and enables other machines to replace more, it is perhaps the most powerful tool for raising human productivity ever invented, and automatically does away with many supervisory jobs. What may be more portentous, it is changing subordinate-management's tasks by eliminating many time-honored functions, such as those of bookkeepers, and by creating many new ones, particularly jobs for systems men with special skills in applying the computer to management science. Some corporations, though loath to discuss the effects of the computer for quotation, regard the displacement of middle management as a harder and more persistent problem than the displacement of line employees, and farsighted ones are thinking in terms of management retraining programs.

But the most important change, because it is basically responsible for all others, is the change at the top. As the power plant of the new so-called information technology, the computer is steadily raising high management's power to make accurate decisions. The world has immemorially underestimated the order of talent needed to run a complex business, particularly a highly competitive enterprise. Compared to the relatively formal problems normally encountered by engineers, physicists and even medicos, the problems confronting the high corporate executive are gnarled and ill-structured. Wherever he looks deeply, he gazes into uncertainty. About the future of the economy he must take the word of soothsayers who usually have been 100 per cent right only when explaining why the other fellow was wrong. He can spend millions to find out precisely what the public wants, only to watch his brave new product flop ignominiously. He may know 786 employees by their first names, but just when he thinks everything at home is proceeding according to plan, some division manager makes another ten-million-dollar mistake.

The unique achievement of the computer is that it is enabling the executive to clear away some of the uncertainty that surrounds him, to subtract some of the variables from the circumstances that fret him, to convert many ill-structured and inherently insoluble problems into well-structured and partly soluble ones, to rely less on hunches and intuition and more on analysis, to behave less as an artist and more as a scientist in disposing of routine matters, and to save his creativity and imagination for more important work.

The word is recentralize

Because the computer does all these things, it is changing the very structure of the US corporation; and this article will look at this consequential change before examining more closely the computer's effect on top and middle management. The machine's power to help US managers control their operations has generated what appears to be nothing less than a pervasive recentralization or reintegration movement. For twenty-five years or so decentralization has been the word for corporations all over the world, and the reason seems obvious enough. As companies grew larger and more complex or more diversified, one man or a small group was no longer able to run them directly. So top managers broke down their organizations functionally, and delegated authority to divisional managers, who were often assigned divisional profit goals, and often were spurred by profit sharing.

The most resplendent example of successful decentralization

doubtless has been the world's largest corporation, General Motors, whose combination of decentralized operations and centralized policy was described by Alfred P. Sloan Jr in recent issues of this magazine. But as one observer has remarked, General Motors decentralized so successfully that it has functioned almost as smoothly as a small homogeneous company. What he meant was that the ideal administrative set-up is provided by the small tight company, in which one man knows everything that is going on and can make all the decisions without cutting red tape, when and as he thinks best. If decentralization was a historical necessity it was also something of a necessary evil, the tribute that a big organization had to pay to the economies of mass production. Although most decentralization has been successful, the near disaster of General Dynamics testifies that making it work is not easy. It also testifies eloquently to the fundamental fact that the top managers of a big company justify themselves to their stockholders and the world only if they can and do manage.

A fundamental reason why one man or a few men could not control large decentralized companies was that the science of gathering and passing on information was not far enough advanced. This is no longer true. In the words of Herbert Simon, professor of administration at the Graduate School of Industrial Administration at Carnegie Tech, just as the cable and wireless once brought far-flung and quasi-autonomous ambassadors and proconsuls under home-office control, so the computer is now radically altering the balance of advantage between centralization and decentralization. It organizes and processes information so swiftly that computerized information systems enable top management to know everything important that happens as soon as it happens in the largest and most dispersed organizations. The general staff can bypass many intermediate functionaries, dispense with much subordinate judgement, and even plan and create for the whole organization by using the computer to simulate the company's activities in dozens or hundreds of hypothetical situations in order to choose the best course. The problem is not how to get information to the top, but how to keep useless information from coming to the top, how to decide on the 'exception' information that management needs to act effectively. That problem, as we shall see, is being solved handily. At all events, whenever a decentralized company used the computer to automate operations, and particularly when it has installed management information systems, it has willy-nilly found itself behaving more like a centralized company.

Recently General Motors itself stirred up systems men with an announcement that it will computerize its world-wide communication system, which connects all GM's far-flung activities with Detroit. The network will be used not only to order autos and parts but to help control inventories and production and to keep Detroit *au courant* with everything relevant happening everywhere. Systems specialists promptly concluded that this was the first step in creating a huge management information system. GM insists that its policy is to remain decentralized; the new network is strictly for communications, and will make for better, not more, control. However, some of GM's divisions, which are huge corporations in their own right, are moving toward centralization by building up integrated data systems of their own. One expert who has observed similar developments in other companies predicts that GM will inevitably find itself pulling its automotive divisions more tightly together.

An outstanding example of the trend is Standard Oil (NJ), the world's number two corporation. As a holding company that owns all or a majority of the stock of more than two hundred 'affiliates', Jersey has been a textbook example of a company that lives by a policy of decentralization. Each affiliate has its own board of directors and officers, and the parent company nominally 'coordinates' the efforts of those affiliates. Actually, the word 'coordinate' has been increasingly a euphemism for 'control', which many companies, particularly international operators, understandably prefer not to use. Among other things, Jersey has always performed the very important *operation* of directing and allocating the flow of petroleum products among its affiliates. In this job, the computer proved indispensable years ago, and since then the machine has made possible a good deal more coordination and standardization of operating practices. As a Jersey official in a symposium sponsored by Chicago's Graduate School of Business and the McKinsey Foundation back in 1959 said

As we minimize differences, something is happening to the concept of decentralization. . . . Why should it continue? Obviously the answer is not so simple, particularly since decentralization has become so institutionalized and will create pressures for its retention. Change must await technological developments.

'Intuition can be structured'

Some of those developments have arrived, and many are on the way. To decide just what should go into a management information system, Melvin Grosz, Jersey's painstaking assistant-controller and head of its computer-systems department, has developed what he calls an Objectives Decomposition Method, or a way of decomposing or analysing management information requirements. 'We've already discovered,' says Grosz, 'that most decisions people consider intuitive today can be found to have an underlying structure if you work long enough.' For three years, using this method, Grosz and his staff have been building up what they call a Uniform Reporting System, and in two years hope to have it transmitting all the important information the company's coordinators will need to cope with the world at large, including forecasts of supply and demand and of financial conditions. Even today the affiliates are kept in line by the computer. Although each affiliate develops its own operating and long-range plans, New York must decide what will be the best combination for the company as a whole. Therefore it appraises the plans by simulation and passes on them accordingly.

International Harvester also has been known as a decentralized company. But its Systems and Data Service Department, which enjoys the status of other major departments, has acquired a reputation for doing very 'advanced' work, and Harvester in effect has been recentralizing. John DeMots, manager of Harvester's systems department says

If you originally decentralized to give responsibility and profit control to a certain level and you are getting good performance, why then you may have no reason for recentralization. But if you decentralized because you lacked information to make timely informed decisions to command and control your organization – if you hadn't time to make the decision centrally and also make it effective – you centralize. Vertically as well as laterally, we think we have achieved a substantial integration of information. And we're just starting.

One of the most ambitious computerized information systems anywhere is being installed at Mead Corporation, sixth in the paper industry, under Vice-President Richard Gilbert, formerly head systems man with McDonnell Aircraft. Mead is a disparate company, with seventeen operations making wood pulp, various kinds of paper, paperboard and containers. Accordingly, it has been highly decentralized. In 1961 the company, on the advice of its accountant, Touche, Ross, Bailey & Smart, decided to install a 'total' system that would include not only process control but a 'real time' management information system – i.e. one that delivers information in time to do something about it. This system, though unfinished, is already tightening up on efficiency, mainly by centralizing primary planning and control functions. Gilbert says

When I first came to Mead, each plant operated with its own data-processing system and bought its own equipment. Now we have coordinated the divisions in systems work and in equipment purchases; everything ties in with the total system. We are thus able to centralize corporate planning functions. At the same time we will measure the performance of various divisions against the corporate plan and provide the information that will let them follow it. We'll set the limits but, of course, we won't tell a manager how to run a plant. We'll centralize the essential things, such as scheduling; but if there is a power failure or flood the mill manager must have the flexibility to take action as he sees best.

As this article went to press, International Paper, largest in the industry, announced that it will set up what it describes as the most comprehensive information and control system ever undertaken in the paper business. IP will expand its present computer installations with 'nearly a score' of IBM 360 machines, complete with visual-display units; thus it will create an integrated system that will both control papermaking processes and provide on-line information to the company's manufacturing, financial, scientific and marketing functions.

More hierarchical than ever?

There is a certain amount of disagreement about just how far recentralization will go and what will happen to it over the long run. A few management experts have argued that computerization would result in more decentralization because subordinate managers, the men on the spot, could use their own computers to make better decisions than anyone else. This argument, though, has largely run aground on the fact that centralized computer systems have already saved millions by company-wide integration of such functions as purchasing, inventory control and scheduling. Another argument goes that responsibility for making money endows subordinate managers with unusual drive, and that computerized recentralization will destroy this valuable asset. The case has some merit, but with important qualifications. If subordinate managers with responsibility have shown commendable drive, they have frequently cherished 'sub-goals' that have not necessarily coincided with the goals of the company as a whole. Experience already suggests that discreet monitoring of their activities by computer systems makes them more sensitive to the company's goals. And if, as many students of management wisely argue, the job of high management is to advise and help rather than boss subordinate managers, it can do so only if it knows a great deal about the work of the man being advised.

Always making allowances for the fact that circumstances alter cases, some say that the combination of highly centralized *policy* control and a certain amount of decentralized *operating* authority is feasible and desirable. Even so, the computer brings shifts in emphasis. US Steel, which has been regarded as a classic example of too much decentralization, is now recentralizing drastically, consolidating seven operating divisions, closing twenty-five sales offices, and coordinating sales and research. But it is also creating five area sales vice-presidents and increasing somewhat the responsibilities of operating and sales middle managers. Norman Ream, head of Lockheed's systems department, believes that management 'philosophy' should govern the degree of centralization. He also thinks that high management's new ability to control a lot of activities may also make for more decentralization of a kind; companies will be more inclined to diversify or to move into products wholly different from their regular line in order to even out cyclical sales fluctuations.

Looking further into the future, Thomas Whisler of the University of Chicago's Graduate School of Business, whose speciality is studying the effect of new technology on business, theorizes that top management will be composed more than ever of formally educated professionals, who as such may not be as organization-minded as today's executives. Thus the corporate high command might become less a military hierarchy and more a partnership. Operations may be centered in the computer, Whisler explains, and creative managerial functions distributed among professional specialists. But he has no clear idea of how this might come about. Meantime, he agrees with those who believe that the computer is centralizing control, and that the management-structure of corporations will be hardly less hierarchical than it is now.

Most of the information at the top manager's disposal has been too inaccurate, incomplete and untimely for well-structured, analytical reasoning. Partly because of this, he has needed a high talent for intuitive judgement, or for assaying variables and unknowns (as women are supposed to) by rules of thumb, shrewd guesses and sharp feelings. The computer is not only enabling but forcing him to think more explicitly and analytically – to formalize his decision-making process and spell out his judgements.

The machine can even show up defects in his problem solving. A systems man has commented

Nothing is more ill-defined than the way some managers arrive at their decisions. One day one of our managers gave me a question he said the computer couldn't solve: 'If two large machines are to be delivered to separate customers on 1 February and I have only one machine on that date, which customer do I ship to?' My answer was that if he told me the process by which *he* arrived at his decision, we could instruct the computer to go through the same process. The trouble with that manager, we soon found out, was that he never knew *how* he arrived at his decisions, and his intuition wasn't good enough to keep him from making mistakes.

The top manager is rapidly discovering that he has to take a deep and continuous interest in the computer, in working closely with systems men, in overcoming middle-management resistance, and in valuing results. Too many, in the past, have turned the whole 'mess' over to a subordinate and forgotten about it. The subordinate, when he found out what could be done with the computer, necessarily began to monkey with the company's structure, job functions and basic ways of doing business. Unless the top executive knows what the subordinate is doing and why, crises are inevitable. Thomas Whisler tells of one controller who had installed computer applications that were largely responsible for turning red ink into black, and had streamlined the company's whole structure. The president, who didn't know what was going on and hardly knew a computer from a water cooler, had meanwhile brought in some ambitious young men to replace retiring division-heads. As a result of the ensuing collison between the new division-heads and the systems people, the company was in turmoil, and its computer program was stalled for two years.

Thanks to the computer's ability to monitor, officers of large and disparate companies are finding it profitable to take a more thoroughgoing interest in their operations than they ever have, and without spending an undue amount of time on them. For several years now Westinghouse has been showing poor profit margins. In a resolute drive to improve the company's productivity, Donald Burnham, its new president, is using his computerized management information system to diagnose weaknesses and cut costs. He has reduced the white-collar staff by some 4000, including a lot of middle managers.

The computer system in another company showed that inventory in one large division had begun to rise inordinately, to around one hundred million dollars, and looked as if it might get out of control. The president immediately took interest.

We asked the guy in charge if that was a valid inventory picture, and he agreed it was. We said it looked about thirty million dollars too high, but he replied that he had an enthusiastic bunch of salesmen who he thought could get rid of the stuff. This attitude was OK, but the overstock held on for four months. That manager is no longer with us.

Many dice, each with a hundred sides

This new mastery of operations gives – or should give – top management more time for its *strategic* work, such as long-range planning, policy making, choosing staff, deciding on new products and capital investments, financing, and public and labor relations. All computer-systems men worth their salt have learned that top management does not need the detailed, day-to-day information that is proving so valuable to subordinate managers. To keep their top executives from being inundated with useless (if interesting) paper, they are striving to provide them only with the 'exception' operating information that demands or justifies action. Indeed, the systems departments of several companies, notably Jersey and Chrysler, are engaged in analysing exactly what their staff executives do, and what information they now need and are likely to need as the supply of relevant facts increases.

What is more, computer-systems men are working hard to help management cope with the baffling variables of the outside world and to master the strategic problems of planning. Eastman Kodak was one of the pioneers in computerized planning. Making a highly perishable product (film) with a highly seasonal (summer) demand, it has stabilized employment by using computers to plan its production and inventories, and to keep the latter adjusted to sales.

One of the important planning tools is simulation, which demonstrates the effect of alternative courses. When an executive is trying to make up his mind, he weighs pros and cons and estimates or guesses on the odds in his favor; simulation simply expands and formalizes this process far beyond the power of any human mind. Nothing is attended with more uncertainty than the process of deciding on expansion and capital investment; as David Hertz of McKinsey and Company has remarked, it is like trying to predict the outcome of a game played with many dice, each with a hundred sides. Hertz has worked out an ingenious simulation process that considers as many as forty variables, such as market size, selling price, market growth rate, share of market, investment required. With the computer he works out the odds on these variables and the likeliest combinations of them; and by repeating the process of selection and computation he arrives at the best bet.

Similar if less sophisticated methods are being used by dozens of companies. Westinghouse employs an alternative investment routine that rates projects by yield and time required to produce the yield, and relates them to the capital available. Much depends on the estimates of return made by the division managers, and part of the technique is to appraise the judgement of division managers. 'Five years from now,' says Lou Hague, director of business systems, 'we'll be able to say manager A has made investments that were right 93 per cent of the time, while manager B has a rating of 72 per cent, and such ratings will help our line management make the final decisions.' Trying to reduce the uncertainty in assaying its external environment, Westinghouse is also building up a store of what it calls directive and environmental information, covering employees, stockholders, customers, government and the economy. 'We are working on a simulation of the company in the real world,' explains Hague. 'It's a tough job, but that isn't stopping us.'

Some companies have begun to use the computer in marketing – not merely for processing orders, but for sales forecasting, distribution planning, pricing and even for buying advertising space. International Harvester's John DeMots says

We are learning how to gauge the market. For the first time we know 90 per cent of what we sell within a few days. We try not only to forecast broad trends but to figure out what industry volume and our own volume will be. Our sales manager, as a result, is channelling his and his staff's energy more effectively.

Uncertainty is infinite

Such advances, computer people believe, will eventually be followed by systems that will command enough pertinent information to answer almost any relevant question put to them. 'The corporate planning technique,' predicts Whisler, 'will then become one of creative interrogation.' An elaborate demonstration of how creative interrogation would work occurred 4 May 1964, at Fort Wayne, Indiana, when representatives of several companies attended a demonstration of a computerized management information device staged by Information Management Facilities Inc. Given a computer with enough information, such a system could not only save untold hours of expensive paper shuffling in the decision-making process, but also generate decisions with more logic behind them. At least two large corporations are installing display systems; and Edward Orenstein, President of Data Display Inc. of St Paul, maker of such systems, predicts that within five years more than 1000 civilian management information systems will be using perhaps 10,000 units.

Thus the job of top manager will be at once easier and harder. He will be faced with less uncertainty in the sense that he will know more about what is going on, but he will have to think harder and more precisely to take advantage of his knowledge.

He will have more time for creative interrogation and long-range strategy; but this will be little if any easier than it is now. Though he will make more analytical judgements, he will need his intuition as much as ever, for ignorance and uncertainty are infinite as space itself, and there will always be plenty to guess about. Moreover, a large part of every such manager's job always will be concerned with human relations, and he must present a figure of esteem to a world whose judgements always are heavily charged with emotion. But all these time-tested faculties and virtues will avail him little if he does not understand how to use the new management tools at his disposal.

The survivors and thrivers

The middle and lower orders of managers seem in for a stormy time. Now middle management is an unavoidably imprecise term, covering very different jobs in different companies; but as a rule it includes all managers below the highest policy level, sometimes even vice-presidents. Nearly six years ago, in what is something of a classic among systems people, Thomas Whisler with Harold J. Leavitt (now of Carnegie Tech) published in the *Harvard Business Review* several speculations on how the new information technology, powered by the computer, would affect management in the 1980s. Among their many prognostications, most of which seem to be turning out well, were two about middle management:

1. Its ranks would be reduced, and business organization structures would consequently be 'flattened'.

2. Many middle management functions would be routinized or formalized, so that many middle managers would in effect move downward.

The first of the two predictions seems to be coming true. The number of middle management jobs relative to output appears to be declining, and for several reasons. One is that white-collar jobs, apparently owing to the computer, are not increasing nearly as fast as they did. Between 1950 and 1960 the average increase was 2·8 per cent a year but last year it was less than 1 per cent. All this probably means fewer supervisory jobs.

The computer is also displacing a lot of middle management by forcing companies to change the nature of the jobs they offer.

Since accounting is often being done by computer as part of systems work, many bookkeeping departments as such are virtually being eliminated, and accountants are broadening into systems work and cost and financial analysis. Functions like credit management, warehouse management, and even sales have been consolidated. One firm, says Thomas Whisler, reduced the number of managerial positions in several divisions by 30 per cent in two years. But, he notes, that this kind of structural flattening is often accompanied by recombination of parts of former jobs into new bundles of responsibility. And

as you might expect, when the smoke of these reorganizations died away, the managers who survived and thrived were those who saw the advantage of this new system early.

The prediction that many middle management positions would be routinized or degraded doesn't seem to be coming off, at least not yet. But intermediate managers are, in some places, being thoroughly monitored by the computer; Lockheed's ADA data-collection system ('"On Line" in "Real Time,"' *Fortune*, April, 1964) prevents supervisors from indulging in 'load balancing', or the practice of transferring some work done from one day to another in daily reports, thus concealing the true capacity of their departments. Before installing data-gathering equipment, Westinghouse rated one factory's production at 85 per cent; after the equipment was installed, the load balancing was discovered, and the plant was rated at 45 per cent; now it is at a true 80 per cent.

Checking up on supervisory management, however, is not quite the same as routinizing or degrading it, and it is hard to come up with specific examples of the latter. What happens, Whisler theorizes, is that a good deal of the average middle manager's job is ordinarily given over to communicating with customers, colleagues, employees; and the computer, by relieving him from the necessity of valuing all information that comes his way, is freeing him for other activities. Norman Ream predicts that

Much middle management will change from clerical and advisory work to short-range planning, in order to free top management for long-range planning.

G. Burck

Nevertheless, the computer is upsetting functions, displacing men and wiping out jobs, and it consequently is generating fear and resistance in middle management. This is one reason why top officers and systems men often prefer not to discuss the effects of the computer realistically; and why company systems men, who must of course get the cooperation of their own middle managers, allude to these men almost deferentially as their customers. A supervisor who has devoted his life to running a department that has become obsolete can be the hardest man of all to shift, and this is why, as we have noted, the realization is growing that displacement of middle managers may be a harder and more persistent problem than the displacement of blue- and white-collar employees.

If technical men are right, more adjustments are in the offing. The day will soon come, they say, when computers will be instructed to make decisions 'heuristically', i.e. by using rules of thumb and reasoning in terms of means and ends; thus the machines will gradually be able to solve not only well structured but badly structured problems, and so will be able to make many decisions now made by middle management. Carnegie Tech's Herbert Simon argues that most decisions governing routine day-to-day physical operation of companies will be programed and automated. Although most of the work in heuristics is being done in schools like Carnegie Tech and MIT, corporations already use the computer heuristically in simulation.

Tomorrow's managers

Now for the other side of the coin. Some ranks of middle management are being swollen by computer and systems men ranging all the way from programmers to specialists in such esoteric techniques as PERT and operations research. They are in short supply everywhere; the metropolitan Sunday papers contain pages of advertisements seeking their talents. These systems people are young, and a large percentage have advanced degrees; many are qualifying for more important jobs. 'We look for broader interests,' says Richard Gilbert. 'Some of our analysts are very able and don't want to be operations research people all their lives.'

Will these people fill a large percentage of tomorrow's top-management posts? In the past forty years a large part of high corporate manpower has been supplied by legal and financial talent, and for obvious reasons. Although these specialists had to master detail, they also had to take a broad, spacious view of their company's problems to understand and rationalize its role in the economy. Roger Blough of US Steel is a good example; as a young Wall Street lawyer assigned in the 1930s to defend US Steel against the charges of the Temporary National Economic Committee's investigation of 'bigness', he learned so much about the industry, both in detail and in the round, that he was soon chief legal talent for the company, and bound for bigger things.

The higher order of systems and computer people should be in an even better position to know about the business than lawyers and treasurers were. They not only will have to understand the company's operating techniques and its relationships with the outside world, they will have to take both an analytical and a creative attitude toward them. 'We think,' says John DeMots, 'we can bring in a young man and assign him to help design several systems, and teach him more about the business than in any other way.' Although the ranks of computer-systems men contain a lot of men who seem 'bloodless' and excessively engrossed in the technicalities of their indubitably fascinating business, some have already ascended to high management posts. The law of averages and their own intellectual growth should take care of others. The computerized world will be an oyster for the young man with brains, judgement, personality, education, ambition – and a good knowledge of computers.

8 A. L. Jacobs and P. Harman

The Scope of Computers in an Airline

A. L. Jacobs and P. Harman, 'The scope of computers in an airline', privately printed for internal circulation by BOAC.

Introduction

In BOAC we are developing one of the most advanced information-handling systems in the world. I use the term information handling deliberately – I could have referred to computers and allied techniques – not only because it happens to be the name of the department, but also because it throws emphasis on the end rather than the means. After all, our job in BOAC is running an airline, not computers. We are therefore only interested in computers as a tool, in what they can do for us, and as a means of getting information and better control over our activities.

What does information handling cover? Well, it has four main divisions. First of all it is responsible for all computer activity in BOAC. Secondly it is responsible for BOAC's communications, ground to ground communications across the world and also air to ground communications. The third arm is concerned with office services. This includes postal activities, registries, archives, typing pools and many similar activities. The fourth area, statistical services, produces statistics for the board and top management.

All these activities, you will appreciate, are related to the handling of information. From now on I shall be speaking solely of the computer and communications activities. The reason why these two major areas are linked together in the same department is very significant and will become apparent later.

Communications

Any airline must have reliable and efficient communications, not only for routine administration messages, but also for reservations and operational purposes. Most airlines use a specialist communications company to provide this service. This is the case with BEA, for example.

However, because of its size and the spread of its network, BOAC has found it economic to have its own network. This crisscrosses the globe serving over two hundred and twenty cities and airports in over seventy countries in all five continents. This is easily the largest privately-owned telegraphic network in the world. It is both faster and more economic than the outside services used by other airlines. The facilities are available to – and are widely used by – BOAC's commonwealth partners.

The Communications branch is also responsible for:

all BOAC's telephone services, including over forty PABX systems.

local VHF radio communications at some seventy airports all over the world. These are needed both for operational contact with aircraft in flight, and to assist with ground handling.

advising on all aspects of in-flight communications and navigational aids.

airport facilities such as closed circuit television systems, flight information services and public address systems.

Out telegraphic network has four nodal points – London, New York, Sydney and Hong Kong. These are places where many circuits come together and where therefore messages have to be routed or 'switched' from one circuit to another.

BOAC is now applying computers to this work – that is to switch messages automatically and to determine optimum routings and loadings. As a result transit times on our circuits have been reduced from hours to minutes, or even seconds, and accuracy has also been vastly improved.

We use two computers in London and a further two in New York for this work. In Sydney our pool partners, Qantas, have introduced two other computers in collaboration with us and this year BOAC's communications agents in Hong Kong are installing two further machines there. BOAC will then have a fully automatic network handling some 175,000 messages a day. You can see now that one of the reasons for linking communications and computers together in our organization is because a communications network like ours depends very much on computer assistance.

Our annual communications budget is some two and a half million pounds made up as follows:

World wide telegraphic network	1·8
Messages sent through other systems	0·2
Telephones	0·35
VHF and other facilities	0·15
Total	2·5

The total BOAC staff employed in communications is some two hundred and fifty.

Computer policies

BOAC got into computers early and by 1965 had two IBM computers operational, mainly on accounting work and statistics, as well as an STC computer giving passenger seat availability information to our main sales outlets in Europe and North America. All these machines are still working. However, in 1965, because of the rapid pace of computer development, it was decided to stand back a little, to take stock of our position, and to try clearly to formulate our long-term objectives with computers, and to prepare a coordinated plan for satisfying them.

In particular we decided that – subject to economic viability –

1. We wanted a *centralized* installation to serve the whole of BOAC from one set of inter-locking records. This would give us enhanced consistency and accuracy.

2. We wanted to *integrate* as far as possible, that is to plan jobs as a whole rather than piecemeal.

3. We wanted to go for *real-time* working. That is, we wanted BOAC staff to have direct access to the computers for feeding in data and requests as events were actually happening. Moreover we wanted responses to come back in seconds, quick enough for them to be used to help make decisions and control the business as the events being reported upon were still open. We did not want to use the computers solely for after the event reporting.

4. We wanted a computer system that could grow with our rapidly increasing volumes and needs up to 1980. We did not want to contend with repeated equipment changes. We wanted to be able to concentrate on the jobs to be done rather than the hardware.

We realized that these were ambitious aims and that it would take a long time to attain them all. Nevertheless we thought the targets were worth aiming for and we are now well on the way.

Equipment and communications

How can we serve a worldwide organization like BOAC from a centralized computer complex, particularly with the requirement to have response times in many cases measurable in seconds?

Let me say at once that real-time working is obviously not needed for all applications. We are currently at an advanced stage in developing it for passenger seat reservations, for passenger check-in, for aircraft loading and for controlling cargo movements. We also intend to introduce it for fare construction and teleticketing at major offices. Longer term we are investigating viability for engineering-maintenance work. There are clearly many other areas which we shall add to this list later on. On the other hand there are still many jobs where such quick responses are not necessary and where therefore more conventional procedures are adequate.

Let me first describe our plan for equipment to satisfy these needs.

We have installed three very large IBM computers at London Airport in a new building which has been purpose-built called BOADICEA House. We are linking these computers by a new network of high grade communication lines to our main offices in Europe and North America. The offices concerned are being equipped with clerk sets. These consist of keyboards, like typewriter keyboards, for feeding in data and requests, together with television screens onto which the responses are flashed back in a few seconds.

Our main centres in Europe and North America are also being equipped with Ferranti Argus computers. These serve as traffic policemen to control the flow of messages on the communication lines and to do local jobs. However, they all work under the control of the large computers at London Airport.

I have just referred to a new network of communication lines. Why? The answer is that BOAC's present telegraphic network, like other such networks, is not fast enough to support the quick responses that we need and that justify the use of television screens. Why are we restricting this plan to Europe and North America at least to start with? Quite simply because it is only in those parts of the world that the necessary high-grade communications yet exist. However, we have plans to extend this system to the Caribbean and Africa quite soon and another of our aims is a direct link with the smaller Qantas computers in Sydney.

To link other parts of the world to BOADICEA, i.e. Africa, Asia and Australasia, we are using BOAC's existing telegraph network. All we have had to do is to install a direct communications link between BOADICEA and our London message-switching computers. This gives BOADICEA direct access to the whole telegraph network.

For example, a person in Singapore wishing to send a message to BOADICEA simply feeds the message into a teleprinter in Singapore. The message then goes on our circuit to Hong Kong, to be automatically switched by the message switching computers in Hong Kong onto the Hong Kong–London circuit. On arrival in London the message is automatically switched by the London message switching computers onto the circuit connecting London to BOADICEA House. It is then fed direct into BOADICEA.

The only differences between stations served by television screens and the new communications network, and those in Africa, Asia and Australasia served by the existing telegraph network, are that the former get a much quicker service, and in the first case whereas access is through typewriter keyboards and television screens, in the latter case it is through conventional teleprinters. But it is essentially a distinction of speed and level of service rather than of principle.

In a way you can see that BOAC has two communications networks – a new fast network for Europe and North America and the existing telegraphic network which serves the whole world. Similarly you can regard it as having two computer systems, if you wish. We have the message switching computers which look after our telegraphic communications and we have BOADICEA, situated at London Airport, with its attendant Argus computers around the world, designed to give us a general service on all other applications.

You can now see why organizationally we have grouped computers and communications together. Not only do communications need computers to handle them but sophisticated real-time computing of the type we have in mind also depends very clearly on first class communications.

Altogether we are currently installing over eight hundred and fifty television type screens and over thirty Argus computers for the local traffic policemen work. In addition there will be two other Argus computers in London to handle cargo control. The network also comprises some three hundred and seventy teleprinters, and will handle some 250,000 messages per day on the new high-speed network and over 100,000 on the existing telegraph network.

As well as IBM for the central computers and Ferranti for the peripheral computers, large orders have also gone to Honeywell for the keyboards, to Kleinschmidt for printers, to Collins for communications equipment, to RCA for maintenance and to STC for installation work.

Reservations

I would now like to tell you what BOADICEA will do for BOAC. A wide range of applications will be covered involving every part of BOAC. I shall start with the passenger seat reservations job as this is the biggest we have undertaken – it has involved some three hundred man-years of development effort – and is one of the first now being implemented.

BOADICEA holds inventory records for all BOAC flights and many pool partner flights for eleven months ahead. It also holds availability and timetable information for hundreds of flights of other airlines.

When a passenger walks into a BOAC office equipped with our television screen sets, it is possible to answer requests on seat availability merely by keying in a few code letters. Responses are available within three seconds, even for stations as far away as Rome and Los Angeles, and include all the flights with seats available which most closely match the passenger's needs.

Once a flight has been selected the seat can be firmly booked through BOADICEA there and then. Indeed this is possible not only for BOAC and pool partner flights but also for flights of other airlines too, BOADICEA then immediately updates its inventories, or, where a sale is for a flight which BOADICEA does not control, sends a message to the other carrier concerned. The message is in such a form that if the other airline has its own computer it is possible to read it straight in.

Conversely where other airlines make requests for space on BOAC flights, the messages concerned are taken directly into BOADICEA which automatically sends a reply. In other words there is no manual intervention, and BOADICEA converses directly with other carriers' computers and reservations centres.

Once a seat has been booked BOADICEA takes in and records details of the passenger, his name, contact address or telephone number, ticket details, arrival information, special meal and seat requests, and so on. Particulars of his complete itinerary are held, covering not only BOAC flights or flights currently booked, but the whole journey, involving perhaps a dozen or more airlines and possibly twenty or thirty more flights. Moreover once such a record is set up in BOADICEA at a given office, it is straightaway available anywhere. So that no matter where a passenger turns up, BOAC knows all about him.

One of the features of this system is that there are no restrictions on the way passengers are handled. Queries can be presented to BOADICEA in random order and the whole system operates in a conversational mode. There should be no need to use any manuals. So far as the reservations agent is concerned he does not know whether the computer is next-door or thousands of miles away.

So far we have been talking of BOAC offices equipped with the television screen sets. For offices further afield, i.e. in Asia, Africa and Australasia, the procedure is very similar but slower. The only difference is that access to and from BOADICEA is through teletype machines of a conventional kind rather than television screens.

There are many other features to this reservation system. Where there is no space on flights which passengers request, BOADICEA automatically displays alternate flights or connecting flights or takes wait-list action. It is possible to book not only airline space but hotels, tours and taxis. You can book skycots and carrycots as well as seats. You can specify special meals or seats. BOADICEA also displays the latest flight information or full details of the places you intend to travel to. Where timetables alter BOADICEA automatically re-books passengers. BOADICEA also produces passenger lists and other information to stations all over the world so that they are fully aware in advance of the passengers and the requirements that they have to handle. Finally BOADICEA tries to optimize revenue, by protecting long-haul journeys against too many short sector bookings.

Other applications

Many other applications are being covered by BOADICEA. They include:

Passenger check-in	Guides clerk, checks reservations. Seat allocation.	integrated with reservations
Weight-and-balance	Controls loading. Dynamic. Approximations. Complex calculations. Trim.	
Flight planning	Optimum time tracks. Fuel calculations.	
Export cargo control	Control goods through new terminal to aircraft. Control storage and loading. Similar to reservations.	
Engineering	Consumables stock control. Component control, including forecast scheduled and unscheduled maintenance.	
In-flight data analyses	Special events and component performance.	
Accounting	Revenue accounting. Tariffs. Pensions and wages.	
Personnel	Selection and development. Inventory of skills.	

Statistics	Component defects. Personnel. Commercial. *Ad hoc.*
Planning.	Timetables. Station loading. Aircraft utilization. Payload and performance. Budgets. Profit and loss statement. Model working.

All aspects of BOAC's work are thus encompassed.

The total computer staff employed covering both operations and development is three hundred and fifty.

Costs

	£m
Computers and peripherals	9·0
Maintenance and other operating costs	12·0
Communication lines	5·5
Development staff	4·0
Buildings and installation costs	3·0
Miscellaneous	2·5
Interest on capital employed	6·0
Total	42·0

Benefits

You can see that BOADICEA is going to cost a great deal. We are also under no illusions on the problems we shall have in installing it and putting it to work for us. There will be major changeover problems, we shall have to get used to new behavioural patterns, many procedures and management functions will need a complete re-thinking.

Computers are never easy to install, and in many respects we shall have novel problems. We are moving concurrently on a wide front, impinging on every area of BOAC's activity. We are linking BOADICEA to BOAC centres all over the world on a twenty-four-hour basis. We intend to use our computers on a conversational basis, with questions and answers proceeding through keyboards and television screens, just as if each user had his own computer at his elbow.

Why are we incurring all these costs and problems? Why are we going into BOADICEA? There are several reasons.

We see BOADICEA, with its ability to handle increasing volumes, and its immunity from many of the problems at least that are associated with ever growing staff numbers, as being one way of combating increasing costs. On the strength of only four or five of the applications I have referred to, we expect BOADICEA to repay its outlay of £42m with savings over the next ten years exceeding £66m, so giving a net saving of about £24m equivalent to a return of over 18 per cent on the capital employed. And this is in terms of displaced staff and equipment only; it takes no account of extra efficiency and the revenue that could result. Much of our work involves peak loads and shift working for which extra staff is not the answer even if it could be found.

Secondly we need BOADICEA to help improve our service to the public. Reservations is a clear example where computer assistance is now essential to handle the volumes we are encountering. The incidence of bookings and cancellations in the twenty-four hours prior to departure is such that it is virtually impossible to keep accurate records manually. With BOADICEA this is all changed; all records are updated at once and in balance. Whereas before late cancellations could not be offered for resale in time, with BOADICEA they are available immediately. A 1 per cent increase in our load factor here seems quite on the cards and would result in a revenue increase of £1·5m p.a.

It is for similar reasons that we need BOADICEA for message switching – without fast communications no airline can operate efficiently – for cargo control and, particularly with the advent of 747s, for departure control. Indeed it is difficult to see how check-in and flight dispatch for these larger aircraft at large airports could take place at all without computer assistance, if frequent delays and congestion are to be avoided.

Finally we need BOADICEA as a management service. BOADICEA will provide management with far more accurate and up-to-date information than is possible by any other means. In addition the computer's ability to carry out complex calculations at high speed and to examine the effects of alternatives, makes the whole decision making process more scientific, both at the tactical level, e.g. determining optimum inventory levels to hold or planning maintenance schedules, and at the strategic level, e.g. deciding the correct number of aircraft and crews needed to operate a given pattern of services. Indeed, without the use of computers it is difficult to see how BOAC could remain competitive in terms of service and efficiency, in view of ever increasing traffic volumes, the complexities of route patterns and the growing tempo of competition and business conditions generally.

Fortunately we are able to afford BOADICEA. We are also quite convinced that BOADICEA is something that neither we nor any other major airline can afford to be without.

9 J. Dearden

Myth of Real-Time Management Information

J. Dearden, 'Myth of real-time management information'
Harvard Business Review, vol. 44, 1966, pp. 123–32.

The latest vogue in computer information systems is the so-called real-time management information system. The general idea is to have in each executive's office a remote computer terminal which is connected to a large-scale computer with a data bank containing all of the relevant information in the company. The data bank, updated continuously, can be 'interrogated' by the manager at any time. Answers to questions are immediately flashed on a screen in his office. Allegedly, a real-time management information system enables the manager to obtain complete and up-to-the-minute information about everything that is happening within the company.

The purpose of this article – aimed at a time span of the next five to seven years – is to raise some serious questions concerning the utility of a real-time information system for top management. I will try to show that it would not be practicable to operate a real-time *management control* system and, moreover, that such a system would not help to solve any of the critical problems even if it could be implemented. I will also try to show that in other areas of top management concern a real-time system is, at best, of marginal value. It is my personal opinion that, of all the ridiculous things that have been foisted on the long-suffering executive in the name of science and progress, the real-time management information system is the silliest.

Meaning of real time

One of the problems in any new field of endeavor is that there is frequently no universally accepted definition for many of the terms. It therefore becomes nearly impossible to question the validity of the concepts underlying the terms because their meanings are different to different people. The term 'real time' is no exception. In fact, in a single issue of one computer magazine, back-to-back articles defined real time differently; and one example, cited in the first article as an illustration of what real-time is *not*, appeared in the second article as an illustration of what a real-time system *is*.

Semantic confusion

One concept of real time is demonstrated by these two quotations:

A real-time management information system, i.e. one that delivers information in time to do something about it (Burck, 1965, p. 106).

A real-time computer system may be defined as one that controls an environment by receiving data, processing them and returning results sufficiently quickly to affect the functioning of the environment at that time (Martin, 1965, p. 378).

The problem with both of these definitions is that they are too broad. *All* management-control systems must be real-time systems under this concept. It would be a little silly to plan to provide management with budget performance reports, for instance, if they were received too late for management to take any action.

The following is a description of real time that comes closer to the concept of real time as it is used by most systems and computer people:

The delays involved in batch processing are often natural delays, and little advantage can be obtained by reducing them. But elimination of the *necessity* for such delays opens new and relatively unexplored possibilities for changing the entire nature of the data-processing system – from a passive recorder of history (which, of course, is valuable for many decisions) to an active participant in the minute-to-minute operations of the organization. It becomes possible to process data in *real-time* – so that the output may be fed back immediately to control current operations. Thus the computer can interact with people on a dynamic basis, obtaining and providing information, recording the decisions of humans, or even making some of these decisions (Martin, 1965, p. 381).

System characteristics

To expand somewhat on this description, the term 'real-time system' as used in this article will mean a computer system with the following characteristics.

1. *Data will be maintained 'on-line'*. In other words, all data used in the system will be directly available to the computer – that is, they will be stored in the computer memory or in random access files attached to the computer. (This is in contrast to data maintained on magnetic tapes, which must be mounted and searched before information is available to the computer.)

2. *Data will be updated as events occur*. (In contrast to the 'batch' process, where changes are accumulated and periodically updated.)

3. *The computer can be interrogated from remote terminals*. This means that the information stored in the computer can be obtained on request from a number of locations at a distance from the place where the data are processed and stored.

Perhaps the most widely known example of a real-time system currently in operation is the American Airlines SABRE system for making plane reservations.

Potential applications

With the new generation of computers, random-access memories have become much less expensive than has been true until now. This fact, coupled with the advances made in data-transmission equipment and techniques, will make many real-time applications economically feasible.

Real-time methods will improve those systems where the lack of up-to-the-minute information has in the past resulted in increased costs or loss of revenue. I believe that many companies will employ real-time methods to control all or part of their logistics (the flow of goods through the company) systems. For example a manufacturer of major household appliances might have raw material and work-in-process inventories in his manufacturing plants, and finished-goods inventories both in company and distributor warehouses and in dealer showrooms. There is a more or less continuous logistics flow all along the route from raw material to retail customer. If all of the data on inventory levels and flows could be maintained centrally and updated and analysed continuously, this would not only solve many of the problems now faced by such a manufacturer, but would make it possible to provide better all-around service with lower inventory levels and lower costs (particularly in transportation and obsolescence).

There are, of course, many other potential applications for real-time management information systems, and I believe that they will be used extensively in the next few years. However, these applications will take place almost exclusively in logistics, and, as I shall explain later on, techniques that may improve a logistics system will not necessarily improve a management-control system. I want to make it clear at this point that I am not opposed to real-time systems *per se*. I believe they have valuable applications in operating situations. I am only opposed to using real-time information systems where they do not apply. The balance of this article will consider top management's use of real-time systems.

Management functions

As used here, the term 'top management' will apply to the president and executive vice-president in centralized companies, plus divisional managers in decentralized companies. In other words, I am considering as top management those people responsible for the full range of a business activity – marketing, production, research and so forth. I am also assuming that the company or division is sufficiently large and complex so that the executive makes only a limited number of operating decisions, if any. I believe that this is a reasonable assumption in considering real-time management information systems. A company where the president makes most of the operating decisions could scarcely be considering a sophisticated and expensive computer installation.

Six categories

This part of the discussion considers, in general terms, the functions of top management. The purpose is to establish how a typical executive might spend his time so that we may later evaluate the extent to which his decision-making can or cannot be helped by real-time computer systems. I have divided top management's functions into six general categories – management control, strategic planning, personnel planning, coordination, operating control and personal appearances. Each is discussed below.

Management control. One of the principal tasks of a manager is to exercise control over the people to whom he has delegated responsibility. Ideally, this control consists of coordinating, directing and motivating subordinates by reviewing and approving an operating plan; by comparing periodically the actual performance against this plan; by evaluating the performance of subordinates; and by taking action with respect to subordinates where and when it becomes necessary.

The formal management control system will, of course, vary with the type and size of business as well as with the type and amount of responsibility delegated to the subordinate. Nevertheless, all effective formal management control systems need three things:

1. A good plan, objective or standard. The manager and the subordinate must agree as to what will constitute satisfactory performance.

2. A system for evaluating actual performance periodically against the plan. This would include both a clear explanation of why variances have occurred and a forecast of future performance.

3. An 'early warning' system to notify management in the event that conditions warrant attention between reporting periods.

Strategic planning. This consists of determining long-range objectives and making the necessary decisions to implement these objectives. Much of top management's strategic planning activity involves reviewing studies made by staff groups. Capital expenditure programs, acquisition proposals and new product programs are examples of studies that fall into this area.

Another phase of strategic planning consists of developing ideas for subordinates to study – that is, instead of waiting for staff or line groups to recommend courses of action, the executive develops ideas of his own as to what the company should be doing.

Personnel planning. This important function of management deals with making decisions on hiring, discharging, promoting, demoting, compensating or changing key personnel. In the broadest sense, this consists of organizational planning. Personnel planning is, of course, related both to management control and strategic planning. Nevertheless, there are so many unique problems associated with personnel planning that I believe it is reasonable to consider it as a separate function.

Coordination. Here management's function is to harmonize the activities of subordinates, especially where it is necessary to solve a problem that cuts across organizational lines. For example, a quality control problem might affect several operating executives, and the solution to this problem might require top management's active participation. In general, this activity tends to be more important at the lower organization levels. The president of a large, decentralized company would perform less of this coordination function than his divisional managers because interdepartmental problems are more common at the divisional level.

Operating control. Almost all top executives perform some operating functions. For example, I know a company president who buys certain major raw materials used by his company. Usually, the operating decisions made by top management are those which are so important to the welfare of the company that the executive believes the responsibility for making them cannot be properly delegated.

Personal appearances. Many top executives spend much time in performing functions that require their making a personal appearance. This can vary from entertaining visiting dignitaries to giving out twenty-five-year watches. (I shall assume the activities involving such personal appearances will not be affected by a real-time management information system.)

Real-time practicality?

The purpose of this part of the article is to examine, in turn, each of the management functions described above (except the last point) to see whether or not it can be improved by a real-time information system.

Management control

I do not see how a real-time system can be *used* in management control. In fact, I believe that any attempt to use real time will considerably weaken even a good management-control system. (In setting objectives or budgets, it may be useful to have a computer available at the time of the budget review to calculate the effects of various alternatives suggested by management. This, however, is not a real-time system, since a computer console need be installed only for the review sessions.)

Calculating performance. In the area of performance evaluation, real-time management information systems are particularly ridiculous. When a division manager agrees to earn, say, $360,000 in 1966, he does not agree to earn $1000 a day or $1000/24 per hour. The only way actual performance can be compared with a budget is to break down the budget into the time periods against which performance is to be measured. If the smallest period is a month (as it usually is), nothing short of a month's actual performance is significant (with the exception of the events picked up by the early warning system to be described below). Why, then, have a computer system that allows the manager to interrogate a memory bank to show him the hour-to-hour or even day-to-day status of performance against plan?

Even assuming objectives could logically be calendarized by day or hour, we run into worse problems in calculating actual performance, and worse still in making the comparison of actual to standard meaningful. If the performance measures involve accounting data (and they most frequently do), the data will never be up-to-date until they are normalized (adjusted) at the end of the accounting period. I will not bore you with the details. Suffice it to say only that a real-time accounting system which yields meaningful results on even a daily basis would be a horrendous and expensive undertaking.

Let us go one step further. Performance reports, to be meaningful, must include an explanation of the variances. This frequently involves considerable effort and often requires the analyst to spend time at the source of the variance in order to determine the cause. Would this be done every day or oftener? Ridiculous! There is one more thing about performance reports. The important message in many reports is the action being taken and the estimated effect of this action. In other words, the projection of future events is the important top management consideration. Will this be built into the real-time system? Since this involves the considered judgement of the subordinate and his staff, I do not see how this could possibly be done even on a daily basis.

Early warning. How about real time for providing an early warning? Here, also, I do not see how it could be of help. Early warning has not been a problem in any top management control system with which I have been acquainted. In most instances, when situations deteriorate to the point where immediate action is required, top management knows about it. As the manager of a division ($100 million a year in sales) said to me, when I asked him how he knew when things might be out of hand in one of his plants: 'That's what the telephone is for.'

In any case, it is possible to prescribe the situations which management should be apprised of immediately, without even relying on a computer. Furthermore, the important thing is to bring the situation to top management's attention *before* something happens. For example, it is important to inform management of a threatened strike. Yet a real-time management information system would pick it up only *after* the strike had occurred.

In summary, then, early-warning systems have been put into operation and have worked satisfactorily without a real-time system. I see nothing in a real-time management information system that would improve the means of early warning, and such a system would certainly be more expensive. (Note that here I am talking about management-control systems. The early-warning techniques of many logistical-control systems, in contrast, could be greatly improved by real-time systems.)

My conclusion on management control is that real-time information cannot be made meaningful – even at an extremely high cost – and that any attempt to do so cannot help but result in a waste of money and management time. Improvements in most management-control systems must come from sources other than real-time information systems.

Strategic planning

Since strategic planning largely involves predicting the long-run future, I fail to see how a real-time management information system will be of appreciable use here. It *is* true that past data are required to forecast future events, but these need hardly be continuously updated and immediately available. Furthermore, much of the preparation of detailed strategic plans is done by staff groups. While these groups may on occasion work with computer models, the models would certainly be stored away, not maintained on line between uses.

Perhaps the most persistent concept of a real-time management information system is the picture of the manager sitting down at his console and interacting with the computer. For example, as a strategic planning idea comes to him, he calls in a simulation model to test it out, or a regression analysis to help him forecast some event; or, again, he asks for all of the information about a certain subject on which he is required to make a decision.

It seems to me that the typical manager would have neither the time nor the inclination to interact with the computer on a day-to-day basis about strategic planning. Problems requiring computer models are likely to be extremely complex. In most instances, the formulation of these problems can be turned over to staff specialists. Furthermore, I think it would be quite expensive to build a series of models to anticipate the manager's needs.

Under any conditions, strategic planning either by the manager alone or by staff groups does not appear to be improved by a real-time system. Models can be fed into the computer and coefficients can be updated as they are used. Between uses, it seems to me, these models would be most economically stored on magnetic tape.

Personnel planning

A real-time management information system does not help the top manager to solve his problems of personnel planning, although the computer can be useful in certain types of personnel-data analysis. About the only advantage to the manager is that information becomes available somewhat more quickly. Instead of calling for the history of a particular individual and waiting for personnel to deliver it, the manager can request this information directly from the computer. Therefore, while a remote console device with a visual display unit *could* be used for retrieving personnel information, the question of whether it *should* be used is one of simple economics. Is the additional cost of storing and maintaining the information, plus the cost of the retrieval devices, worth the convenience?

Coordination

The coordination function is very similar to the management-control function with respect to potential real-time applicability. A manager wants to know right away when there is an interdepartmental problem that will require his attention. As is the case with early-warning systems developed for management control, a real-time system is not necessary (or even useful, in most cases) to convey this information. Further, I cannot see how a real-time management information system could be used in the solution of these coordination problems, except in unusual cases.

Operating control

There is no question that real-time methods are useful in certain types of operating systems, particularly in logistics systems (see McGarrah, 1966). To the extent that a top executive retains certain operating-control functions, there is a possibility that he may be able to use a real-time information system. Because of the necessity of doing other things, however, most executives will be able to spend only a limited amount of time on operating functions. This means generally that they must work on the 'exception' principle. Under most conditions, therefore, it would seem much more economical for a subordinate to monitor the real-time information and inform the top executives when a decision has to be made.

It is very difficult to generalize about this situation. Here, again, it appears to be one of simple economics. How much is a real-time system worth to the manager in relation to what it is costing? I cannot believe that there would be many instances where a manager would be concerned with operating problems to the extent that a real-time information system operating from his office would be justified.

Reporting by computer

In recent months, there have been experiments to replace traditional published reports by utilizing consoles and display devices to report information directly to management. Although these techniques, strictly speaking, are not real-time, they bear such a close relationship to real-time systems that it will be useful to consider them here.

Modus operandi

The general idea is that the information contained in the management reports would be stored in the computer memory so that the manager could ask for only the information he needed. This request would be made from the computer console, and the information would be flashed on a screen in his office. For example, a manager could ask for a report on how sales compared with quota. After looking at this, he could then ask for data on the sales of the particular regions that were below quota and, subsequently, for detail of the districts that were out of line.

The benefits claimed for this type of reporting are as follows:

1. The manager will receive only the information he wants.

2. Each manager can obtain the information in the format in which he wants it. In other words, each manager can design his own reports. One manager may use graphs almost exclusively, while another may use tabulation.

3. The information can be assembled in whatever way the manager wants it – that is, one manager may want sales by areas,

and another may want it by product line. Furthermore, the manager can have the data processed in any way that he wants.

4. The information will be received more quickly.

Important considerations

Before installing such a system, it seems to me, a number of things should be taken into account.

First, what advantage, if any, does this system have over a well-designed reporting system? Since the storage and retrieval of data in a computer do not add anything that could not be obtained in a traditional reporting system, the benefits must be related to convenience. Is there enough additional convenience to justify the additional cost?

Second, is it possible that for many executives such a system will be more of a nuisance than a convenience? It may be much easier for them to open a notebook and read the information needed, since in a well-designed system the information is reported in levels of details so that only data of interest need be examined.

Finally, will the saving in time be of any value?

It seems to me that the two main considerations in installing such a system are the economics and the desires of the particular executive. There is one further possibility, however, that should be carefully considered. What will be the impact on the lower-level executives? If these people do not know the kind of information their superiors are using to measure their performance, will this not create human-relations problems?

Without going into details, I can see many problems being created if this is not handled correctly. With a regular reporting system, the subordinate knows exactly what information his superior is receiving – and when he receives it – concerning his performance. Furthermore, the subordinate receives the information *first*. Any deviations in this relationship can cause problems, and the use of a computer to retrieve varying kinds of information from a data base is a deviation from this relationship.

Three fallacies

If management information on a real-time basis is so impractical and uneconomic, why are so many people evidently enamored with this concept? I believe that the alleged benefits of real-time management information systems are based on three major fallacies.

Improved control

Just about every manager feels, at some time, that he does not really have control of his company. Many managers feel this way frequently. This is natural, since complete control is just about impossible even with the best management-control system. Since most companies have management-control systems that are far from optimum, there is little wonder that a feeling of insecurity exists. In the face of this feeling of insecurity, the promise of 'knowing everything that is happening as soon as it happens' has an overpowering appeal.

As explained previously, real-time will not improve management control and, consequently, will not help to eliminate the insecurity that exists. What is usually needed is a combination of improved management-control systems and better selection and training of personnel. Even at best, however, the executive will have to accept responsibility for what other people do, without having full control over their actions.

'Scientific management'

There appears to be considerable sentiment to the effect that the scientific way to manage is to use a computer. This fallacy implies that the executive with a computer console in his office is a scientific manager who uses man–machine communication to extend his ability into new, heretofore unavailable, realms of decision-making.

I believe that it is nonsense to expect most managers to communicate directly with a computer. Every manager and every business is different. If a manager has the necessary training and wishes to do so, it may be helpful for him to use a computer to test out some of his ideas. To say, however, that *all* managers should do this, or that this is 'scientific management', is ridiculous. A manager has to allocate his time so that he spends it on those areas where his contribution is greatest. If a computer is useful for testing out his ideas in a given situation, there is no reason why he should have to do it personally. The assignment can just as easily be turned over to a staff group. In other words, where a computer is helpful in solving some management problems, there is no reason for the manager to have any direct contact with the machine.

In most instances, the computer is of best use where there are complex problems to be solved. The formulation of a solution to these complex problems can generally be done best by a staff group. Not only are staff personnel better qualified (they are selected for these qualifications), but they have the uninterrupted time to do it. It seems to me that there is nothing wrong with a manager spending his time managing and letting others play 'Liberace at the console'.

Logistics similarity

This fallacy is the belief that management-control systems are merely higher manifestations of logistics systems.

The fact is that the typical real-time system, either in operation or being planned, is a *logistics* system. In such a system, for example, a production plan is developed and the degree of allowable variances established in a centralized computer installation. The actual production is constantly compared to plan; and when a deviation exceeds the established norm, this fact is communicated to the appropriate source. On receiving this information, action is always taken. Either the schedules are changed or the deficiency is somehow made up.

Notice that speed in handling and transmitting vast amounts of information is essential. This is the critical problem that limits many manual logistics systems; and the computer, particularly with real-time applications, goes a long way toward solving the speed problem.

In contrast, speed in processing and transmitting large amounts of data is *not* a critical problem in *management-control* systems. Consequently, the improvements that real-time techniques may effect in logistics systems cannot be extrapolated into management-control systems.

The critical problems in management control are (a) determining the level of objectives, (b) determining when a deviation from the objective requires action and (c) deciding what particular action should be taken. The higher in the organizational hierarchy the manager is positioned, the more critical these three problems tend to become. For example, they are usually much more difficult in planning divisional profit budgets than plant expense budgets. In some instances the computer can help the manager with these problems, but I do not see how it can solve them for him. Furthermore, the use of computers in solving these problems has nothing to do with real-time.

Short-term view

While real-time management information systems may be very useful in improving certain kinds of operating systems, particularly complex logistics systems, they will be of little use in improving management control. This is particularly true in the short-range time span of the next five to seven years.

The following is a checklist of questions that I believe the manager should have answers to before letting anyone install a remote computer terminal and a visual display screen in his office:

1. What will the total incremental cost of the equipment and programming be? (Be sure to consider the cost of continuing systems and programming work that the real-time systems will involve.)

2. Exactly how will this equipment be used? (Be sure to obtain a complete description of the proposed uses and the date when each application will become operational.)

3. Exactly how will each of these uses improve the ability to make decisions? In particular, how will the management-control system be improved?

With precise answers to these three questions, it seems to me that a manager can decide whether or not a remote terminal and visual display device should be installed. Do not be surprised, however, if the answer is negative.

Long-range outlook

What are the prospects of real-time systems, say, fifteen or twenty years from now? Some experts believe that, by that time, staff assistance to top management will have largely disappeared. Not only will the staff have disappeared, but so will most of the paper that flows through present organizations. A manager in the year 1985 or so will sit in his paperless, peopleless office with his computer terminal and make decisions based on information and analyses displayed on a screen in his office.

Caution urged

It seems to me that, at the present time, the long-term potential of real-time management information systems is completely unknown. No one can say with any degree of certainty that the prediction cited above is incorrect. After all, fifteen or twenty years is a long time away, and the concept of a manager using a computer to replace his staff is not beyond the realm of theoretical possibility. On the other hand, this concept could be a complete pipedream.

Under any circumstances, many significant changes in technology, organization and managerial personnel will be required before this prediction could be a reality for business in general. As a result, if such changes do occur, they will come slowly, and there will be ample opportunity for business executives to adjust to them. For example, I believe there is little danger of a company president waking up some morning to find his chief competitor has installed a computer-based, decision-making system so effective that it will run him out of business.

I believe all executives should be open-minded to suggestions for any improvements in management information systems, but they should require evidence that any proposed real-time management information system will actually increase their effectiveness. Above all, no one should rush into this now because of its future potential.

The present state of real-time management information systems has been compared to that of the transportation field at the beginning of the Model-T era. At that time, only visionaries had any idea of how transportation would be revolutionized by the automobile. It would have been foolish, however, for a businessman to get rid of his horse-drawn vehicles just because some visionaries said that trucks would take over completely in twenty years.

It seems to me that this is the identical situation now. Even if the most revolutionary changes will eventually take place in management information systems twenty years hence, it would be silly for business executives to scrap present methods until they are positive the new methods are better.

References

BURCK, G. (1965), *The Computer Age*, Harper & Row.
MCGARRAH, R. E. (1966), 'Logistics for the international manufacturer', *Harvard Bus. Rev.*, vol. 44, no. 2, pp. 156–66.
MARTIN, E. W. Jr (1965), *Electronic Data Processing*, Richard D. Irwin.
MARTIN, J. (1965), *Programming Real-Time Computer Systems*, Prentice-Hall.

Part Four
Scanning the Business Environment

The business environment generates a vast amount of information from competitors, suppliers, consumers, the government and other sources. Some of this information is 'relevant', most is not. How can a business set about filtering this information?

The *filter* problem, that is the problem of providing management with relevant information, is the major problem facing information technologists. Progress in this area over the last decade has been slow, despite the 'great leap forward' of the 1950s.

Reading 10 is an epilogue to a doctoral thesis designed to discover how management retrieves information from the environment. The author concludes that this function 'just grows', it is seldom designed. The scanning function is uncoordinated and its crucial role in decision-making is seldom given due weight. Several constructive suggestions for designing a scanning mechanism are put forward. The author makes the interesting suggestion that once the need for environmental information is recognized, external economies will create a service industry to satisfy the need.

10 F. J. Aguilar

Scanning the Business Environment:
Some Practical Considerations

Excerpts from F. J. Aguilar, *Scanning the Business Environment*,
Collier-Macmillan, 1967, pp. 183–208.

Up to now, discussion has focused almost exclusively on 'what is happening' in the scanning activities by which top management gains information about opportunities for and threats to its company in the outside environment – information that could serve management in making decisions of strategic and long-term importance. Scanning activities were examined generally in a statistical survey and specifically in a number of case situations. The primary objective of this study is limited to descriptive analysis. The position taken was that description must precede prescription in the case of any relatively unexplored problem, a category into which strategic scanning undoubtedly fits.

It would be difficult, however, in the course of a protracted investigation of scanning not to note techniques and practices that appear to work well and others that appear to work poorly. One is also bound to encounter various intriguing ideas for improvements expressed by individuals directly concerned with the process. Much more understanding of 'what is happening' is necessary before 'what should happen' can be adequately treated, but there is no valid reason why we should not anticipate this next step at least in a tentative way.

Accordingly, this chapter will be devoted to some practical considerations that top management might profitably weigh in seeking to improve scanning. These will be discussed under the following headings: integration of scanning activities, appraisal of scanning activities, building the 'scanning organization' and looking beyond the firm.

Integration of scanning activities

One of the major problems is the fractionalization of an organization's scanning activities. This problem manifests itself in two ways: (1) in the failure of individuals and units to gather reasonably accessible information that is important for others in their organization; and (2) in the failure of decision-makers to receive relevant information *already* residing in the company. These consequences are particularly noticeable with respect to communications across divisional lines. As a practical matter, it would seem that the potentially greatest *initial* improvement to scanning for many companies might lie, not in the gathering of completely new bodies of information, but rather in the improved application of existing efforts and the improved utilization of current informational inputs through coordination and integration.

The reasons for fractionalization of scanning arose from a very basic feature in all complex organizations – namely, division of labor. [...] That some fractionalization is inevitable was indicated by Ely Devons in the following comment, which applies to scanning as well as planning:

> Every attempt at planning reveals these two problems: first, the need to split up the field to be covered so that each administrative unit can deal efficiently with its own sector; and second, the need to secure that the actions of these separate units all fit into the general plan. But the implementation of these principles always leads to a conflict. For the first requires delegation and devolution, so that plans can be manageable and realistic; and the second requires centralization, so that plans can be coordinated (1950, p. 14).

Whereas each company situation will call for its own particular solution to the problem of fractionalization, three basic elements will undoubtedly be included in most proposals for improvement:

1. Coordination through explicit assignment.
2. Coordination through planning.
3. Coordination through internal communication.

Coordination through explicit assignment

Coordination through explicit assignment must start with the men at the top, the company's most influential men. What it means, in essence, is that senior managers should, to the extent possible, be made formally responsible for seeing that strategic information is collected in their departments and for marshalling this information in such a way that meaningful implications can be shared with other interested members of the top executive group. If, as seems likely, merely assigning this responsibility does not get results, there are ways of educating and assisting executives to do a better job. It should be emphasized that marshalling of *strategic* information is the area where improvement seems most needed. From the limited field observation, it appeared that senior executives were aware of the need of marshalling key-*operating* information from the outside environment. They were more likely to have difficulty turning their attention to information with *long-range* or *strategic* implications.

One dysfunctional consequence of failure to assign specific responsibility for assembling strategic information to influential executives is where divisional executives count on the corporate planning group to monitor long-range trends in their own industries, whereas the planners see their mission as being exclusively concerned with new fields into which the company might diversify.

A recent major restructuring of the top-management organization in one of the world's largest chemical companies (Imperial Chemicals Industries Ltd, or ICI) both attested to the widespread need for improved coordination of the total strategic-scanning job, and illustrated a possible solution especially designed to fit the needs of large, complex companies where scanning requirements are vast. ICI's reorganization was motivated in part by top management's realization that it was losing its ability to keep properly informed with respect to all the company's different business activities. Headed by a working board of directors, the company established what were called 'control groups' of three or four directors for each of the company's major divisions. Each control group was responsible for monitoring the operations, plans and strategies of its respective division, and for relating them to corporate plans and strategies. Further integration was effected by having senior directors hold membership in several related control groups. As a result, the whole business came under the purview of three senior directors, who in turn worked closely with the chief policy and strategy maker, the chairman of the board. The important principle to be noted in this arrangement was that specific individuals in top management were held accountable for each of the different sectors of the business in such a way as to funnel strategic information to the top, and, presumably, to permit a reasonably effective dissemination of top management's policies *and interests* back down the line.

The assignment of responsibility for assembling and considering strategic information is, however, probably not sufficient in itself, especially where executives hold busy operating-line positions. Routine, immediate, familiar and programmed considerations tend to crowd out strategic, long-range, unfamiliar and unprogrammed considerations. Yet, it is important to have the active participation of higher-level executives in assembling and interpreting strategic data because of their intimate familiarity with the business or part of the business.

Where success in gaining the active participation of operating-line executives in obtaining strategic information occurs, it appears to stem from two conditions: (1) executives are made aware of the kinds of information and considerations which strategy formulation requires, and (2) they are provided with assistance in performing this task.

The first point regarding education would seem self-evident, except that it is so often overlooked. Telling key subordinate managers what is wanted is perhaps all right; getting them actively involved is better, for example a research manager might become sensitive to broad strategic considerations as a result of his participation on a management team project, or where key division managers participate on management task teams. In short, there would appear to be significant merit in the practice of at least temporarily assigning important executives to formal search activities involving strategic issues.

Under the usual operating pressures found in most companies, awareness of strategic-information needs on the part of an operating executive may not be enough; he will probably need assistance if he is to make his maximum contribution. Such assistance was often provided by a small staff unit of one or several persons responsible for helping key executives identify and obtain strategic information.

The presence of such staff assistance lends continuity and expertise to the scanning task. In addition, staff assistants can extend the ground covered by high-level executives. In one large European company headed by an executive board, each member was assisted full-time by a promising subordinate manager for a period of two years. This arrangement seemed to offer several benefits to the strategic scanning process. Obviously, as the assistant learned the problems and activities of the top executive, he was able to contribute considerably to the latter's scanning efforts. Furthermore, when the middle-manager assistant returned to the field, he was able to improve the scanning efforts in the unit to which he went. This second impact tended to increase in importance as each of these men rose within the company ranks.

The provision of staff assistance was, however, not without pitfalls. One common problem found was that many such staff units, particularly those several echelons below the top organizational level, became more or less disconnected from the heart of corporate strategy making. That is to say, difficulties followed when units were unaware of top management's real interests. In one company, for example, the following dysfunctional chain of events was set in motion:

1. A corporate development staff unit explored areas falling outside the limits of top management's interests.

2. The unit's efforts and proposals were repeatedly rejected.

3. The approach of the frustrated unit shifted from trying to inform top management to trying to sell or defend its findings.

4. Top management became disenchanted with the unit because of its 'irrelevant' contributions and also, possibly, because of its increasingly defensive attitude. At this point, the ability of this discredited unit to contribute to the scanning process was doubtful, even if it were to encounter useful information.

One apparently successful means of averting such difficulties was to tie the staff unit closely to top management. For some units, such as a long-range planning staff, the tie-in was often accomplished by having the high-level executives actively participate in the staff's deliberations. For other units, such as an acquisitions staff, the tie-in was often accomplished by holding a top-level executive responsible for the staff's work. The basic principle or aim in all cases was to insure that expert, specialized staffs were somehow guided to perform in such a way that their output would coincide with the demands of the top managers. For this result to be achieved, there had to be feedback – continuous or frequent rather than occasional – from top management to the staff regarding the value to the former of the latter's current scanning activities.

Coordination through planning

The subject of long-range planning procedures has been widely dealt with in recent years and thus will not be discussed here (see Ewing, 1958; Branch, 1962; Steiner, 1963; Scott, 1965; Ansoff, 1965; Steiner and Cannon, 1966). It should suffice to point out that formal long-range planning, properly executed, facilitates and encourages strategic scanning in several important ways:

1. By defining the scanning responsibilities for all important units of the company, thus providing motivation.

2. By defining the objectives and critical issues to be considered, thus giving direction.

3. By enlarging awareness of the activities and interests among executives in the company, thus encouraging communications.

Like coordination by explicit assignment, coordination through planning is facilitated by the use of staff men. (The same will be found true of coordination through communication.) Not all these staffs are similarly organized, of course. Each high-level executive may need staff support to help him with his new – or rather newly emphasized – strategic scanning responsibilites, but usually such support can be given by one assistant. In contrast, the planning staff will be a separate unit, sometimes quite large, and only top corporate and perhaps divisional executives or executive committees should have such staffs reporting to them.

Coordination through communications

Basic to coordination of scanning is the process of internal communication, and anything that helps to improve the exchange of information among the various decision-making centers will make scanning much more fruitful. For example, top-management meetings can be made more productive. Other means – such as staff coordinators and visual aids – may also be adopted to facilitate the useful exchange of strategic information.

Several companies tried to encourage the flow of information by *requiring* extensive reporting through memoranda and meetings. These efforts undoubtedly increased the flow of words and paper, but one could question whether they increased actual *communications* – i.e. the perception and understanding of a message by the receiver. The problem was one of timing. Information was typically contributed within a company *when it was available and of interest to the source*. But information made its greatest impact *when it was relevant to the receiver*. When these two moments failed to coincide, as often was the case, the transmission of information tended to result in an ineffective communication.

One senior executive in one of these companies explained that in practice a manager sought information in meetings with the 'sources' (i.e. fellow managers) rather than by any attempt to review the 'mass of stale memos in the file'. He added that whoever had originated the communication could usually recall the information or its whereabouts. This statement points out an important function of management meetings. It also suggests that emphasis in such meetings should be given to a disclosure of the informational needs of each member rather than of information which happens to be prominently available at the moment. That is, *more concern should be given to exploring what information people want than to presenting information they happen to have*. The transfer of relevant information to the needy party will follow naturally enough.

The problem of timing was also reduced when companies were able to make known – perhaps through a corporate plan – the different issues and considerations that might become relevant in the *future*. In this way, the receiver of internal communications could *anticipate* the usefulness of the information, even though he was not currently interested in the particular point. He could then either learn the information or at least file it in an appropriate place for later consideration.

In general, the larger and more complex the company, the

greater the need for means to facilitate the communication of relevant external information. Many of the larger companies studied had staff members who were primarily concerned with recognizing and communicating, or causing the communication of, important information. (A distinction should be kept in mind between the staff assistant mentioned earlier and the information coordinator being considered here. The staff assistant was responsible for helping a line decision-maker and was interested in communications primarily as these involved information affecting his own, or his superior's, problems. The information coordinator was responsible primarily for *moving* information to appropriate decision-making points within the organization.)

One of the most fruitful instances observed of the use of staff-information coordinators involved coordination of technical information by senior-service technical specialists. (In one case, the staff coordinator even had the authority to call and to chair meetings of the managers in charge of the various technical line units.) To act in this staff capacity, senior middle-level executives were transferred from their former line positions. Utilizing their talents in this way not only helped to solve the communication problem, but appeared to be a gainful way to employ experienced older men who were near retirement.

More difficult to assess was the formal or *de facto* transfer of senior top-level executives to positions as staff coordinators of strategic (and other) information. Depending on the man and the respect in which he was held, such an assignment might work well. One large company had a senior marketing vice-president whose position was redefined in such a way that his principal responsibility became that of obtaining market information from both outside and inside sources. Interestingly, he was regarded as an excellent source of strategic information not only by members of top management but by the divisional managers as well. However, there was some evidence that high-ranking men given such assignments might find it difficult to maintain respect and influence. One reason for this difficulty stems from the fact that this kind of position has frequently been used in the past as a polite way to put a senior executive out to pasture, and a stigma understandably has become attached to this role. Thus, though transfer of high-ranking men to the coordinator's role seems to offer great potential value, circumstances may preclude a successful application of this arrangement. Not only must there be a man who could fit the role, but also favorable attitudes must exist on the part of high-level line executives. Since these requirements will rarely be met in combination, use of *top-level* coordinators can be considered the exception rather than the rule.

For top management itself, perhaps one of the most comprehensive and potentially useful aides for bringing together the results of the many scanning activities in the company was the use of a central information collection and display point, sometimes referred to as the 'corporate information-presentation room'. In this location were gathered and displayed through charts, graphs, tables, models and so on, the various critical data and information for top management's consideration and review.[1]

One of the principal values of such a room was in just placing the relevant information at top management's fingertips. Roby and Lanzetta indicated the importance of this step in their comments on group performance:

The dispersal of information may be as critical a factor as the sheer amount of information that must be relayed. This is, where several pieces of information must be obtained ... it is generally more effective if the information can be obtained from a single source (1956).

A second possible benefit from such a center would be to use it as a point where the different informational inputs could be

---

1. A series of photographs of one such display room is shown by Branch (1962, p. 128, plates 1–3). Further testimony regarding the importance of using visual-display techniques and the extent to which the practice may be carried is given in the following comment: 'A number of corporations have taken advantage of the decision-center concept. DuPont is a well-known example of a company which has used it for both long- and short-range planning purposes.... DuPont's decision center is a room that makes use of a tramrail system and a hierarchy of charts which allows rapid pin-pointing of operating problem areas.

'The importance of visual-display techniques in increasing the effectiveness and efficiency of presentations cannot be overstressed. For instance, I M C [International Minerals and Chemical Corporation] has been able to justify extensive use of "visuals" to the degree that the Strategic Planning Department has its own graphic analysts and the corporation retains a consultant to increase the effectiveness of executive presentations.' Smalter and Ruggles (1966).

truly integrated. The meaning and importance of this procedure are brought out by the following comment:

> In this respect, industry can learn much from military or governmental intelligence organizations, where inputs from many different sources are brought together in a central intelligence office for comparative study. This practice has proved how much can be learned from relating two dissimilar bits of information, neither of which could have told a significant story by itself.

Some integration of information will naturally take place in the course of top management's exposure to the full array of company data. But the task of specifically bringing together the various informational inputs for comparative study might well be assigned to special staff assistants.

Appraisal of scanning efforts

Before top management can place itself in a position to improve the coordination of scanning as advocated in the previous section, some assessment must be made of scanning activities as currently conducted within a company. Three approaches to self-appraisal seem to merit particular discussion:

1. Analysis of past performance.

2. Examination of the congruence between the *interests* of key executives and the *information* that is tendered to them for purposes of strategic decision-making.

3. Re-assessment of the firm's informational *needs*.

The first of these approaches has been found fruitful in many situations. The second can be advocated as a means of helping to extirpate a frequently encountered shortcoming. The third presents rich possibilities too often overlooked or underplayed.

Evaluation of past performance

Probably one of the most obvious procedures for appraising a company's scanning activities would be evaluating the results of past performance. An apparently useful approach followed in one company involved a review of specific previous major decisions. This review began with an appraisal of the relative successfulness of the decision. Next an attempt was made to determine the critical information which – by its presence or absence, its accuracy or its inaccuracy – appeared to contribute to success or failure. Following these steps, consideration was given to why the critical information was or was not obtained, and finally to what could be done to reinforce positive elements and to overcome deficiencies.

The value of some such approach would seem self-evident. Yet only two out of the forty-one companies studied followed such a procedure, and then only to a limited extent. Several reasons might account for this finding.

Possibly, the single most important reason was that top management in most companies had simply not considered the need to make a formal appraisal of its own scanning activities. Also, several difficulties tend to belie the apparent simplicity of performing an historical appraisal. For example, determination of whether or not a decision is 'correct' is not easy, even after the fact. Decisions must be based on the expected outcome of future events, and the actual occurrence of an unexpected outcome does not mean that the earlier assessment was ill-judged. This is true whether results turn out much more or much less favorable than expected. In other words, a successful outcome is not proof of a wise decision, nor is an unsuccessful outcome proof of a poor decision.

Furthermore, the passage of time diminishes the possibility of determining just what did take place in the decision-making effort. Thus, an important preliminary step to this procedure would be to document the decision-making process in detail *at the time* the decision is being made, in anticipation of its eventual review. But what complications might be expected from such a procedure? Will not executives tend to hedge the record with qualifications? Will the threat of review cause executives to make more conservative decisions – a change which may be far from desirable?

Closely related is the danger that the performance appraisals may become or may be perceived as 'witch hunts'. The difficulty of convincing everyone that the purpose of an appraisal review is *to learn* and *not to cast blame* may well be the biggest stumbling block to successful adoption of this procedure. Yet this difficulty is not totally insurmountable, and management would be well advised to try, over time, to introduce some variation of this procedure.

One obvious limitation to the usefulness of appraising past performance is that past performance must be relevant to future needs. Often, however, management must evaluate newly-proposed scanning activities never before attempted. This problem was seen in Gemca when it introduced scanning for new-business opportunities. One approach that could prove useful in judging the value of projected as well as of existing scanning activities is described below.

Information/interest/influence congruence

The concept of information/interest/influence congruence rests on a simple premise: that scanning for strategic information by staffs and lower-level managers is useless unless the information obtained is both wanted by and understood by the executives at or near the top who decide the company's long-term policies, strategies and plans. In other words, unless the information passed up fits the interests of the executives who have power and influence, then the acquisition of tidings, no matter how important, tends to be of little consequence.

The rule of striving for congruence between the interests of the strategy-makers and the substance of strategic information scanned will not guarantee the quality either of the scanning process or of the information obtained. But such a rule will help to ensure that the fruits of scanning, such as they are, will be used in the decision-making process. In the author's opinion, one of the key problems acting to discourage the development of formal scanning activities was the failure to consider carefully beforehand exactly *what information* key managers would be interested in using – or, at least, in considering for use – as they prepare to make their strategic decisions.

Although the rule of information/interest/influence congruence is easy enough to state, its application is not so simple. Difficulties multiply, especially in large, complex firms where a whole team of managers may be engaged in strategy-making and the varying interests of numerous influential people must consequently be considered. Compounding the difficulty is the fact that the subordinate scanners (for instance, a planning staff) must also consider the relative weight that each of the policy-makers may exert over a particular decision, and even the influence that one policy-maker may exert on the native or natural primary interests of another.

Establishing congruence among information, interest and influence is extremely important, as stated above, to avoid the waste of getting information that will not be used. But total dedication to this goal may well have a major dysfunctional consequence where key executives' interests differ from a firm's informational needs. That is, too much emphasis may be given to supplying an executive with information he wants, and conversely not enough to supplying information he may need but does not recognize as important. In other words, staff members can also serve top management in educating them as to what information should be considered in making long-term strategic and policy decisions. The dilemma for the staff member is to introduce as much useful but as yet unappreciated information as he can, but not so much as to discredit his efforts in the eyes of the top managers being served. This problem for the staff scanner can be lessened to the extent that top management educates itself as to what information is needed for strategic decisions.

Needed versus desired information

A great danger in evaluating a company's scanning activities is that much thought will be given to improving the means of getting information already obtained and little or no attention will be paid to reassessing just what information the company really has to have and should be seeking. Failure to take stock of new or changing needs for information was a fault all too frequently encountered among the companies investigated for this study.

The reasons for this lopsided emphasis are undoubtedly many and complex, but one of them would certainly be the propensity of most people to prefer the familiar to the unfamiliar – to refine accepted and accustomed practices instead of exploring questionable and uncharted ground. The question as to just what new kinds of information might be needed would often not be raised until circumstances had made it painfully clear that existing data-inputs were inadequate. By then it would be late – perhaps too late.

How can a management go about identifying areas of important information that it may have overlooked? With this problem the usefulness of defining just which activities are most critical to success for a firm in a certain industry or market should be noted. This ought to help focus attention on the key or payoff areas where the competitive battle may be either lost or won. Another useful approach is to try to identify underlying trends in the industry that affect the product or its market. As new products or markets are added, new identification should be made of new payoff areas and trends. Moreover a fresh look should be taken at scanning activities in the firm to make sure that these are kept in tune with changing needs.

To make sure that scanning ranges widely enough, time could profitably be devoted to devising and answering some broad 'what if . . .' questions. For example, what if there is a downturn in the economy or an upturn accompanied by serious inflation? What if science brings us new sources of power or substitute raw materials? What if sociological trends like urban congestion and air and water pollution require major changes in our means of transportation and our processes of production? What if the population explosion becomes exaggerated or dramatically reversed? What if the cold war gets hot enough to require rationing of certain scarce commodities that are important to our firm?

As these examples suggest, it is generally useful to look beyond local industry trends to the much broader environments of economics, science and technology, social and demographic developments, and so on. When the answer to one of these 'what if' questions suggests or indicates a possible significant impingement on the future development of the firm, then some thought should at least be given to monitoring the relevant activities or trends as part of the firm's scanning activities.

Building the 'scanning organization'

Clearly, top managers must participate heavily in the strategic scanning effort, not only by seeking information themselves, but also by making sure that their subordinates are getting the right quantitity and quality of information, in view of what is needed and what is available. This task, properly done, demands more time than top management can give it.

As a consequence, for many of the more complex situations (such as can be found in most larger companies), much, if not most, of the burden of developing, performing and controlling scanning activities must be entrusted to subordinate executives. The proper staffing of such positions in the companies studied was far too often unsuccessful. The difficulties found appeared to stem from top management's failure to consider either the specific capabilities or the propensities of the persons selected for this job.

It would seem almost trite to say that search should preferably be performed by someone who knows the subject matter under study and the key sources of information, if this rule were not so often violated. For example, in company after company one could find diversification studies where the executives in charge knew little about the industry being searched. What is more, in over half the instances noted, the remaining members of the search team were similarly ignorant. It would appear that such individuals begin with three strikes against them. First, they do not know what information exists. Second, they do not have the contacts to get the information. Third, they do not have the capabilities to assess the implications of much of the information that they do receive.

A second consideration, not always appreciated, is that scanning assignments should take into account the natural propensity of the individual. Simply stated, some individuals make good scanners and others do not. Certainly top management wants a man with intelligence, experience, ability and interest. But there is another essential quality – sensitivity. One executive colorfully highlighted the importance of this factor with a smile: 'Effective searching requires exposure. But like a photograph, exposure is not enough; the impression also depends on the film's sensitivity.' Jerome Bruner has referred to this characteristic as 'intuitive familiarity', defining it as a quality 'that gives [a person] a sense of what combinations are likely to have predictive effectiveness and which are absurd.' (1962, p. 21).

How does top management find or train such men? At least for the present, we probably can do no better than to heed Herbert A. Simon's answer to this question, where he comments on the selection of decision-makers:

To some limited extent we have found out how to assess human qualities by formal testing. In the main, however, we select a good decision-maker for an organizational position by looking for a man who has done a pretty good job of decision-making in some other organizational position that is almost equally taxing. This is a simple-minded approach (1960, p. 12).

In many cases, the 'best' person to perform or to direct scanning by virtue of his aptitude, knowledge, experience or availability is not well-known by members of top management or perhaps not yet of proven competence in their eyes. In situations of this sort, where the decision-makers may find it difficult to place confidence in the scanner or in the information he obtains (especially where the latter runs contrary to expectations), the need arises to find a means of validating the information. Somewhere along the line, then, critical information should get a seal of approval by someone in whom the top executives have confidence. Otherwise, top management is apt to spend its precious time in arguing over the facts – that is, whether something is true or not – rather than in analysing the problem to which the facts pertain. Obviously, in the realm of strategic matters, the idea of 100 per cent validation is absurd.

Involvement by top management in strategic scanning must be long-term, if for no other reason than that results are often slow in coming. On the basis of experiences of many companies with implementing corporate long-range planning, 'set-up time' could well require at least two years. Dr D. D. Otto, manager of the commercial precalculation and planning department of Philips (Eindhoven), a company with one of the most comprehensive planning and information retrieval systems in existence, said in 1964 at a seminar on planning, 'After thirteen years of intensive effort to develop our system, the company has probably only attained about 75 per cent of its original objectives in terms of performance.'

Whereas top management is exhorted to be patient in waiting for results from scanning activities, a similar exhortation should not be extended to the line people who are expected to contribute to these efforts. The development of scanning activities should proceed so that managers *down the line* can recognize benefits to them *at each step*. It is not enough for top management to envisage an *ultimate* usefulness to these people: the intervening steps – and particularly the first steps – must seem to 'pay their own way'. Otherwise, there is a danger that subordinates will view the scanning assignment as 'just one more half-baked management scheme detracting from the job to be done'. Such an initial or transitional impact could lead to lasting organizational resentment and resistance.

Beyond the firm

Results of a company's scanning efforts depend largely on conditions outside the company that affect the quantity, quality and availability of information. But to say that scanning depends on outside factors is not to imply that these outside factors are entirely beyond the influence and control of the business community. In fact, not only can the businessman help to create an environment more auspicious for scanning, in many instances he is the only one who can effect the necessary changes.

The point is a simple one. Briefly stated, the more businessmen become actively concerned with obtaining useful external information, the higher will be the quality, quantity and availability of external information. This result, in turn, will enhance the potential achievement of a given level of scanning efforts. Several reasons can be cited for this conclusion. First, increased attention to and experience in scanning should lead to new and improved techniques of seeking, obtaining and handling external information. As a relatively unexplored area of activity, scanning should exhibit dramatic changes as man's ingenuity is brought to the task. Second, increased demands for information should bring about more extensive and reliable 'facilities' (e.g. publications, government statistics, archives) for its collection, distribution, presentation and retrieval. Third, increased experience in disclosing and exchanging information should accelerate the spread of these practices, thereby making much more industry data available.

Needless to say, opportunities for improving the conditions for environmental scanning are almost without limit. Of these opportunities, some can be realized, at least in part, through action by a single firm. Others require concerted effort by several or many companies. Still others must await action by major institutions outside the industrial community – e.g. government or the press. Even in the latter case, however, these outside institutions will respond faster if businessmen are active in pressing their needs.

Of the contributions that a single firm can make to improving the environment for scanning, perhaps none is more important than public and semi-public disclosure of its own performance and future plans. The United States businessman has typically been far ahead of his counterpart in other countries in terms of his permissive attitudes toward the *public* disclosure of information. This is to be applauded, for the disclosure of facts and intentions helps to establish a common basis for premises by others and thereby helps to lessen major miscalculations. It is not enough to know what a future market demand might be if the decision-maker does not have some idea of how competitors (actual and potential) might behave with respect to this market. As evidence, one has only to recall the over-capacity that has plagued the various process industries because of a lack of such information.

Naturally, there are limits to what can and should be revealed. But has business reached the limits of open disclosure?[2] The answer is probably 'no'. In many cases, much more could be stated without transgressing the obvious rule that 'disclosures that would lose or reduce a competitive advantage would not be in the stockholder's overall best interest and, of course, should be avoided' (Bevis, 1966, p. 155).

Of the contributions to improved scanning that depend on concerted action by many firms, one of the most important is strengthening the informal information 'network'. [. . .]

One possibility might be the establishment of an industry committee that could try to define the critical issues, threats and opportunities for the whole of an industrial sector (e.g. plastic films). Much might be gained if the vast interpretative powers of an industry's outstanding managers could be focused on their vital common as well as parochial interests. Membership on such

2. The words 'public' and 'open' modifying 'disclosure' were stressed for what should be obvious legal reasons.

a committee might include, in addition to leading industry figures, persons from related industries, the financial community and government. Support might be provided by a staff of economists, scientists, social anthropologists and so forth, who would represent a 'strategy staff' for the industry.

This line of reasoning may be summed up by comparing the industrial or business sector with more structured bodies. Metaphorically, there seems to be a need to add a head to the man, or a government to the nation.

As to improvements in scanning that depend on action of outside institutions, probably the greatest potential lies within the province of government, especially at the national and supranational levels. One might mention first the output of more usable statistics. In this connection one must applaud the recent introduction by the Commerce Department of input/output tables for the US economy. The potential usefulness of these data was pointed out in the following introductory comments accompanying the first set of tables.

Input/output analysis has a variety of applications including such diverse uses as evaluating an individual firm's sales potential and probing the implications of broad economic programs. For example, a businessman can compare his company's marketing position with that of the industry as a whole and note possible areas of additional market potential. Moreover, while companies frequently know the industries which use their products and services, they less frequently know the industries which use the products and services of their customers. Furthermore, their knowledge diminishes rapidly as these relationships are extended to the customer's customers, and so on. An approach, such as input/output, which traces these myriad purchase and sale relationships permits an understanding of the probable changes in demand for the products of any given industry that may result from expected changes in other industries or markets which are seemingly unrelated.

Input/output is a powerful tool for analysing changes in the economy because it provides a series of links between the demands of final markets and the outputs of industries. Consequently, it brings into focus the possible repercussions of changes in gross national product or its components on the output of each of the industries. For example, it permits identifying the industries which are affected directly and indirectly (and the extent to which they are affected) by specified changes in consumer expenditures, by increasing exports or imports, by changes in the level of defence expenditures, or by an expansion of Federal road-building programs (1964).[3]

A more radical step that a government might take would be the introduction of a strictly limited type of national economic planning. The desirability of government planning has been a hotly debated issue for many years and is one on which this study does not presume to make any final judgement. However, recognition must be given to the value of the increased flow of relevant information that usually accompanies planning efforts. Time and again, executives responsible for gathering long-range external information in semi-planned economies (such as that of France and Japan) extolled the value of the government's planning statistics and the explicit codification of the government's policies and intentions. These comments should not be dismissed as the 'brain-washed attitudes of a French businessman', as one cynic called them. In fact, most of the favorable comments came from managers in non-planning countries whose companies were involved in world-wide operations.

National planning generally exhibits a number of distinguishable features:

1. It determines what *is* happening.

2. It predicts what *would* happen, based on current trends, in the absence of deliberate action.

3. It sets goals on targets and requires action consistent with its view of what *should* happen.

These features may be characterized as (1) recording, (2) forecasting and (3) directing the allocation of resources.

Much of the controversy over national planning revolves about the wisdom of directing allocation, and not about recording or predicting. But is there any compelling reason why the more acceptable activities cannot be divorced from the less acceptable? Would not reports about what is happening and predictions about what will be happening prove very helpful to the businessman in

3. The initial tables break down the economy into eighty-six industrial groups. Professor Wassily W. Leontief, acknowledged originator of the conceptual framework, was reported to desire further breakdown into four hundred and fifty to five hundred industries.

determining what he *wants* to do, in the absence of state directions telling him how he *can or must* perform?

Obviously, opponents of national planning will see a risk that recording and predicting will prove to be only the thin entering wedge, to be followed by directing. But if this possible development is recognized and if the danger of it is agreed to, then it can be guarded against. The alternative – of doing nothing – is even bleaker.

Summary

From the above suggestions, it is perhaps possible to sense some of the exciting new vistas that might be opened up as more attention is given to the challenge of viewing and searching outside the firm. Improvement in scanning for external information can be fostered in several ways. The opportunities for greatest immediate improvement undoubtedly lie within the company: in deciding what kinds of information are needed; in organizing for getting these data; and finally in facilitating the proper use of information at all levels but especially at the top.

Over and above these areas of potential improvement lie some broader possibilities for improving the generation and distribution of important external information about an industry and even about the social, political, scientific and economic setting within which that industry operates. There is a role here for publications and a potential role for the statistician and economist, whether in the industry itself, the financial community or the government. There is even a possible role for a limited type of government planning – i.e. planning confined to releasing information that would be useful as a guide to free enterprise.

Improvements in any and all of these areas will certainly enhance an organization's ability to look for distant troubles and treasures.

References

Ansoff, H. I. (1965), *Corporate Strategy*, McGraw-Hill.
Bevis, H. W. (1966), *Corporate Financial Reporting in a Competitive Economy*, Macmillan Co.
Branch, M. C. (1962), *The Corporate Planning Process*, American Management Association.

Bruner, J. (1962), *On Knowing: Essays for the Left Hand*, Harvard University Press.

Devons, E. (1950), *Planning and Practice*, Cambridge University Press.

Ewing, D. (ed.) (1958), *Long-Range Planning for Management*, Harper & Row.

Roby, T. B., and Lanzetta, J. T. (1956), 'Work-group structure: communications and group performance', *Sociometry*, vol. 19, no. 2, p. 112.

Scott, B. W. (1965), *Long-Range Planning in American Industry*, American Management Association.

Simon, H. J. (1960), *The New Science of Management Decision*, Harper & Row.

Smalter, D. J. and Ruggles, R. L. (1966), 'Six business lessons from the Pentagon', *Harvard Bus. Rev.*, vol. 44, no. 2, pp. 64–75.

Steiner, G. A. (ed.) (1963), *Managerial Long-Range Planning*, McGraw-Hill.

Steiner, G. A., and Carron, W. M. (eds.) (1966), *Multinational Corporate Planning*, Macmillan Co.

U.S. Department of Commerce (1964), 'The inter-industry structure of the United States', *Survey current Bus.*, pp. 11–29.

Part Five
Evaluating Management Information Systems

It has been suggested that if an English economist in 1830 had been able to calculate a cost-benefit analysis on the subsequent history of railways, they would never have been built. The *private* cost would have exceeded the *private* benefit to the owners. Yet the railways provided an enormous *social* benefit to the nation. Perhaps the same situation applies to business computers.

Several attempts have been made to evaluate business computers and they all make for gloomy reading (see Reading 5 for example). Few business computer systems can be *proved* to pay off. The catch is in the word 'prove'. Conventional cost-accounting systems are not suited to the type of cost-benefit analysis required for evaluating computers.

Reading 11 discusses the various approaches to evaluating computers and emphasizes the crucial distinction between the cost-saving and the cost-benefit approach.

Reading 12 emphasizes the importance of applying profit standards to computer operation. Several practical schemes for effecting this are put forward. An interesting method of pricing-out computer work is suggested.

Reading 13 presents an ambitious attempt to evaluate a management information system using simulation methods. It seems a pity that this interesting approach has not been followed up.

Reading 14 examines the economics of time-sharing. The authors report a dramatic improvement in the time required for program development, but caution against the high cost of down-time. The interesting problem of pricing time-shared systems is discussed.

Reading 15 tests Grosch's Law regarding the relation between speed and cost of computing. The law is validated.

11 T. W. McRae

The Evaluation of Investment in Computers

T. W. McRae, 'The evaluation of investment in computers', *Abacus*, vol. 6, 1970, pp. 56–70.

Introduction

When an organization buys an electronic digital computer it is making an investment. An expenditure of present resources to provide a future income.

For various reasons, which shall be examined later, conventional methods of evaluating investments are not wholly suited to evaluating computers. The computer is a difficult investment to evaluate because the income from the computer is not as clearly defined as it is with most other investments. This article will attempt to classify the output from the computer into several categories. This classification will be used to suggest those categories where evaluation is feasible and those categories where it is not and a logical sequence of steps for evaluating the computer will be suggested.

The problem

In 1967 the United States spent $3·96 billion on computer hardware. The expenditure on software and associated equipment was probably almost double this figure. The total value of investment in computer hardware in the United Kingdom approached £750m at the end of 1967. An increase of almost one-third on the previous year. The investment in computers in both countries is likely to reach 10 per cent of total manufacturing investment by the early 1970s.

This is a massive expenditure of resources. How is it known that the resulting benefit will justify the cost? How do we know that alternative methods cannot achieve the same results at lower cost? It is surely a remarkable tribute to the marketing skills of the computer manufacturers that this question has gone unanswered for so long.

A careful search of the literature by the author and several o his colleagues, with the aid of a professional search organization (the National Computer Centre) netted a mere thimbleful of viable *ex-post* justifications of the economic viability of the computer. *Ex-post* is emphasized because there are a large number of *ex-ante* claims, that is, claims made *before the computer system is installed*. The latter, of course, proves nothing,

The absence of *ex-post* evidence of the computer's economic viability does not prove that the computer is a poor investment. It simply suggests that a viable method for evaluating the computer has not been developed.

The following pages will not attempt the exceedingly ambitious objective of devising such a method. It has the more modest aim of providing an economic framework within which a viable method can be developed. This may seem a rather limited objective, but our review of the literature suggests that many writers believe they are tackling the whole problem of computer evaluation when they are only tackling part of it. An economic review is needed to piece these various studies together – and show what problems still remain to be solved.

The conventional approach to evaluating an investment

A computer is a production good and not a consumption good. A production good is acquired, not for itself alone, but because it helps to produce consumption goods. Buildings, plant and machinery, furnishings, etc. are production goods. The value of a production good depends upon the value of the goods and services produced by the production good. A cold summer diminishes the value of ice cream and so the value of ice-cream making machines declines.

In recent years a good deal has been written on the valuation of production goods. All of the methods suggested relate the estimated future income stream from the investment to the present cost. Many variations on this basic theme have been suggested. The best known being the discounted cash-flow method popularized by Merrett and Sykes (1963).

The net cash-flow generated by the investment $£p_1, £p_2, £p_3, \ldots,$

£p_n in years 1 to n is discounted to a fixed point in time at the appropriate opportunity cost of capital r, to give

$$\sum_1^n \frac{p_i}{1+r} i = £P.$$

If $£P > £K$, when $£K$ is the cost of the investment then $£(P-K)$ gives us the net present value of the future profit-stream generated by the investment. The analysis may have to be modified for risk. Can this approach be applied to evaluating an investment in a computer?

The output from a computer is a set of numeric, alphabetic and other symbols (for example a graph on a cathode ray tube). Can we estimate the value of these symbols and so indirectly evaluate the computer? This is the central problem in evaluating computer systems.

A definition of data and information

It has been noted that the output from a computer is a set of symbols. In this section these symbols will be classified into two categories, one of which shall be called data and the other information.

Data are any non-random set of symbols. A sender and a receiver agree on a set of rules, and a dictionary attaching meaning to given configurations of symbols. They can then communicate meaning to one another by transmitting data over a channel. This data need not be concerned with a *decision*. A good part of the multifarious book-keeping transactions recorded in business organizations are not used as inputs to decision processes. In the remainder of this article the word *information* will be used to define data which is used as an input to a decision process. All of the output from a computer system can be allocated to one or other of these two categories, or to both, since data and information are often produced as a joint product.[1]

Popell (1966, p. 182) carried out an interesting survey of the allocation of computer time in various industries in the US. This tabulation is shown in Table I.

1. Joint products are defined in economics as products which can be produced more cheaply jointly than separately, i.e. paraffin and petrol, meat and hides.

Table 1 Allocation of Computer Time in Various Industries in the USA

	Percentage					
	Insurance	Banks	Petrol	Transport	Retail	Manufacture
Accounting	89	98	36	55	66	43
Decision-making	3	2	7	12	6	10
Sales forecasting	0	0	5	2	2	8
Production control	0	0	3	9	4	13
Information retrieval	4	0	3	12	0	8
Engineering	0	0	20	2	0	7
Simulation	0	0	17	1	0	1
Other	4	0	9	7	22	10

A very considerable proportion of computer time is devoted to generating data. This is unlikely to come as a surprise to the reader, but it is important for later analysis. It will be seen that the evaluation of data presents a relatively simple problem compared to the evaluation of information.

In summary; we define data as any set of meaningful symbols, and information as data which is used as input to a decision process. All of the output from a computer system can be defined as data or information or both.

Why not leave evaluation to the free market?

The problem then, is quite straightforward. How are data and information evaluated? But before tackling this problem, it would be useful to take a brief look at one body of opinion that refuses to admit that there is a problem!

They advocate leaving the evaluation of computers to the free-market pricing mechanism. Their argument runs as follows. Any cost-plus system of pricing is inefficient. It is best to leave price to be determined by the free market. Set up your computer centre as an autonomous unit and let it charge what the market will bear. There is sufficient outside competition to keep it on its toes. If it makes a profit the surplus funds can go to expanding the computer centre – it can even take on outside work if it wants to. If it makes a loss, it will have to contract its services, and eventually go out of business. Either way, the economic viability of the computer is tested against the objective measure of the free market. The argument sounds convincing, and for this reason is often advocated (but rather less frequently adopted) in management circles. But, of course, this method, *simply shifts the valuation problem from the computer department to the customer*. It does not solve the problem of computer evaluation.

However, although it contributes nothing to the problem of evaluation, this method does shift the locus of decision to a more *impartial* point in the organization. The computer customer is less likely to be committed to the computer, and so better able to provide an impartial verdict on its comparative performance.

The conclusion is that the let-the-computer-stand-on-its-own-feet school makes no contribution to the evaluation problem.

Cost-effective versus cost-benefit

Economists have devised two methods for evaluating the efficiency of a system. One of these is called the *cost-effective* approach (see Stratton, 1968), the other the *cost-benefit* approach. It is most important to be clear on the distinction between these methods before examining the literature on computer evaluation.

A system is defined as a set of inter-related elements which absorbs material from its environment, processes this material, and returns the material, modified in some way, back into the environment. A computer complex qualifies as a system under this definition. It draws in raw data from its environment, sorts, collates, adds, etc. this data, and returns it in the modified form of reports, back into its environment.

The cost-effective method is the easier method of evaluating a system. The cost-effective method assumes the outputs from a system to be fixed in quantity and quality. It then explores the comparative cost of various methods of producing this fixed output. That system which can produce the fixed output at lowest cost is selected as being the most *efficient* system, i.e. it provides the lowest input/output ratio.

For example, the annual cost of processing the company payroll might be £x. An alternative system is suggested using a different combination of hardware, etc. costing £y. The cost-effective approach assumes that 'the company payroll' is a fixed quantity of printed symbols which can be produced by either method. If £y < £x we select the new method, if £y > £x we retain the old. This may seem naïve, but as we shall demonstrate later, most of the existing literature on computer evaluation adopts this approach. An alternative method of evaluating a system is to use the cost-benefit approach.

The cost-effective approach assumed that although the inputs to a system were variable, the output was fixed. The cost-benefit approach (see Prest and Turvey, 1965) removes this latter constraint. The cost-benefit approach allows both the inputs and the outputs from the several systems to vary, and then attempts to measure which of these systems is the most efficient, that is, which system has the lowest input/output ratio; for instance, if in the previous example the new method provided a more sophisticated cost analysis of payroll. Even if £y > £x, one might adopt the new system if it was considered that the improved cost analysis exceeded £(y−x).

The literature on the evaluation of computers is bedevilled by the failure of authors to distinguish between the cost-effective and the cost-benefit approach. Frequently, a cost-effective approach to one system is compared to a cost-benefit approach to another (see Kalscheuer, 1968, p. 47), or a writer despairs of ever being able to evaluate the computer when he means that he despairs of finding a cost-benefit formula, although a cost-effective formula might be perfectly adequate, for example Callahan (1967).

A brief review of the literature

A good deal has been written on the evaluation of computers and information systems. Most of the literature is descriptive and of little value. Many articles are inconclusive, for example; in short, in most companies today there exists no method of measuring the performance of computer equipment or the computer section as a whole (Callahan 1967, p. 84). Many articles are negative and pessimistic: 'the experts say that no computer has ever been worth it' (Gill 1962). 'Striking a balance between cost and value appears to have eluded the analysts. The problem increases in complexity with each advance in technology and technique' (Brenner 1965, p. 22). Scientific attempts at evaluation are rare. The shining exceptions being the work on computer comparison by writers such as Meredith-Smith (1968) and Knight (1966).

Most writers adopt the cost-effective approach although few appreciate the crucial distinction between cost-effectiveness and cost-benefit. A classic example of the cost-effective approach is Janes's paper (1963) on evaluating computers in the UK government service. He discounts estimated-cost savings to a fixed date and states that the computer will be paid for out of direct staff savings. The aim is an annual average return of 10 per cent on investment in computers. He comments that 'within a government service increased efficiency does not produce increased profit but increased savings'. However he qualifies this remark later when he states that '... if better management information is put forward as a reason, then there should either be an attempt to quantify the benefits to be obtained or, alternatively, the improvement in management information must be defined ... and priced' (p. 291). He does not suggest how this can be done.

Many other articles describe the cost-saving approach. Kalscheuer (1968) is a recent example. The several articles which purport to prove Grosch's Law relating cost and speed of computing are all cost-effective in approach (see Knight, 1966). Bauer and Hill's excellent article on the economics of time-sharing (1967) adopts a cost-effective stance and all of those interesting articles which attempt to devise benchmarks for comparing the efficiency of various computer systems use the cost-effective approach. Meredith-Smith (1968) has a useful summary.

Several articles make tentative but rather inconclusive moves in the direction of evaluating the benefits of information. Axsmith (1965) lists four 'roads to computer profits'. Three of these are incremental benefits, reduced working capital, improved use of resource capacity, improved decision-making, only one is cost-effective – reduced administration costs.

Several writers have listed the value of improved resource utilization resulting from computer output. Dessau claims that a Stockholm hospital saved $800,000 a year by using a computer to speed up patient turnaround from fifteen to fourteen days (1966). BOAC justify their expensive time-share reservation system on the basis of increasing average flight utilization. There are many other articles of this type. The improved speed of the information network allows an increased utilization of a given factor of production. With respect to this type of evaluation Bedford and Onsi (1966) make the interesting point that information is traditionally supplied and *evaluated* by the accountant. The accountant is not likely to appreciate the uses and therefore the benefits of the information he produces. Therefore the accountant will tend to evaluate information systems as *data*-generating systems and use cost-effective methods of evaluation. He may not appreciate the incremental value of improved resource utilization which is not under his control.

The classic paper on evaluating short-term information is Boyd and Krasnow's 'Economic evaluation of management information' (1963). The authors distinguish between the cost-saving and cost-benefit approach, and they attempt to evolve a methodology for evaluating the 'length of the planning period . . . and second the magnitude of the information transmission delays' (p. 12). A simple production model is developed incorporating four production shops, three components and two products.

The experimenter exerts control over the simulation by setting parameters for the physical system, the information processing system and the environment. He is also free to independently set the cost elements of the accounting structure, which govern the absolute level of the financial results (p. 11).

The authors simulate this simple model on a computer under various sets of conditions. They consider that 'for a firm of the type represented, perhaps the best single overall measurement of physical performance is that of delivery time' (p. 18). By altering one parameter of the model at a time the authors are able to evaluate the effects of altering the planning period or information lag. They arrive at conclusions such as the following. 'The value of this change, from a one-month to a two-week planning cycle, is in the order of $19,000' (p. 22) or 'a comparison of earnings between runs two and three places a value of about $16,000 on this reduction in information delays' (p. 22). They conclude that 'the extension of this method to useful economic evaluation of proposed systems in real firms will depend on how successfully the critical dynamics of the real enterprise can be described in model form' (p. 23). The current popularity of system model-building might suggest that the Boyd–Krasnow approach deserves a wider application than it seems to have received. The importance of the method is that it provides a *practical* mechanism for equating the marginal cost of information to its marginal value and so introduces the concept of optimality into investment in information systems.

Every article quoted above discusses the problem of evaluating data or information *in the short term*. A computer can also, at least theoretically, provide input to long-term decision procedures. How is the benefit of long-term information evaluated?

Finally, the celebrated McKinsey reports on computer evaluation should be noted (see Garrity, 1963). These reports are quoted (but seldom discussed) more widely than any other papers in the literature. The first report (1963) reaches important conclusions but does not provide the information by which these conclusions can be validated. An audit of twenty-seven computer installations revealed that nine were 'unmistakeably successful' and eighteen 'marginal at best'. 'For every dollar laid out ... the typical lead company's annual return is $1·30' (Garrity, 1963, p. 7). The 1968 report does not attempt to measure the return on computer investment.

The conditions under which the cost-effective method of evaluating is viable

In the previous section it was noted that most attempts at evaluating a computer system have used the cost-effective method. The cost-effective method assumes that the purpose of the computer system is to produce a given quantum of symbols within a given time-period. Various data-processing configurations can achieve this objective, the configuration chosen being the one which produces the required output at lowest cost. Since most of the costs of data processing are direct costs, it is relatively easy to calculate the historical cost of a computer system for a given period. When this method is viable it is by far the best method to use since it avoids the very tricky problem of evaluating information. Therefore, we must ask ourselves under what conditions the cost-effective method is a viable method of evaluation.

To answer this question it is necessary to return to the earlier discussion of computer output. The reader will recall that all of the output from the computer system was allocated into the two classes *data* and *information*. Data is sent outside the business system to customers, suppliers, the government and so on. Information is used as an input to business decisions which can modify the business in one way or another. It can be concluded that since data is a *final* good, produced for itself alone, and not, like information, as *intermediate* good, to be used as an input to a further process, it *can be evaluated by using cost-effective methods*. If all of the output from a computer installation is data, there is no need to look further for a viable method of evaluation.

Now it is clear from the studies of Poppel (1966) and others (see Hooper, 1967) that a large proportion of the output from commercial computer-systems consists of data. This being so, the problem of evaluation resolves itself into a simple exercise in comparative costing, and avoids the difficult problem of evaluating information.

The problems of evaluating information

How can information be evaluated? Stigler (1961), Lave (1963), Nelson and Winter (1964) and others have defined information as a reduction in uncertainty, and evaluated this reduction in uncertainty to arrive at a value for information. This is an interesting and useful approach under rather highly constrained conditions, but it is not, I think, of much use in evaluating the varied stream of information flowing from a computer.

Information, by our definition, is an input to a decision process. To evaluate information in this context it is necessary to know the outcome, X_1, of the decision without this particular piece of information and the outcome, X_2, of the decision after this piece of information is made available. If state X_1 is identical to state X_2 the information has no value. If state X_2 provides higher profit or lower costs than state X_1 then this difference gives us the value of the information. If state X_2 provides lower profits or higher costs than state X_1, the information has negative value, and is better without it.

Now this method of evaluation sounds simple enough in theory but, with the exception of one important class of problem which shall be described, it can seldom be applied in practice. The method runs up against one of the oldest and most intractable problems in economic theory. We are required to impute a given increment of income or cost to a given increment of information. But suppose there are several increments of information used in solving the problem? How do we impute the increment of income £i_1 to piece of information I_1, £i_2 to piece of information I_2 and so on? The theory (see Stonier and Hague, 1964) is simple, the practical application formidably difficult. The decision-maker is being asked to forecast the various outcomes of a decision when each piece of information in turn is suppressed, and to evaluate each of these outcomes when the actual results of the decision may not be known for months, or even years, if ever. Thus it is rarely possible to evaluate an individual piece of information when a decision depends upon several pieces of information.

Fortunately, however, there is one important class of decisions to which these conditions do not apply.

Asset utilization

There is one class of business decision where the computer is making an important and growing contribution. This is in the area of *asset utilization*. This type of problem has two subclasses. In the first class the capacity utilization of an asset of fixed capacity can be increased by speeding up the information network controlling the system. In the second class the average amount invested in an asset can be reduced by similar means. Examples of the first class are airline and hotel reservation systems, equipment leasing, staff allocation. Examples of the second class, inventory control, debtors control and cash-flow analysis.

A wide range of business computer applications fall into this category. Which is fortunate, because I believe that this is one of the few situations where the benefit of information *can* be evaluated with a reasonable degree of accuracy. For example, by placing the airline seat-reservation records on a computer and providing data links between the computer and a large number of airline reservation offices, the average capacity utilization of the aircraft can be improved. In the case of BOAC, for example, a 1 per cent improvement in utilization from say, 55 per cent to 56 per cent, would improve profit by around £800,000 in one year.

In every application of this type, a fixed block of resources must be acquired prior to the period of operation. A large part of the total cost of the resources is therefore fixed relative to the utilization level attained during the period. The key to profitable operation is high capacity usage. Almost invariably the demand for the resource, hotel beds, bus seats, hired typists, etc. comes from a large number of independent consumers each of whom requires a relatively small part of the total resource available. In addition, the consumer is usually able to cancel or alter his demand at little cost and at short notice.

Under such conditions, it is most important to keep the records of the 'state of play' of the system up-to-date. This puts a high premium on the rapid and accurate transmission and analysis of information. In addition, since the only variable affected is capacity utilization, the benefit of the improved information flow can be calculated without too much difficulty. In the alternative case of a reduction in the average value of an asset, such as inventory, debtors or cash, the evaluation process is even simpler. A more frequent surveillance of inventory will reduce the value of the safety stock carried, or a more accurate prediction of cash flow will allow rearrangement of payment and receipt dates to reduce oscillation in the cash balance or overdraft.

Many of the most profitable applications of the computer lie in this area, and the benefits of improved information can be measured by the reduction in the average value of the investment in the designated asset.

It can be seen, therefore, that where information from a computer is used to improve the utilization of a designated asset, the evaluation of the information is feasible.

Evaluation in the long term

In most of the previous examples speed was the attribute which provided the incremental benefit. The faster feedback cycle on the utilization of beds, aeroplane seats or inventory, increased the utilization of capacity or decreased the average investment in the asset. Notice that these are examples of decision-making in the short term. How is information affecting decisions in the longer term evaluated?

Dearden (1968) has made an important contribution to this topic by introducing the concept of the time-span of decision (see Jaques, 1963, ch. 6). The minimum time-span *after* a decision is taken *before* it is worthwhile monitoring that decision. Dearden comments: 'the longer the minimum time-span the less important will be the effect of automating the capture, processing, transmission and publication of financial-control information.' The point has been well taken, and has implications far outside the limited field of financial control.

We can identify three distinct phases in the development of the use of the computer in business. In the earliest stage the computer is simply a data-generating device and cost-effective methods of evaluation are adequate. In the second, current, stage of development computers are being widely used for short-term decision-making on the utilization of assets. I have argued that evaluation of this type of output is feasible. The third stage, the use of computers in long-term decision-making, has hardly arrived.[2] When we reach this stage the evaluation of the incremental benefits will prove exceedingly difficult. The time-span of decision is long, therefore the *speed* of the computer is of less importance, while the period before the decision can be evaluated may be of the order of several years. Also the information from the computer is likely to be only one of many inputs to the decision-process.

It will, therefore, be practically impossible to evaluate the *benefits* of computer output used in long-term decision-making. However, for the foreseeable future this type of output will account for only a tiny fraction of total computer output and much of this fraction will be produced as a joint product with data and short-term information which is needed for other purposes. So long as most, and in many cases, all, of the output from

2. In 1966 R. H. Brady interviewed a hundred 'top managers' in the United States. In not one instance did he find them using a computer for decision-making although they all had access to a computer (Brady, 1966).

the computer falls into the category of data or short-term information, the problem of evaluating the computer is not insurmountable. I think a good case can be made out in support of the proposition that it is in these two areas that the computer will *always* be of most use in business.

Data and information as joint products

Where data and information are produced as joint products, as when the input to an invoice procedure is used for sales analysis, the *incremental* cost of the information is usually close to zero, since the data must be produced whether or not the later information analysis is tacked on to it. When evaluating information care must be taken not to double count the cost of joint products.

A basic approach to evaluating the computer

It is now possible to piece together the various strands of argument set out in the previous pages to arrive at a basic approach to evaluating a computer-based information system.

1. Identify all of the reports generated by the computer. Find out how many of these reports are *joint reports*. Two or more reports are joint reports if it is cheaper to produce them jointly than separately.

2. Classify the reports listed under (1) as either data or information or both.

3. Calculate the opportunity cost of the computer system, i.e. calculate the total of those costs which would *not* be incurred if the computer system did not exist.

4. Calculate the cheapest alternative cost of producing the reports classified under data in (2).

5. If £p, the opportunity cost of the present system is less than £a, the alternative cost of producing the 'data' reports within a given time-constraint, then the evaluation process stops here. The computer is justified on cost-effective grounds. There is no need to proceed to the more difficult stage of evaluating information.

6. If £$p >$ £a, the computer cannot be justified on cost-effective grounds. Therefore it must be determined whether the incremental cost £$(p-a)$ can be justified on cost-benefit grounds. Does

the speed, accuracy, etc. of the information provided by the computer provide a benefit in excess of £$(p-a)$? This decision is made by evaluating the benefit of the 'information' reports listed under (2). If these reports control the short-term utilization of assets, it has been proved that an approximate evaluation is feasible. Usually a very rough evaluation is sufficient to clinch the matter one way or the other. It is only necessary to estimate whether one figure is larger than another. A *precise* calculation of the *difference* is not required. If the benefit clearly exceeds £$(p-a)$, the evaluation stops here. The computer is justified on cost-benefit grounds. But suppose the costs still exceed the benefit? What is the next step?

7. If, at this stage, the costs far exceed the benefits, it is improbable that the computer is a viable investment. If, however, the costs are only slightly in excess of the benefit, the case is 'not proven'. I do not see that any amount of economic or mathematical ingenuity can be of help. For reasons set out earlier in this article, I do not see that a meaningful evaluation can be placed on reports which determine activities far in the future, or reports that are only one of many to a decision-process. Fortunately, this category of report, which is mainly of the 'one-off' variety, accounts for only a small part of current computer output. This completes the suggested approach to evaluating *the output* from the computer. But there is another set of effects generated by the computer which also has economic implications.

Costs and benefits not connected with the output from the computer

So far it has been attempted to evaluate the computer by evaluating the costs and/or benefits of the *output* from the computer. However, the computer will affect the organization into which it is introduced in a variety of ways which are not connected with the *output* from the computer. These effects can be called *non-output* effects. Several of these non-output effects are likely to have economic implications, that is, they may alter costs or revenue.

Non-output effects can be classified into two broad categories. *External* effects which are mainly concerned with improving the image of the company in the outside world, and *internal* effects on such things as distribution of authority, work satisfaction and so forth.

There can be no doubt that the publicity derived from introducing a sophisticated computer system has an economic value. This is, for example, one of the simplest ways of persuading the general public that the company is sympathetic to modern management techniques. A system such as BOADICEA has certainly improved the image of BOAC. But what is the precise economic value of the improved image? How many more passengers use BOAC because they are impressed with the company developing a sophisticated computer system? I do not believe that this type of benefit can be evaluated.

The outlook is rather more optimistic when we turn to *internal* non-output effects. Mann and Williams (1960), Tuthill (1966), Mumford and Ward (1968) and others have shown the influence of the computer on the human side of the organization.

The interdependency of information flow and command structure is well known. An alteration of one inevitably has repercussions on the other. A change in command structure is likely to affect the efficiency of the organization. The introduction of a more highly automated information system can affect the work content of clerical staff. The work tends to become less discretionary as elementary decision routines are automated. Thus job satisfaction will decrease for some and increase for others (Mumford and Ward, 1968, ch. 12). The computer can set up role strain between line and staff management and affect management attitudes to such things as control and education. All of which can in turn affect the morale of the organization. Also the social cost of implementing change which is borne by the staff, and the families of staff, directly concerned with developing the system, must not be forgotten.

Many of these non-output effects are likely to alter the efficiency of the organization; to increase or reduce costs and profits. This being so, a rigorous method of evaluating the computer ought to take them into account. Can these effects be evaluated? This brings contact with the very difficult problem of costing social change (Likert, 1961, ch. 5). Some success has been achieved in costing changes in such things as the rate of staff turnover, but the near impossibility of *proving* the connection between social cause and social effect makes significant progress in this area very difficult. However, some research is in progress on the problem, for example by the Institute for Social Research, University of Michigan and the Manchester Business School.

It should be noticed that some of these non-output effects (i.e. improved market image) are positive, while others (i.e. reduced work satisfaction) are negative. Since every computer evaluation examined in this article ignores these effects, they implicitly assume that the positive and negative effects cancel each other out, but this is improbable.

Conclusion

This article set out to review the literature on the evaluation of computer-based information systems and to suggest where evaluation is feasible and where it is not. The classical approach of economists to evaluating a production good is to evaluate the services generated by the production good. This article identified two distinct outputs from the computer: information and data. Information was defined as being an input to a decision-process within the firm, data as all other outputs from the computer. In the early stages of computer use most of the output can be classified as data while information is often produced as a joint product with data. Since data is a final good, produced for itself alone, the conclusion is that cost-effective (cost-saving) methods of evaluation are adequate.

If a significant proportion of computer time is spent on producing information an attempt should be made to evaluate the incremental benefits of this information. Distinction between long- and short-term decision-processes was made, concluding that most computer-output provides input to short-term decisions affecting the utilization of assets. Analytical and heuristic methods are available for assessing the incremental value of information in this area. Thus up to this point the evaluation of computer-based information systems is feasible. A good part of current (1970) computer output falls into one or other of the previous categories. Other forms of information present formidable problems of evaluation. Fortunately, this category accounts for only a small portion of current computer output.

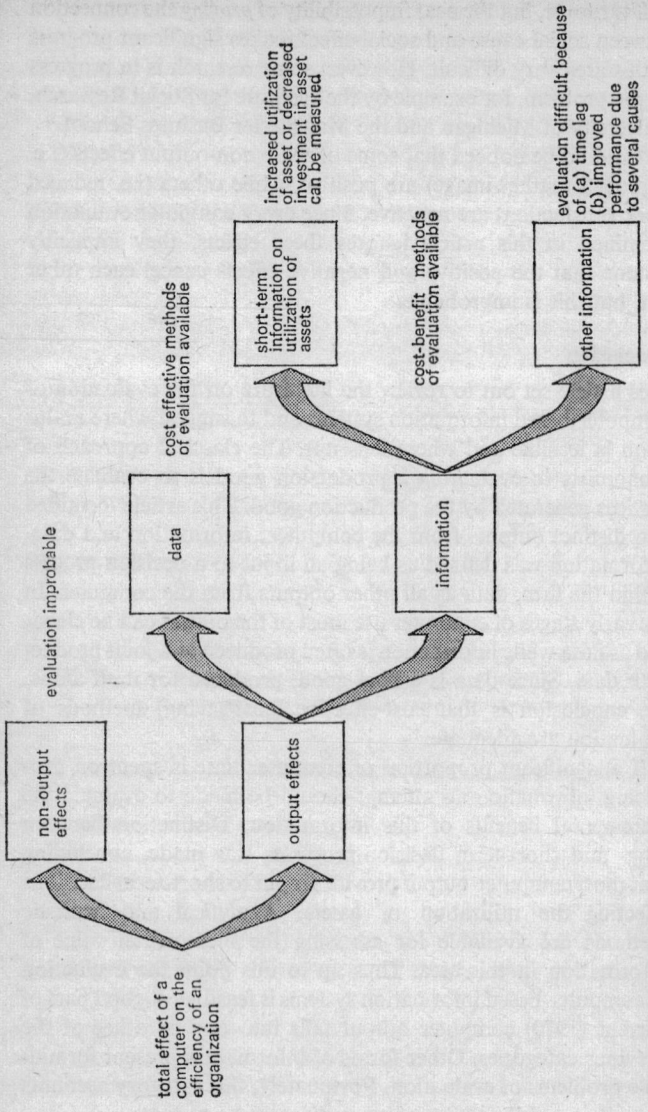

Figure 1 Tree diagram illustrating suggested approach to evaluating computer system

- total effect of a computer on the efficiency of an organization
  - non-output effects — *evaluation improbable*
  - output effects
    - data — *cost effective methods of evaluation available*
    - information
      - short-term information on utilization of assets — *increased utilization of asset or decreased investment in asset can be measured*
      - cost-benefit methods of evaluation available
      - other information — *evaluation difficult because of (a) time lag (b) improved performance due to several causes*

The discussion was deliberately limited to the problem of evaluating the *output* from the computer. However, by altering the information flow, the computer has a wide ranging impact on work contact, organization structure, attitudes to change, the company image and so forth. Many of these effects have economic implications. Unfortunately, it is not known how to measure these effects or how to evaluate them in economic terms.

The conclusion is that if we ignore the effects noted in the last paragraph, the evaluation of *current* computer based information systems is not as formidable as some writers have suggested. However, as the proportion of computer time devoted to generating information increases, so the difficulty of evaluating computer-based information systems will also tend to increase. Figure 1 presents a graphical model of the suggested approach.

References

BAUER, W. F., and HILL, R. H. (1967), 'Economics of time-shared computing systems', *Datamation*, pp. 41–9.

BEDFORD, N. D., and ONSI, M. (1966), 'Measuring the value of information', *Manag. Services*, vol. 3, no. 1, pp. 15–22.

BOYD, D. F., and KRASNOW, H. S. (1963), 'Economic evaluation of management information systems', *IBM Systems J.*, vol. 2, no. 2, pp. 2–23.

BRADY, R. H. (1967), 'Computers in top-level decision-making', *Harvard Bus. Rev.*, vol. 45, no. 4, pp. 67–76.

BRENNER, J. R. (1965), 'Towards a value theory of information' in A. B. Frielnik (ed.) *Economics of ADP*, North-Holland Publishing Co.

Business Management STAFF (1965), 'How to make sure your computer pays off', *Bus. Manag.*, vol. 95, no. 10, pp. 37–41, 96, 98.

CALLAHAN, J. R. (1967), 'Management by objective: economical use of computers', *Computers and Automation*.

DEARDEN, J. (1968), 'Time-span in management control', *Finan. Exec.*, vol. 36, no. 8, pp. 23–30.

DESSAU, E. (1966), 'EDP in hospitals', *Computer Survey*, vol. 5, p. 73.

GARRITY, J. T. (1963), 'Top management and computer profits', *Harvard Bus. Rev.*, vol. 41, no. 4, pp. 6–12, 172–4.

GILL, W. A. (1962), 'Economic considerations in the use of electronic computers', *Computers and Automation*.

HOOPER, D. W. (1967), 'Computer survey questionnaire', *Computer Survey*, vol. 6, no. 3, p. 200.

JANES, J. D. W. (1963), 'Measuring the profitability of a computer system', *Computer Bull.*, vol. 7, no. 1, p. 284.

JAQUES, E. (1963), *Equitable Payment*, Heinemann.

KALSCHEUER, H. D. (1968), 'Profitability measurement of MISs', *Europ. Bus.*, no. 17, pp. 47–51.

KNIGHT, K. E. (1966), 'Changes in computer performance', *Datamation*, pp. 40–54.

LAVE, L. B. (1963), 'The value of better information in the raisin industry', *Econometrica*, vol. 31, no. 1–2, pp. 151–64.

LIKERT, R. (1961), *New Patterns in Management*, McGraw-Hill.

MANN, F. C., and WILLIAMS, L. K. (1960), 'Observations on the dynamics of a change to EDP equipment', *Admin. Sci. Q.*, vol. 5, no. 2, pp. 217–56.

MEREDITH-SMITH, J. (1968), 'Computer performance evaluation', *Computer Bull.*, vol. 12, no. 5, p. 13.

MUMFORD, E., and WARD, T. B. (1968), *Computers: Planning for People*, Batsford.

NELSON, R. R., and WINTER, S. G. (1964) 'The weather-forecasting systems', *Q.J. Econ.*, vol. 78, no. 3, pp. 420–41.

POPELL, S. D. (1966), *Computer Time-Sharing*, Prentice-Hall.

PREST, A. R., and TURVEY, R. (1965), 'Cost-benefit analysis: a survey', *Econ. J.*, vol. 75, no. 12, pp. 685–735.

STIGLER, J. J. (1961), 'The economics of information', *J. Pol. Econ.*, vol. 69, no. 3, pp. 213–25.

STONIER, A. W., and HAGUE, D. C. (1967), *A Textbook of Economic Theory*, Longmans.

TUTHILL, D. W. (1966), 'The thrust of information technology on management', *Finan. Exec.*, vol. 34, no. 1.

12 Staff of *Business Management*

How to Make Sure Your Computer Pays Off

Staff of *Business Management*, 'How to make sure your computer pays off', *Business Management*, vol. 95, 1965, pp. 37–41, 96, 98.

In 1960, a well-known midwestern firm computerized its inventory system. Its aim was twofold: to reduce the time its warehouses took to fill orders from its retail soft-goods stores and to reduce the amount of inventory the warehouses had to carry.

In the ensuing five years, the firm's sales have increased 28 per cent and its pre-tax profit 18 per cent. Management could not be happier.

Yet it has little reason to be. For, in the same period its expenditures for computer equipment have jumped a whopping 870 per cent, and its expenditures for computer operations have gone up 310 per cent. What's worse, in the inventory area at least, the computer has made no contribution to the company's profits. In fact, the computer hasn't even come close to accomplishing what it was supposed to accomplish.

Why not? Although the company can fill orders much more quickly than it once did, its retail outlets aren't taking advantage of the new system. Instead, they're placing their orders several days later than they used to. Result: The company's warehouses haven't benefited.

To top it all off, serious tension has arisen between the company's computer and warehouse personnel. The latter say the new system isn't fulfilling its goals. In answer, the computer people recently rented additional equipment (at $60,000 a year) to further reduce the time it takes to fill an order.

Obviously, however, the new equipment isn't helping. The firm's retail outlets still aren't placing their orders any faster.

This true story comes from Douglas J. Axsmith, a senior associate of McKinsey & Company, the New York-based management consulting firm. Axsmith's speciality is providing advice on the design of large-scale, business-oriented computer systems. Among other companies, he's counselled two well-known oil firms, a major airline and a famous beverage manufacturer.

The heart of the matter

The story illustrates what he considers one of the most important facts about business's current use of computers: many firms aren't making their computers pay off. Those that are obtaining a profit from their computers aren't obtaining all they should.

As he puts it:

Although the potential for obtaining profits from computers is great, it is often being realized only partially, if at all. Recent surveys show that companies obtaining a profit from their computers are getting, at the most, only half of what they should be getting.

Why aren't these companies doing better? Why are some companies obtaining no profit at all?

There are several reasons. In some companies, top management has little interest in computer operations. In other companies, computer personnel are not as competent as they should be. In still other companies, neither top management nor computer personnel have made a real effort to plan and control their computer's use.

To Axsmith's mind, the last reason is, in many ways, the most important.

In company after company you'll find there is a lack of sound, economic knowledge as to whether the computer is returning a profit and, if so, how much profit.

Management assumes the computer is profitable, but it is operating on faith rather than fact. It is not applying to its computer the same return on investment criteria that it applies to research projects or other expensive investments.

Take one company I know. If you asked why it had rented a particular computer, you would be handed a carefully documented pamphlet comparing the equipment of various computer manufacturers. If you asked what it was doing with its computer and how it was doing it, you would again be presented with impressive documentation. But if you asked why it was using the computer in these ways – how it had justified these particular applications – you would be met with blank stares.

I once asked the company just this question. That is what the computer people told me: 'Well, we don't have any formal method for choosing applications. Sometimes, management asks us if we can do such and such. If we have free machine-time, we do it. Other times, we suggest various projects on our own. If we're turned down, we may do them anyway.'

I then asked the company for its estimates on what its various applications were costing. It turned out there weren't any estimates.

Go to other companies and ask how much their computers are earning or saving, and you're apt to get answers like these: 'Well, we don't know how much we've saved, but our business has changed so much that we're certain our costs would be much higher if we didn't have a computer.' Or 'Our operating costs are probably higher than they used to be, but the new information we produce is allowing management to make better decisions.' In short, management often assumes its computer is profitable. But it has little evidence to support its assumption.

Some further proof of Axsmith's charge: the American Management Association recently made a survey of 288 companies that use computers. Of these 288 companies, 253 said their computer operations were successful. Yet only 112 of the 288 had goals precise enough to be measured. And not one mentioned the exact amount of savings it hoped to achieve.

Four roads to profit

In Axsmith's opinion, unprofitable computer operations shouldn't exist. He emphasizes that there are four important ways in which a computer can increase profits. They include:

1. Reduction in administrative costs. By reducing the amount of paper work you must handle or the number of employees needed to handle it, a computer can slash your administrative costs by 30 per cent to 50 per cent annually. The precise amount of savings will depend on how sophisticated your computer system is, how carefully you strive to achieve savings, and what industry you're in. Thus, banks, insurance firms and utilities are in an especially good position to achieve savings because they handle so much paper work.

2. Reduction in working capital requirements. If you apply your computer to your sales order-shipping-billing cycle, it can speed up cash flow and thereby reduce your investment in accounts

receivable. It can also reduce your investment in raw material, in-process or finished goods inventories. How? By providing faster notice of sales demand and thus enabling you to carry lower inventory. Or by providing better production-scheduling information and thus enabling you to abbreviate your in-process manufacturing time. Or by centralizing your order-processing and thus enabling you to draw on inventory from all your warehouses and reduce the amount you must keep in any one of them.

3. Better use of company resources. When a computer plans schedules or provides information for controlling the use of manufacturing equipment, sales forces or other costly resources, substantial savings are possible. How substantial depends primarily on the scope of the resources rather than the improved degree of control. Thus, a 2 per cent improvement in the use of a resource costing $5 million a year would generate a profit increase of $100,000.

4. Better corporate decisions. A computer can swiftly analyse past sales-data and help management make more accurate sales forecasts. Or it can help management decide whether to produce a new product or enter a new market. Axsmith says:

Profit increases through better decision making are potentially the most significant. But, to date, this has been the least exploited area of computer profitability, partly because of the high cost of implementing quantitative decision-making techniques and the considerable time they take.

To achieve profits or savings in one or more of these areas, says the management consultant, you must successfully manage the economics of your computer system. To effect such management, you must:

1. Evaluate the potential benefits of any given computer application before implementing it.

2. Establish sound methods for controlling the application and measuring its actual benefits.

3. Institute a profit-oriented method for distributing the cost of the application.

Axsmith emphasizes that:

Top management must *force* its computer department to take these steps. The computer department is not likely to take them on its own.

The reasons are simple. Computer people are not apt to be familiar with a business as a whole, and they are even less apt to be oriented to its need to make a profit.

Instead, they're likely to be oriented solely to their own department. They will want to build the best possible computer system. That may or may not be the system that will contribute most to company profits.

In other words, computer people are not apt to ask a vice-president of sales, 'What information can we provide you about your customers that will help you increase company profits?' Instead, they're likely to ask, 'Give us all the information you have about your customers. We will keep all of it on the computer.' This, regardless of the cost of keeping the information or the likelihood that it will contribute to profits.

Here then, in more detail, is what top management must force its computer department to do to help maximize profits.

Evaluate potential benefits of all proposed applications

Axsmith says that:

Few companies make any real effort to do this. Too often, they take a 'How can we miss?' attitude.

This is a serious mistake. Failure to specify and quantify in detail all potential savings will keep you from properly deploying your manpower so as to actually achieve the savings. It will also keep you from following up to make sure what you hoped to save actually has been saved.

What's needed?

Obviously some method of estimating the impact of a proposed application. In making this estimate, you must first assay the odds you'll achieve tangible benefits.

Too many companies, he says, fumble this job. If they decide to print all their invoices by computer, they assume they will no longer need invoice typists. Or if they centralize and automate their order processing, they assume they can eliminate the clerical personnel in their sales offices.

Staff of *Business Management*

Axsmith points out:

Matters seldom work out quite so neatly. Invoice typists do more than type invoices. Clerical personnel in a sales office do more than clerical work. Both groups make special reports, trace errors or just answer the phone.

Because of this, you must identify *all* the work performed in the areas you plan to computerize, figure how many people must be retained to handle this work and estimate your savings accordingly. Otherwise, you may overestimate your savings substantially.

Axsmith says estimating how much a computer is likely to reduce your working capital requirements or improve your use of corporate resources is even more difficult than estimating how much it will reduce your administrative costs. That's mainly because you will have several options.

For example, suppose computerization gives you better and faster sales forecasts, enabling you to fill orders more quickly. You can then do one of two things: fill the orders more quickly and be paid sooner. Or plan your manufacturing operations more efficiently and perhaps cut overtime work. Thus, the course you take will help determine where and when you will achieve savings.

Because these decisions and estimates are difficult to make in advance, some companies don't even try. In this area especially, a 'How can we miss?' attitude prevails.

This, he emphasizes, is the wrong way out. Even if you can't estimate precisely how much your working capital requirements will be reduced or to what extent your corporate resources will be better used, you can estimate the minimum amount of savings you must achieve if the computer application is to be worth its cost. You can also estimate the amount of time it will take to achieve these minimum savings.

For example, if it will cost $20,000 to implement an application and you want to recover this sum in five years, you know you must achieve minimum annual savings of $4000. Whether you can do so will depend, of course, on the nature of the procedure to be computerized. Axsmith says that:

It's important that these estimates be a joint effort on the part of your computer people and the people whose operations will be computerized.

This will not only result in more accurate estimates, but also prevent arguments later on.

If you're considering computerizing some corporate procedure, you must also estimate the intangible benefits you're likely to achieve. Such benefits may include more timely cost reports or more detailed market breakdowns. Knowing the intangible benefits you're likely to derive will be especially important if you're trying to decide between two applications whose tangible benefits seem equal.

Estimating intangible benefits requires two steps, Axsmith says.

Again, one involves gaining agreement on the minimum amount of savings that must be achieved. You can probably do this by estimating the application's initial and operating costs, then applying a return on investment percentage to these costs.

For example, a better sales report will cost $50,000. This sales report may enable you to drop unprofitable customers or unprofitable products or take some other action to improve profits. If you take one or more such steps, what are your annual savings likely to be? If you require a 10 per cent annual return on investment but figure you won't get more than 5 per cent, you may want to abandon the project. (What return on investment percentage you apply will depend on your own needs and desires. Obviously, however, one possibility is whatever percentage you apply to other corporate ventures.)

The second step involves determining what must happen if the savings are to be realized and ascertaining how likely it is that these things will happen. Axsmith thinks that:

This step is harder than the first. That's partly because it requires a fairly broad knowledge of the business, partly because it requires thinking the project through from beginning to end.

But this step must be taken. You remember the midwestern firm that has realized no benefit from its computerized inventory system. Why has it failed? Because it assumed, without checking, that its retail outlets would continue to place their orders on the same days they had always placed them. The entire success of the project hinged on the accuracy of this assumption. When it proved inaccurate, the company didn't benefit.

You can implement this step by checking your assumptions with the line managers in your own firm. Axsmith's opinion is that line managers will be more willing to check assumptions than to answer questions like 'How much would computerizing such and such a procedure be worth to you?'

You'll also do well to check the experiences of outsiders, such as management consulting firms or other businesses. Axsmith is

a great believer in attending data processing conferences. You can pick up a lot of valuable information. In particular, you can find out whether other firms have tried any of the applications you're considering, whether they fell on their faces, and if so, why.

Control your applications and measure their actual benefits

Why establish a method for controlling a computer application and measuring its effect on profit? There are several reasons.

One reason is to enable you to detect, as quickly as possible, applications that are not returning the minimum savings you have decided they must return. As Axsmith says:

One of the real advantages of a measurement and control system is that it enables a company to go backward. If an application doesn't pay off, the company can return to its manual system. And don't think this hasn't happened. One major airline has done just that with part of its accounting system – and wisely so.

A second reason is to enable you to make sure you obtain the savings you expect when you expect them.

A third reason is to enable you to check your estimates of an application's initial cost. For, if these estimates are wrong, so will your operating cost estimates be wrong. (You will also learn, of course, how to make future estimates more accurately.)

To achieve these objectives, you will have to set up a formal system for controlling the application and measuring its results. Axsmith says this system must meet the following requirements:

1. It must include a formal method for estimating costs.

Many companies complain that they seriously underestimated the time and money it would take to computerize a given procedure. The reason they went wrong is usually simple. Different people estimated different parts of the process in different ways. How they made their estimates, no one knows. Often, they themselves don't remember.

The solution to this problem is also simple. Take all the quantitative information you have about a given application before you implement it. For example, you'll know the various kinds of information that will be contained in each computer input – a man's name, job title, salary bracket and so forth, to cite one possibility.

Multiply each bit of this quantitative data by the same amount of time – say, half a week. In other words, estimate that it will take you half a week to write, edit and so forth each kind of information that will go into and come out of the computer.

Finally, keep a record of how long it actually does take. Over a period of time, you will learn how accurate your estimates are. You can then anticipate probable errors in future estimates.

The key to this method, of course, is to first make a mechanical estimate – estimate that each kind of input and output will take the same amount of time.

2. It must include plans for achieving tangible benefits on a definite schedule and agreements from responsible line managers that it is possible to meet this schedule.

3. It must include a procedure for determining whether the application produces intangible benefits and a method for measuring their impact.

What procedure? That will depend on the company and on the procedure being computerized. The consultant suggests:

But take this example. A computerized sales report will cost $20,000. This sales report will enable a company to do several things – redeploy its salesmen, perhaps, so as to increase sales, or drop an unprofitable product. Suppose the company takes these and other steps, then keeps track of the results. The measurement of the effectiveness of the sales report will be whether any one of these steps or some combination of them enables the company to recover its $20,000 in a given period of time.

4. It must require weekly reports from each computer analyst and programer, showing how he is spending his time.

These reports should state what computer application each man is working on and precisely what he is doing – analysing, designing, programing or whatever.

Such reports will not only result in better future estimates of the time a particular application may require, but, very frankly, they will also result in less goofing off in your computer department.

In addition, your control system should require monthly *progress* reports on each project in process. These reports should contain detailed figures on the time and cost required by the projects and should go to top management.

5. It should require an estimate of the future cost of a procedure if it were not computerized.

Often, it takes several years for a computer application to achieve predicted savings. In order to estimate these savings accurately, you must avoid comparing the cost of a computer application with the *present* cost of your manual system. Instead, you must compare it with the likely *future* cost of the manual system.

This requires that you establish some formula for determining how the manual system's cost is likely to change over a period of, say, four years. Axsmith advises:

If you're considering computerizing a billing system you might estimate the future cost of the manual system by estimating your future number of orders and multiplying their total by the cost of handling one order. In making estimates in this or any other area, you should, of course, seek the advice of the line managers whose procedures are to be computerized.

To measure your future savings, you need only subtract the cost of the application from what you have decided the future cost of the manual system would have been.

Axsmith emphasizes that any competent computer manager can establish a formal method for controlling and measuring computer applications. It's up to top management to see that he does so.

Institute a profit-oriented costing method

What departments in your company should pay for your computer operations?

Companies handle this problem in several different ways. In Axsmith's opinion the best way is a little-used one. It's called the fixed-variable costing method, and it works like this:

Before an application is begun, the computer department and the department that will benefit from the application determine the present (and future) cost of the present system. The computer department then pays the cost of setting up and implementing the application, but charges the other department what the old manual system cost. At the same time, the computer department is credited with any savings the application achieves. Once these cumulative savings have enabled the computer department to recover its investment, it starts charging the other department the actual cost of the application.

Axsmith says this method offers any corporation three distinct advantages.

First, company departments are *not* charged the high initial cost of implementing a computer application. This helps overcome any reluctance they may feel about computerization of their departments.

Second, the computer department is forced to be brutally realistic in estimating costs and savings. Reason: It's going to pay for a given application until the initial cost has been recovered.

Third, if the computer department slightly inflates its cost estimates, it can build a reserve fund to pay for research work, short-term losses and so forth. (Obviously, this slight inflation must not boost the cost of the computer application above the cost of the system it is replacing.)

In short this method forces a computer department to operate like any other profit-making business. This, in turn will help its operations contribute to the profits of the company as a whole.

I know of only two firms that use this method. One's a division of one of the big automobile manufacturers. The other is a division of a beverage manufacturer. Both have been successful with it.

Let's assume your company successfully takes these three steps. How long will it take you to profit from a given computer application? How long will it take you to recover your investment in the application?

Axsmith says the time required to achieve a profit depends on the time it takes to implement the application and the type of profit it returns – reductions in administrative costs or whatever.

In general, he points out, reductions in administrative costs are achieved through attrition or transfer of personnel.

In my experience if these reductions are well planned, they can be achieved as rapidly as the attrition rate allows. Thus, the time it takes to achieve savings will be equal to the time it takes to implement the application, plus the time it takes to achieve a reduction in personnel.

Staff of *Business Management*

By contrast, savings in working capital requirements or resource utilization often begin as soon as an application is implemented. 'However,' cautions Axsmith, 'don't assume this will be the case without checking. If you do, you may achieve no savings at all.'

Why? Because savings in these areas will be realized only if policies in effect before the application was implemented remain in effect afterwards. Or if advantage is taken of the benefits the application provides.

For example, suppose a computer increases the utilization of a machine and, by means of improved scheduling, reduces in-process manufacturing time, too. If the extra manufacturing time provided by the computer is not used to advantage, there will be no savings.

Profit obtained from better corporate decisions often comes in the form of 'avoided losses'. In other words, a computer analysis causes management to decide against a course of action it ordinarily would have taken. Thus, the analysis may persuade management not to build a new plant because the plant's profit potential would be small.

It's difficult to assign a specific dollar value to such avoided losses. But a company can increase its accuracy by using the discounted cash flow method to estimate these losses. If possible, this method should be part of the computer analysis itself.

Four years is typical

The length of time it takes to recover an investment in a computer application will always depend on the cost of implementing the application and the time it takes to implement it, plus the savings the application achieves and the time it takes to achieve these savings. For this reason, recovery time will vary from application to application. Axsmith says that:

Despite this variance surveys show there is a remarkable consistency in the length of time it takes to recover an investment in an overall mix of applications. With companies that have installed a computer for the first time, the payback period ranges between three and a half and five years. Most companies make the grade in approximately four years.

When companies replace or add to their equipment the payback period drops to about one year. That's because the equipment coming out these days, such as the IBM 360 or the RCA Spectra 70, is very efficient and very compatible. In other words, it permits easy conversion of existing computer programs.

How, then, to sum up? Says Axsmith:

Computers can pay for themselves. But, to date, there's been a disappointing gap between their performance and their potentiality. The way to narrow this gap is not only to search for more applications with high payout but also to improve control and measurement of existing applications.

This job poses no major technical problems. The barriers to it are solely emotional. These barriers can be overcome. How? One, top management must insist on control and measurement of its computer applications. And two, in implementing this control and measurement process, computer departments must work closely with departments they serve.

13 D. F. Boyd and H. J. Krasnow

Economic Evaluation of Management Information Systems

D. F. Boyd and H. J. Krasnow, 'Economic evaluation of management information systems', *IBM Systems Journal*, vol. 2, 1963, pp. 2-23.

The evaluation of data-processing systems has traditionally rested upon the notion of cost displacement. This approach is a natural outgrowth of viewing such systems as essentially productive. However, significant economic benefits of many recent systems accrue from the so-called intangible benefits to management. Thus, the nature of current information systems suggests that they be viewed, for purposes of economic evaluation, in a broader context than that of a producing machine.

Here we view the contribution of an information system in maintaining control over a business system operating in a changing environment. This view implies a criterion of evaluation related to the dynamic performance of the firm. We hypothesize that better information will lead to better control which in turn will yield improved total performance. The control objective of the firm is to respond to the environmental demands in an economically efficient manner. The effectiveness of an information processing system in satisfying this objective may be evaluated by:

1. An accounting measurement of the financial performance of the firm over time in the face of changing demand (environment).

2. The accuracy, completeness and timeliness with which that demand is satisfied.

These measures, being more complex, are more difficult to estimate than cost-displacement and require an adequate model of the firm itself.

The objectives of the current study were, first, to define a method suitable for the economic evaluation of information systems when viewed in this manner; and second, to demonstrate its technical feasibility by applying it to a hypothetical firm.

Description of the method

The importance of the dynamic behavior of the firm to its own well being has been shown and it has been demonstrated that this behavior can be simulated (Forrester, 1961). Advanced information systems, which are often intimately and extensively involved in control, have also been successfully simulated. The problem then, is to relate the mechanics of the information system to the dynamics of the business firm within a single model.

The simple firm performs an economic function upon which its existence is based. (The modern corporation, of course, often performs many such functions.) A minimal set of activities is required in order to perform this function: we designate this set and its inter-relationships as the *physical system*. In a manufacturing firm the elements of the physical system are the production processes and the resources which produce the end product. In a service firm, the physical system is composed of those activities and their associated resources which directly provide the customer with service.

A total representation of the firm requires, in addition to the physical system, a second part referred to as the *information-processing system*. The latter encompasses all activities of the firm whose direct or indirect function is to control the physical system (Figure 1). In a real firm there are, of course, activities which do not fall within either of these two categories (for example, janitorial services). These activities are of little interest for the purposes at hand, and appear only as fixed or variable cost elements within the accounting structure.

The information-processing system is broader in concept than any existing data-processing system, the latter serving as a component of the former. The information-processing system can be represented by the following basic elements and their inter-relationships:

Sensor. This type of element originates all data input to the information-processing system. It includes both manual and machine-generated input. It reports the occurrence of an event within the physical system (or perhaps within the environment).[1] A segment of a physical system is shown in Figure 2. Sensors record all possible events, the receipt of material into inventory, disbursements from inventory, and the receipt of requisitions (demand) for inventory.

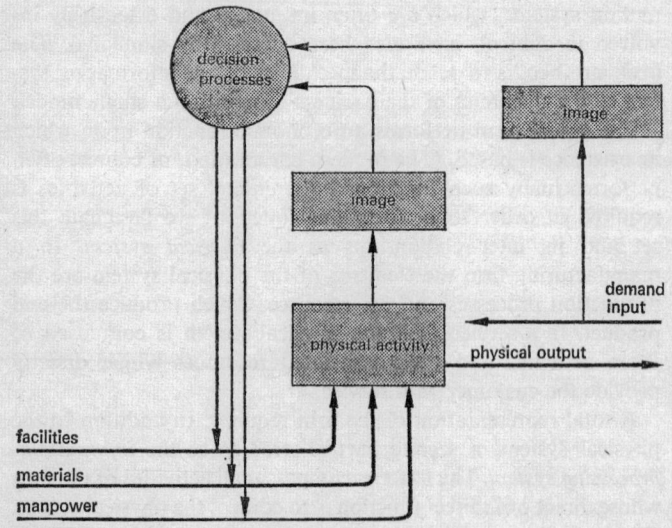

Figure 1 Elements of a dynamic model

Input transmission. Sensed data are subject to delay and/or distortion during transmission. All delays associated with input are imagined to occur at this point (i.e. sensing alone is complete, accurate and instantaneous).

Image. The end result of data input and most conventional processing, whether machine or manual, is an image. In Figure 2, the image of the true inventory is the inventory record. Images

1. The model described in this paper is entirely discrete in nature. If one wished to describe continuous events within the physical system of a model (e.g. flow processes), sensors would report the *rate* of occurrence of such events.

can be classified as levels (e.g. inventory) or rates (e.g. the arrival rate of inventory requisitions). If applied to continuous flow measurements, level images would be the time integral of one or more rate images. With appropriate sensors, images can be provided which describe any activity within the physical system. However, they are distorted as a result of input transmission delays and may be biased by the random or systematic loss of sensed data during transmission.

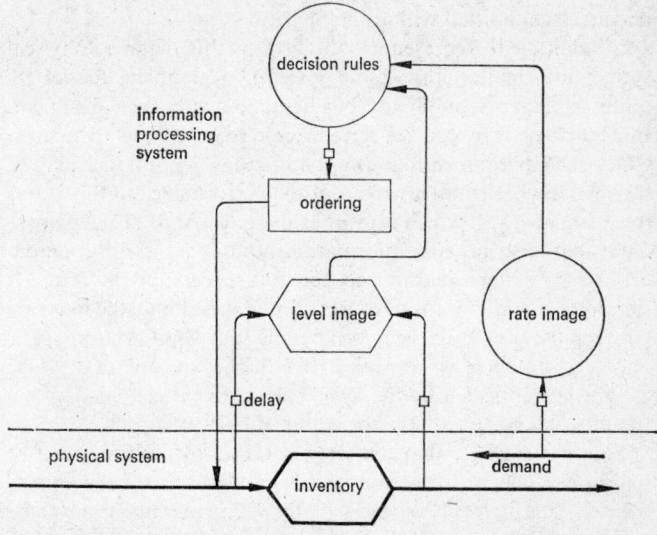

Figure 2 Segment of a dynamic model

Decision process. This is a crucial element of the information-processing system. The term is used in the broadest possible sense to encompass all decision-making related to the control of the physical system. Decision processes can function with the aid of much or little information; with information which is accurate or distorted, timely or outdated. The information upon which the decision process depends (all of the information available to it) is contained in images. The decision process has no direct contact either with the physical system or the environment. In the example of Figure 2, the decision to order additional material for inventory utilizes images of the current requisitioning rate and inventory level.

Output transmission. The result of a decision is a command which will ultimately produce some change in the activities of the physical system. A single time delay is associated with both the decision-making process and the transmission of its commands. In Figure 2, the command is in the form of an order for additional material. More generally, commands take the form of an adjustment to the resources committed within the physical system.

In addition to representing the firm in this manner (physical system–information processing system), a complete model requires explicit recognition of the interaction with its environment. In particular, it recognizes certain basic requirements (demands) which the environment places upon it and which it undertakes to satisfy. One basic measurement of the performance of the firm is the adequacy with which it satisfies these demands. The environment may also provide information inputs to the information-processing system relevant to the future demand pattern. (It should be noted that for purposes of model building, the interface between the firm and its environment is somewhat arbitrary. The crucial distinction is between that which can and that which cannot be controlled by the firm. The former is classified within the physical system; the latter within the environment.)

Figure 3 suggests that the representation of the firm has two interfaces: one with its environment and one with the experimenter. This figure also suggests the experimenter may change the parameters governing the environment and the information-processing and physical systems. In order to measure the results of these changes, he must make comprehensive observations regarding the performance of the simulated firm. The mechanism for accomplishing this observation has been designated the *accounting structure* because of the central role of financial accounting for performance evaluation. Cost is a critical element of performance and must be considered in any overall evaluation. Conventional accounting procedures are introduced for this purpose. The complete accounting structure is capable of providing any desired data concerning the operation of the model, including data which are entirely independent of cost. No errors or time delays are introduced. In this sense it is perfect and provides an accurate and unbiased appraisal of the performance of the firm.

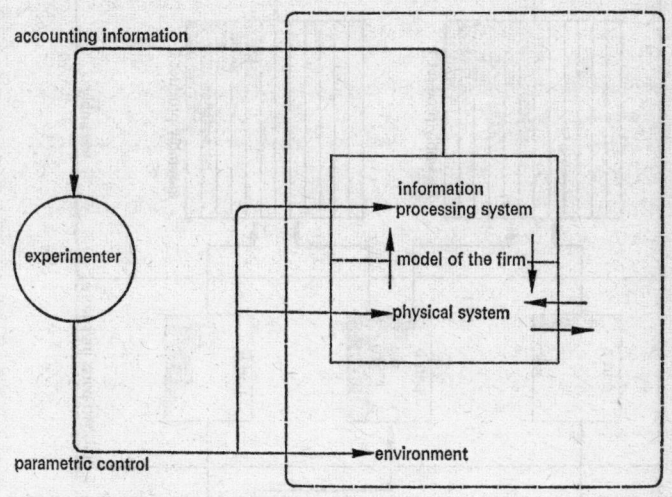

Figure 3 Interfaces in the simulation

A specific model

We will now describe a specific model of a simple, hypothetical manufacturing firm.

The physical system of the model shown in Figure 4 incorporates as much as possible of the dynamic complexity found in a typical manufacturing operation within a nominally simple model. Thus, a basic assumption is made that the general dynamic characteristics of a system can be adequately represented without the introduction of the large number of individual elements actually present. The components of the physical system are now described.

Two end products are manufactured, designated as Products 1 and 2. Both products are assembled and shipped to customer order. Three finished parts (Parts A, B, C) provide all of the components for the assembled products, in accordance with the Bills of Material shown in Table 1.

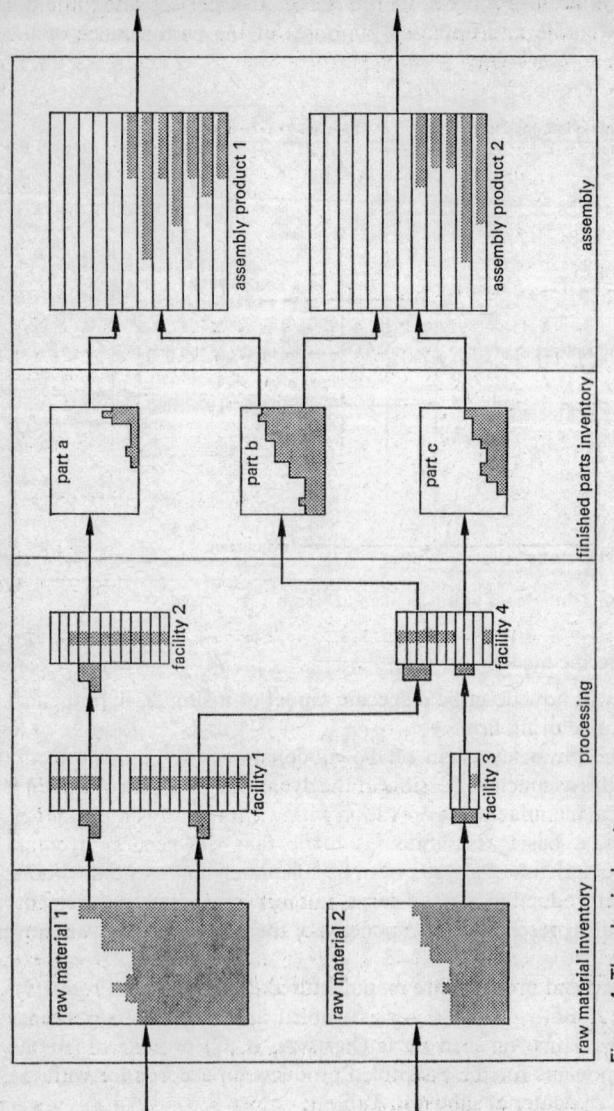

Figure 4 The physical system

It can be seen that Part B is common to both products, introducing a conflict situation (with its related decision problems) of the type often found in practice.

Table 1 Bills of Material

	Units		
	Part	A	B	C
Product 1		1	2	
Product 2			1	1

The activities of the physical system are distributed over three stages of manufacturing: raw material procurement, parts processing (fabrication) and assembly and shipping. This introduces much of the dynamic complexity of the model, since overall response is dependent upon actions taken somewhat independently within each stage. Accurate control will require good planning to coordinate the activities within different stages. These activities are:

Raw material procurement. Inspection, receipt and storage of raw material.

Processing. Requisitioning of raw material. Set-up of a facility unit for processing a particular part. Processing a part on a facility unit (fabrication operation). Scrapping a part on a facility. Movement of partially finished parts to next operation. Movement of finished parts into inventory. Storage of finished parts in inventory.

Assembly and shipping. Requisitioning of finished parts required for assembly of an order. Movement of parts to assembly area. Assembly. Scrapping of parts during assembly. Requisitioning and movement of replacement parts. Shipment of completed orders.

The scale of an activity (e.g. time to perform, rate of occurrence, etc.) is either dependent upon other activities and therefore determined by the simulation (for example, number of parts in inventory); or it is a parameter of the physical system controllable by the experimenter (for example, time to assemble one unit of Product 1). In the latter case, the value may be specified determinately as a constant or a function, or stochastically as a random function.

The performance of an activity requires the commitment of one or more resources. Several activities have been structured so that they compete for the same resources, thereby creating typical conflict situations which can only be resolved by rational decisions. The resources available in the model are:

Processing manpower. Men within the processing stage are entirely interchangeable, and may work on any valid operation, or remain idle.

Assembly manpower. Men within the assembly stage may assemble orders for either product. However, no transfer of men between the assembly and processing stage is permitted.

Processing facilities. Each facility within the processing stage possesses a discrete number of units of capacity. A processing operation commits one man and one unit of facility to the processing of one part. The facility units must be set up prior to processing, however successive units of the same part may be processed on the same set-up.

Material. The finished parts used in the assembly of the two products are fabricated from two raw materials. Two of the finished parts (Part A and Part B) compete for Raw Material 1.

The prime objective in constructing the information-processing system was to provide sufficient capability to permit effective dynamic control over the physical system. Within this context, the emphasis was placed upon building a conventional structure which could plausibly incorporate a range of data system types. Figure 5 is a schematic of the complete model depicting, among others, all of the major features of the information-processing system.

Hierarchical aspects of an information-processing system in the large firm are included. Decision-making occurs at various

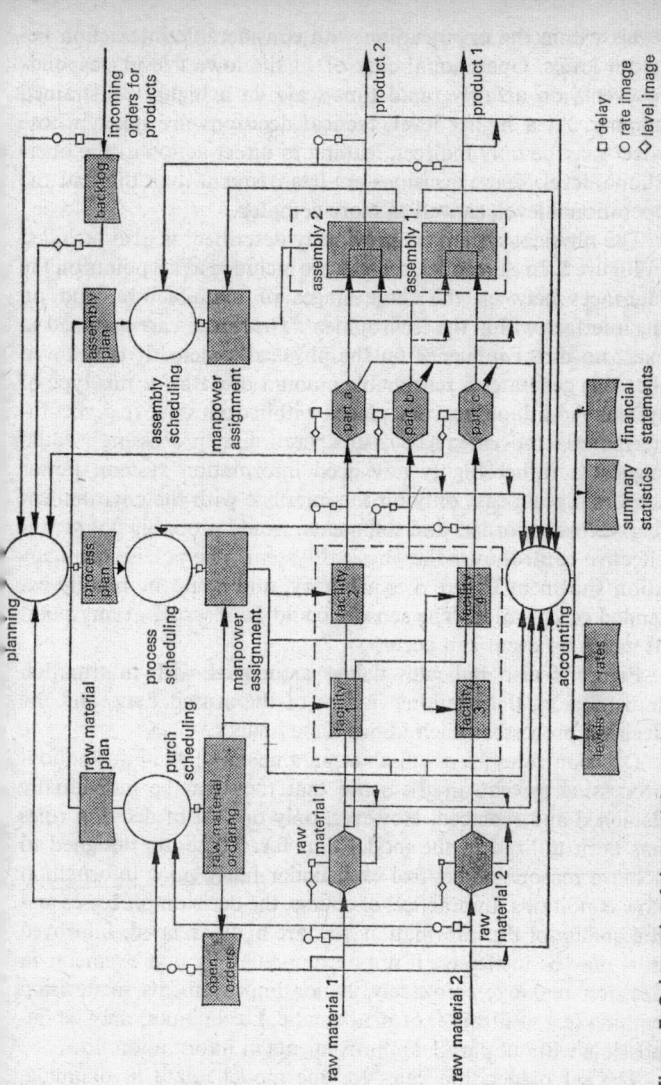

Figure 5 Schematic of the model

levels within the organization with considerable interaction between levels. Operational control, at the lowest level, responds to events on a fairly rapid time-scale, in a highly constrained manner. At a higher level, tactical decisions are taken whose effect may be only indirect, leading to direct action at the operational level. These decisions are less frequent than those at the operational level, as well as more complex.

The physical system, as previously described, is also included in Figure 5. In the model, sensors are included at all points on the interfaces between the three stages of manufacture, and on the interface within the environment. The sensors are assumed to exert no direct influence on the physical system. It is believed that this generates a reasonable amount of data for this type of system. Additional sensors, placed within each stage (e.g. recording material movements between operations in processing), would suggest a rather highly advanced information system. Fewer sensors placed, say, only on the interface with the environment (e.g. recording orders and shipments) would probably not permit effective control over the physical system. The precise configuration shown in Figure 5 is arbitrary, and could be readily extended or curtailed. The sensors could be inserted at any point at which an event can occur.

Figure 5 also indicates delays associated with information transmission, the resulting images of the sensed data, and the decision processes which utilize these images.

Decision rules are themselves parameters of the information-processing system, in the sense that they can be individually detached and replaced. However, only one set of decision rules has been utilized in the model thus far. These are designed to achieve reasonable control even under fairly poor information flow conditions. In practice, of course, the decision processes and the quality of the information flow are highly related. Improved flow may be ineffective if not accompanied by improvements in decision making; conversely, major improvements in decision making (e.g. utilization of mathematical techniques) may be impossible without parallel improvements in information flow.

The set of decision rules for the model relate to planning, purchasing and manpower assignment. Descriptions follow:

Planning. This is the mechanism which permits the model to adjust to, and perhaps anticipate, systematic changes in customer demand. The crucial element in planning is projection of shipping requirements for the next two months, based upon the past pattern of orders and the current backlog of unstarted orders. Exponential smoothing is employed to generate the forecast of future orders, and the backlog is distributed to future requirements in an exponential manner. Once shipping requirements are established, they are used as the planning base at all three stages of manufacture. An assembly plan is produced from the shipping requirement by adjusting for assembly lead time. The processing plan and the raw-material plans are generated from the assembly plan by the necessary parts explosions, adjustments for excess inventories, lead times and scrap losses.

Purchasing. The raw material plan provides the basis for ordering raw material. Orders are placed periodically, at a time determined by the availability of a new plan. This time is later than the nominal date of the plan, due to the delay implicit in the planning process. (For example, the plan stating requirements for the months of January and February might not be available until the second week in January.) Before ordering, therefore, the plan must be updated for material received since the start of the month, and for any currently open orders. Allowance is also made for the possibility of receiving defective material. The actual order quantity is determined so as to cover requirements through an entire period (month) until the expected receipt of the next order.

Manpower assignment. In the processing stage, the plan is used once each week to generate a scheduled load. The plan is first adjusted for parts produced since the first of the month, and is then extended in accordance with the work content (standard time) remaining in the month for each production operation. The available work force is then assigned to each operation (part to be processed on a facility) in proportion to the computed work loads and subject to the limitations set by facility capacities. Existing set-ups are not considered in arriving at this decision. The implementation of the decision will permit reassigned men to complete the operation on which they are currently engaged before moving to their new assignment. In the assembly stage, the assignment procedure (between products) is identical except that there are no facility constraints to be observed. Each stage makes assignments based on its own work force, with no exchanges permitted. The planning process is insensitive to local conditions prevailing 'on the floor'. As a result, it is possible for assignments to be made to operations for which material is perhaps temporarily unavailable. In such cases, it is desirable to consider reassigning the men to other idle facilities for which material may be available. The decision determines the number and location of idle men, and reassigns them in sequence to the remaining operations to the limit of facility capacity. In the assembly stage, this decision merely transfers idle men to the alternate product unless idleness is observed for both products.

As previously noted, the commands associated with the foregoing decision processes consist of purchase orders, which generate new material, and manpower assignments. All of the decisions are time triggered, although it would be equally straightforward to utilize event-triggering. The lengths of the planning period (month) and the manpower assignment review period (week) are fully adjustable, as are all of the delays associated with decision making and implementation.

The interactions between the firm and its environment are limited. They consist of the following items:

Customer orders. An input to the physical system. The properties of an order are: it is for a single product; it specifies the quantity (number of units) required; it is held within the physical system until filled.

Product shipments. An output of the physical system. No partial shipments are made. Orders are shipped as soon as completed.

Purchase orders. An output of the information processing system. Each order is for a single raw material, specifying the quantity desired.

Receipt of raw material. An input to the physical system. The environment imposes a delay (lead time) upon the filling of purchase orders. At the end of this delay, material is entered into the physical system.

The nature of the interface between the model of the firm and the experimenter is indicated in Figure 3. Communicating the results of the simulation is the role of the accounting structure. It provides a wide variety of data needed for evaluation. Cost factors are a critical element of performance, and are incorporated in a fairly complete set of conventional financial statements. Direct data are also provided on all relevant features of the physical system (e.g. inventory levels, manpower utilization) and of the information processing system (e.g. shipping requirements, scheduled loads by operation in man-hours). Some of the data are provided as a function of time (i.e. periodically), some as a single aggregate measure for the entire simulation period.

The experimenter exerts control over the simulation by setting parameters for the physical system, the information-processing system and the environment. He is also free to independently set the cost elements (e.g. labor rates, material prices) of the accounting structure, which govern the absolute level of the financial results. The major controllable features of the model are summarized in Table 2. For stochastic variables the parameters are in the form of a probability distribution.

In addition to direct variation of system parameters, the experimenter may introduce more basic changes. Decision rules can be modified or entirely replaced without disturbing other parts of the model. It is also possible, though not quite as straightforward, to modify the structure of the physical system. For example, the flow of parts in the processing stage could be changed, or the material-usage specifications could be altered.

Description of the simulation runs

The experimental approach that is chosen depends entirely upon what one wishes to learn about the total system. It is possible to vary the parameters of the information-processing system in order to evaluate the relative worth of a spectrum of data processing capabilities; or evaluate alternative decision-processes. Alternatively one can vary the parameters of the physical system to suggest the range of industry characteristics for which a given information handling capability is worth while. As in all simulation work, a systematic approach to experimentation is desirable. In particular, statistically designed experiments offer the best prospect of achieving soundly based conclusions at minimum cost in computer time.

Table 2 Parameters which can be Controlled by the Experimenter

Sub-system	Parameter	Stochastic
Physical	Set-up times	Yes
	Processing and assembly times	Yes
	Material movement times	Yes
	Rejection rates	Yes
	Size of work forces	No
	Facility capacities	No
Information processing	Input transmission delays	Yes
	Command delays	Yes
	Decision parameters	
	Planning	
	Length of period	No
	Fastest smoothing constant	No
	Backlog distribution constant	No
	Processing and assembly lead times	No
	Inventory safety margins	No
	Planned manpower assignment	
	Standard times	No
	Purchasing	
	Scrap allowance	No
Environment	Purchase order lead time	Yes
	Customer order arrival rate	Yes
	Customer order quantity	Yes

We turn to the second purpose of this paper, which is to demonstrate the feasibility of the method for the economic evaluation of certain 'intangible' benefits of improved information systems. For this purpose six simulation runs were selected.

These runs were based on manipulating two aspects of the information-processing system: first, the length of the planning period together with a related implementation delay; and second, the magnitude of information transmission delays.

The model contains a series of decision-rule algorithms beginning with the generation of a sales forecast and continuing on through the detailed scheduling and assignment of materials and manpower. These algorithms are applied periodically and new plans and schedules are generated based on the sensing of new demand information as well as 'accomplishment-to-date' in the physical system. These algorithms closely parallel typical planning and scheduling sequences in a real manufacturing enterprise.

Thus, increasing the frequency of the planning cycle specifically implies the availability of information systems of increased capacity and sophistication.

Table 3 lists the characteristics of the three planning cycles used in the feasibility runs. The slow cycle corresponds to once-a-month, medium to every-two-weeks, and fast to once-a-week planning and scheduling. The implementation delay (output transmission delay) represents the time lag between the availability of the basic new planning information and actually putting the plan into effect.

Table 3 Planning Cycles

Characteristic	Slow	Medium	Fast
Length of period	1 month	2 weeks	1 week
Implementation delay	7 days	4 days	2 days

The second aspect of the information-processing system chosen for manipulation was that of information time-lags (input transmission delays). The information-processing system senses various aspects of the environment and physical system through more or less distorted images. A principal distorting influence is that of information delays. For example, it may be necessary to write today's purchase orders based on last week's inventory figures.

Two sets of such delays were used in the feasibility runs as indicated in Table 4. In the slow set, incoming orders and shipping and receiving status are sensed through a one-week time lag and in-plant movements are assigned a two- or three-day delay as shown. In the fast set, the first category delays were reduced to one day and the in-plant delays to zero. (The latter change implies some type of on-line production monitoring system.)

Table 4 Information Delays

Information category	Slow	Fast
Incoming orders for products Open purchase orders for raw material Product shipments Raw material receipts	1 week	1 day
Part movements, finished parts to assembly	3 days	0
Raw material movements into process Finished part movements into inventory	2 days	0

Three values of the planning cycle and two sets of information lags yield six combinations which were the basis for the feasibility runs. Three of these runs (as designated in Table 5) will be described in some detail.

Table 5 Parameter Combinations for Simulation Runs

		Planning cycle		
		Slow	Medium	Fast
Information delays	Slow	(1)	(2)	
	Fast		(3)	

The activity which initiates the internal functioning of the simulation model is the stream of incoming orders for products. This demand pattern is also the most direct means for loading and testing the management-control capabilities of the model. A prime function of the management is, in a broad sense, to respond in an effective way to the demand pattern. As noted above, the purpose of the feasibility runs was to determine whether significant differences in performance would result from changes in selected aspects of the information-processing system. In order to amplify any such differences, a severe response requirement was placed on the model through the demand pattern. This was accomplished by imposing an abrupt change in the product demand mix.

Figure 6 is a graphical representation of the demand pattern used for all six of the feasibility runs. The initial level of demand for Product 1 is at the rate of twenty orders per week, and for Product 2 ninety-five orders per week. At the end of the first four weeks of simulated operation, Product 1 orders rise suddenly to fifty per week, while Product 2 orders drop suddenly to fifteen per week. Demand remains at these levels for the balance of the sixteen-week period simulated.

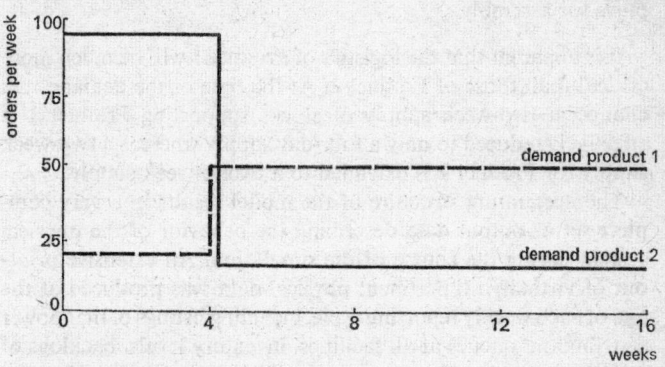

Figure 6 Demand pattern

Prior to starting each run, the model was initialized by providing a stock of raw materials and finished parts in the proportions required to supply the processing and assembly functions at the initial demand mix. The amount of the initial raw-material stock was adjusted between runs so as to be compatible with the planning cycle used.

In addition, the forecasting algorithm was given 'historical' demand levels which also reflected the initial demand mix.

The effect of these initializing values was to put the modelled enterprise approximately in the condition of having operated for an extended period at the initial demand mix and of having no expectation that this would change.

The nature of the management-response problem presented can be anticipated by an examination of the demand pattern. When the abrupt change in demand mix occurs at the end of the fourth week, there are three major problems:

1. The nature of the change in demand must be assessed and extrapolated in the form of new sales forecasts.

2. Raw material orders must be initiated to rebalance the raw material inventory to fit the new mix. Early action is especially critical here due to the substantial procurement lead times.

3. Processing manpower assignments must be shifted in order to supply the finished parts inventory with a new mix of finished parts for assembly.

It is apparent that the logistics of Product 1 will be much more critical than those of Product 2. At the time of the demand mix change, a two-week supply of stocks supporting Product 1 is effectively reduced to only a four-day supply whereas a two-week supply for Product 2 is extended to a twelve-week supply.

The accounting structure of the model results in a very complete set of output data describing the behavior of the physical system during the course of the simulation. An extensive printout of virtually all pertinent physical-data was produced at the end of each weekly reporting cycle, including listings of manpower distribution, queues at all facilities, inventory levels, backlogs of unfilled orders, product shipments and raw material receipts.

As mentioned earlier, the total accounting structure contains a financial cost accounting framework which provides a set of standard costs for the evaluation of finished products and all raw material and in-process inventories. These standard costs are a function of input parameters specifying material costs, wage rates, labor standards, standard burden rate, etc. Table 6 is a tabulation of the parameter values used in the feasibility runs.

At each reporting cycle the pertinent physical rates and levels are sensed and extended by the appropriate actual and standard cost values to produce a set of conventional financial statements including a manufacturing expense statement, an income statement, a statement of cash flow, and an abbreviated balance sheet tabulating current assets. Table 7 illustrates the form of these statements.

Table 6 Accounting Parameter Values

Category	Detail	Value
Product selling prices	Product 1	$325
	Product 2	$215
Raw material costs	Raw material 1	$20
	Raw material 2	$95
Direct labor standards	Wage rate	$2·50 per hour
	Standard work content	
	Facility 1, Part A	5 hours
	Facility 1, Part B	4 hours
	Facility 2, Part A	10 hours
	Facility 3, Part C	1 hour
	Facility 4, Part B	2 hours
	Facility 4, Part C	1 hour
Standard burden	Burden rate (on D L)	70%
Fixed-cost assumptions	Depreciation charge	$4000 per month
	Selling and administration expenses	$20,000 per month

Results of simulation runs

Perhaps the most direct indication of the response of the physical system to product demand is given by a comparison of the actual shipments of finished products with the demand pattern. Figure 7 gives this comparison.

In all the graphs of Figure 7, there is an initial rise from zero shipments which reflects the initializing phase of the run during which the assembly operation is loaded from the finished parts inventory. This process only affects shipments for the first two weeks.

In the case of Run 1 it will be noted that shipment of Product 1 responded rapidly to the demand step with shipment actually exceeding the new level by the seventh week.

This rapid initial response reflects the fact that assembly is 'to order'. During the eleventh and twelfth weeks, however, Product 1 shipments dropped sharply. Shipment did not again match the demand rate until the sixteenth week.

Table 7 Form of Weekly Financial Statement

Manufacturing expense statement

Raw material purchases	$xxxx	
Direct labor expense	xxxx	
Indirect expense	xxxx	
Depreciation	xxxx	
Total expense		$xxxxx
Deduct inventory increase/decrease		
Change in raw material inventory	$xxxx	
Change in in-process inventory	xxxx	
Change in finished parts inventory	xxxx	
Change in assembly inventory	xxxx	
Net change in inventories		xxxxx
Cost of goods sold		$xxxxx

Income statement

Sales		$xxxxx
Deduct:		
Standard cost of goods sold	$xxxxx	
Manufacturing cost variance	xxx	
Cost of goods sold		xxxxx
Gross profit on sales		xxxx
Less selling and administration expense		xxxx
Net profit/loss on operations		$xxxx

Cash flow $xxxx

Balance sheet

Cash		$xxxxx
Inventories	$xxxx	
In-process	xxxx	
Finished parts	xxxx	
Assembly	xxxx	
Total inventories		xxxxx
Total current assets		$xxxxx

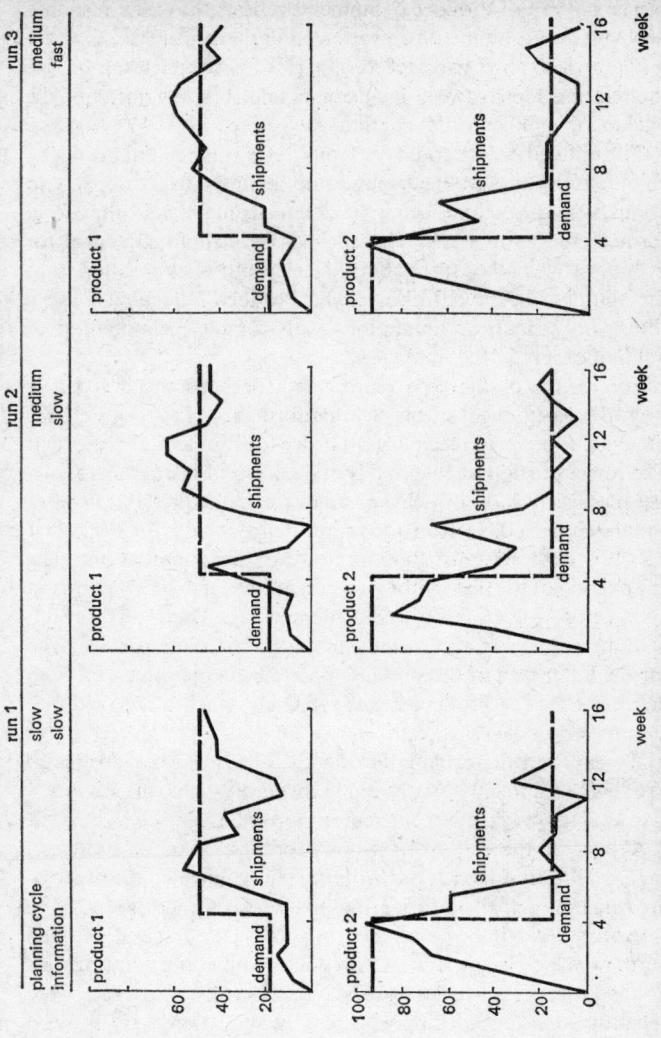

Figure 7 Comparison of demand and shipment

The pattern of Product 2 shipments reflects the easier response problem posed by the downward step in demand.

Figure 8 displays two aspects of performance which summarize the relationships between the demand and shipping patterns, the backlog of unfilled orders and delivery time.

The unfilled orders graph for Run 1 reflects the initial Product 1 shipping response to the demand step, with the backlog rising to about fifty units and being held approximately at that level through the tenth week. The abrupt rise in unfilled orders for Product 1 which begins at about the eleventh week resulted from the shipping lag noted above. The Product 2 backlog pattern shows only small accumulations with complete elimination of unfilled orders in the final weeks.

For a firm of the type represented, perhaps the best single overall measurement of physical performance is that of delivery time, i.e. time from receipt of an order to shipment of the order. The lower portion of Figure 8 is in the form of histograms showing the distribution of delivery times for the entire sixteen-week simulated period. In Run 1, average delivery time for Product 1 was 12·1 days. The distribution, however, is a bimodal one. The left portion of the histogram is representative of delivery performance before the eleventh-week shipping lag. The right portion, with an average of about eighteen days, represents performance for the latter part of the simulated period. As might be expected, delivery time for Product 2 was relatively much better, with an average of $4\frac{1}{2}$ days.

We can find the explanation for the eleventh-week decline in Product 1 shipments by observing inventory behavior. Figure 9 is a week-by-week plot of inventory levels.

A part of the initial draw-down of raw material shown in Figure 9 for all runs reflects the initial phase in which the processing function is loaded during the first week of operation.

In Run 1, it will be noted that raw-material outages developed during the fifth, sixth and seventh weeks with corresponding dips in the in-process stock. Finished part stocks, however, were generally sufficient to support assembly and shipping.

A shipment of Raw Material 1 was received during the seventh week, but the quantity was not adequate to support the new demand level for parts A and B. During the tenth week the stock

Figure 8 Order backlog and delivery time

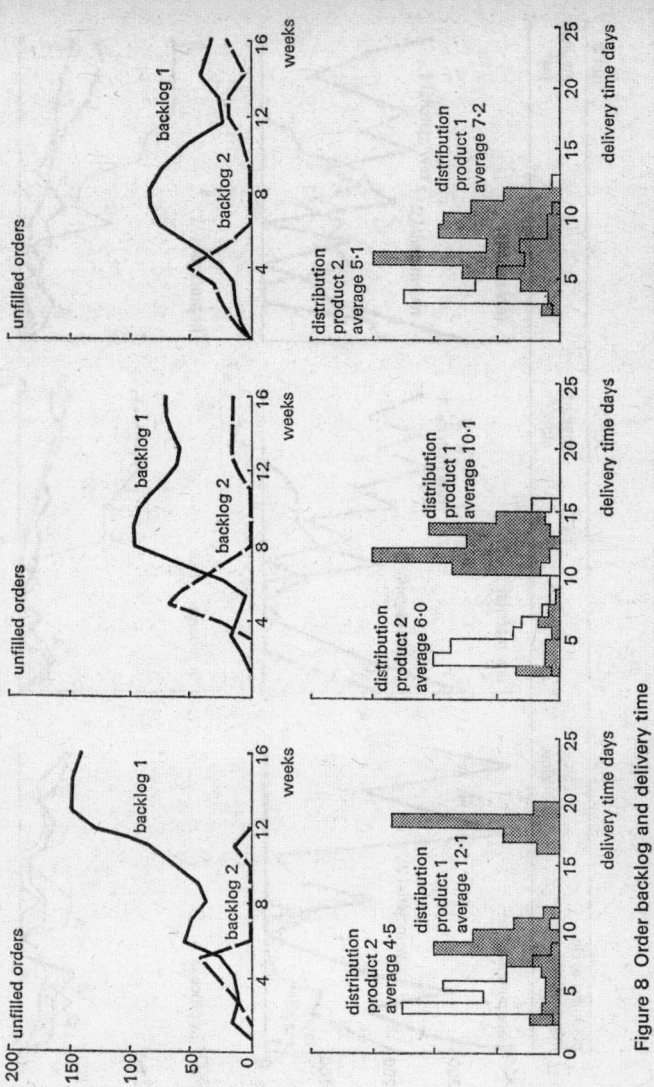

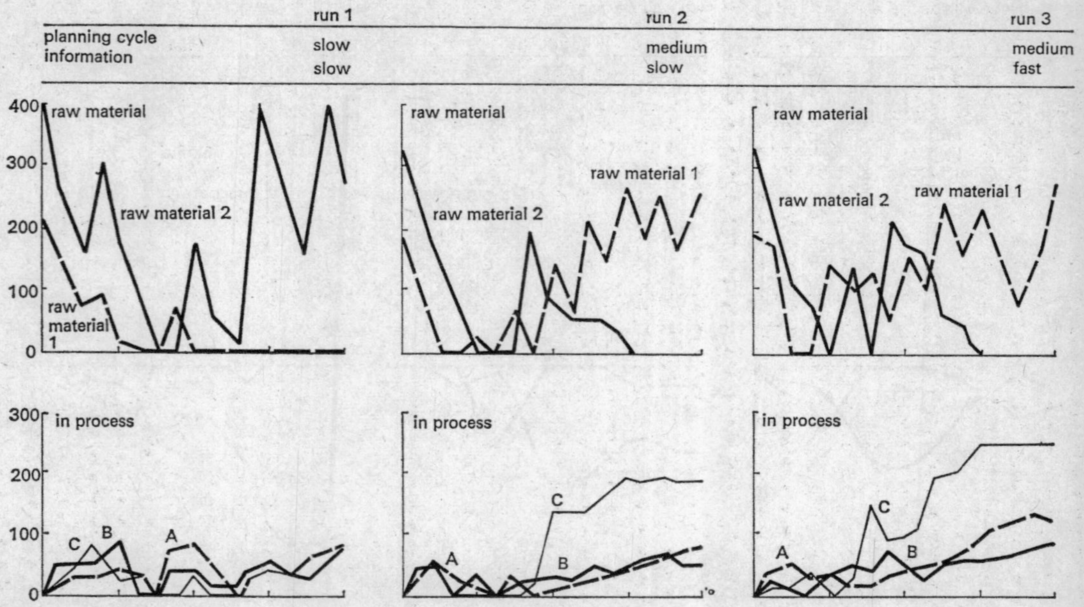

run 1
run 2
run 3
planning cycle
information
slow
slow
medium
slow
medium
fast
raw material
raw material 2
raw material 1
in process
A
B
C
400
300
200
100
0

Figure 9 Inventories

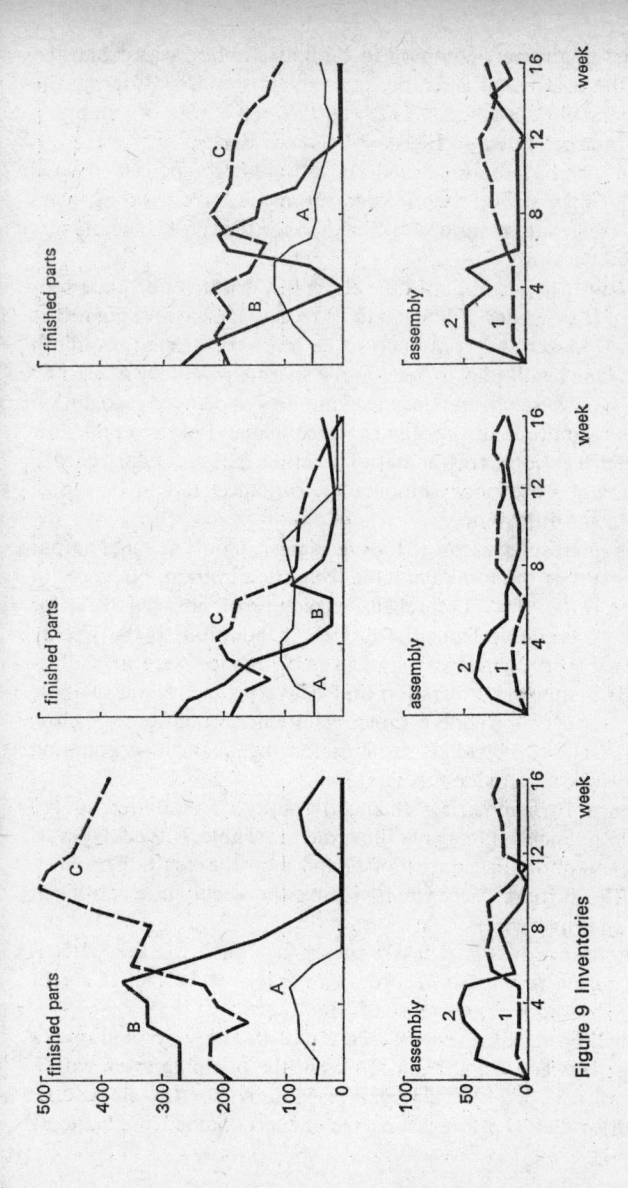

of Part B, the part common to both assemblies, was exhausted with the result that assembly was largely shut down during the tenth and eleventh weeks. This was reflected in the poor shipping performance shown in Figure 7 for those weeks.

The material outages noted above were accompanied by substantial idleness of the work force during the corresponding intervals. As a result, manpower utilization for the run as a whole was only 77 per cent.

In Run 1 it was not until the eleventh week that adequate supplies of Raw Material 1 began to be received. Excessive quantities of Raw Material 2 continued to be received through the ninth week. One result may be seen in the soaring inventory of Part C.

Both of these phenomena are symptoms of delayed recognition of the magnitude of the change in the demand pattern and slow corrective action in raw material ordering. The secondary effects, as shown, were poor shipping performance and low average manpower utilization.

The run results discussed thus far represent only selected output values out of the total available from the program, but serve to illustrate the very comprehensive picture of physical behavior which is available from the model. In addition to the weekly values, two measures of physical performance were also illustrated: manpower utilization and delivery time. None of these data, however, provide a direct economic evaluation, which is our present objective. It remains for the financial accounting framework to provide this vital link.

Figure 10 summarizes financial results as tabulated in the weekly financial statements illustrated in Table 7. Weekly levels of income and expense are plotted and show the resulting profit or loss. The current assets graph pictures the weekly fluctuations in cash and inventories.

Cumulative financial performance in Run 1 for the sixteen-week period resulted in recording a net loss of $23,600. Current assets showed a net decrease of $7600.

It will be recalled from Table 5 that the only key parameter change between Runs 1 and 2 was in the planning cycle with a medium (two-week) cycle being substituted for the slow (one-month) cycle. The forecasting technique remained the same as

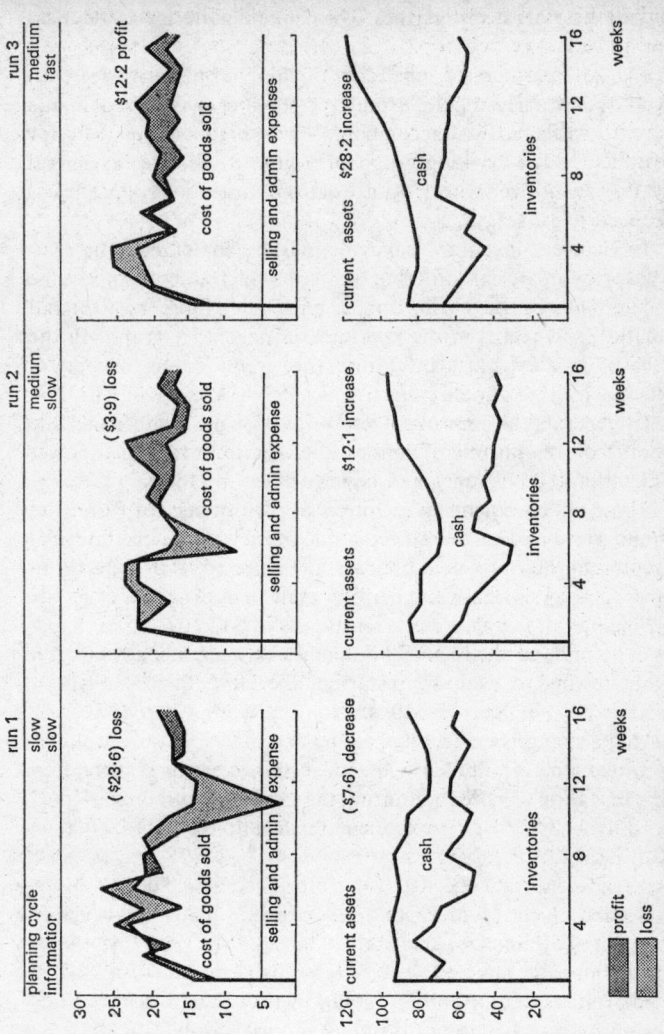

Figure 10 Financial results

did all the other decision rules. The demand pattern was identical for all runs.

Figure 7 permits a comparison of shipping performance with Run 1. An early dip in Product 1 shipments occurred in the seventh week but was accompanied by a high shipping rate for Product 2. The backlog graph of Figure 8 indicates a general improvement over Run 1. Run 2 delivery time for Product 1 was reduced to 10·1 days.

In Figure 9 inventory behavior may be compared. The two-week raw material ordering pattern which accompanies the medium planning cycle in Run 2 is reflected in more frequent and smaller 'saw-teeth' in the raw-material inventory graph. In the case of finished parts inventory, the over-shooting of Part C stock, which was noted in Run 1, is much less severe in Run 2.

In general, the improved responses of Run 2 shortened the period of readjustment and resulted in improved manpower utilization (82 per cent), and better delivery performance.

These improvements in the physical performance of Run 2 are summarized and cast in an economic framework by the financial accounting output which appears in Figure 10. Run 2 performance for the sixteen-week period resulted in a net loss of only $3900 and an increase in current assets of $12,100.

In comparing the financial outcomes between Runs 1 and 2, it is interesting to examine results in the eleventh week. Run 1 recorded a net loss of $10,500 for the week whereas Run 2, having accomplished its rebalancing and material 'turn-around', recorded a net profit of $4800 with sustained earnings thereafter. It is revealing to note that during the same eleventh week, Run 2 actually had a lower investment in inventories ($41,200) than Run 1 ($62,200).

At the eleventh week, Run 1 inventories consisted largely of the unneeded inventory of Part C and unfinished materials, whereas, Run 2 had attained a reasonable balance of the right inventories throughout the physical system. It seems clear that Run 2 benefited from better inventory management which in turn resulted in improved utilization of facilities and manpower.

The demand pattern was identical for both runs and thus presented the same hazards and opportunities. Run 2 management was no more 'intelligent' (the decision rules were unchanged), but was simply made more effective through the improved response capability permitted by the shorter planning cycle. The value of this change from a one-month to a two-week planning cycle is of the order of $19,000 (reduction in loss from Run 1 to Run 2), in the model context for the period shown.

In Run 3, the planning was kept at the medium (two-week) frequency as in Run 2, and the reduced information lags of the fast set were substituted for the slow lags.

A comparison of earnings between Runs 2 and 3 places a value of about $16,000 on this reduction in information delays.

The financial results for the runs described above, together with results for the other three runs, are summarized in Table 8.

Table 8 Summary of Profit or Loss

		Planning Cycle		
		Slow	Medium	Fast
Information delays	Slow	($23,600) Loss	($3900) Loss	$11,500 Profit
	Fast	($1100) Loss	$12,200 Profit	$24,000 Profit

It will be seen that, within this very limited exploration, a continuous improvement in performance resulted from either an increase in planning frequency or a reduction in information delays.

Since there is stochastic 'noise' in the model, statistical significance was tested by introducing a different random number sequence in repeat runs. The differences in economic performance described above, were shown to be highly significant in the statistical sense.

Summary and concluding observations

This paper has defined a method for evaluation of some major 'intangible' aspects of an information processing system in terms of its contribution to the dynamic control of a firm as measured by the overall economic performance of the firm.

Application of the method has been demonstrated by a series of simulations carried out using a specific model of a hypothetical firm.

The feasibility of the method has been tested to the extent that selected parameter changes which are representative of 'improved' information processing have been reflected in significant improvements in overall economic performance of the modelled firm.

The extension of this method to useful economic evaluation of proposed systems in real firms will depend on how successfully the critical dynamics of the real enterprise can be described in model form. In addition, there is a need for fuller understanding of the effects of selective aggregation and/or scaling down of the multiple characteristics of the real firm, since some degree of abstraction will always be required to obtain models of manageable size.

Results such as those described in this paper, together with the current rapid rate of development in modeling and simulation techniques, serve to strengthen the authors' belief that the method described shows significant promise for eventual extension to useful evaluation of real information-processing systems.

Reference

FORRESTER, J. W. (1961), *Industrial Dynamics*, MIT Press.

14 W. F. Bauer and R. H. Hill

Economics of Time-Shared Computing Systems

W. F. Bauer and R. H. Hill, 'Economics of time-shared computing systems', *Datamation*, vol. 13, 1967, pp. 41–9.

Time-shared systems will undoubtedly cause a greater attention to large-scale, centralized computer complexes. Since the physical location of the computer is relatively unimportant, why not locate the equipment centrally and derive the benefits of that centralization? This tendency to centralize plus the requirements for reliability and expandability in time-shared systems will, in turn, generate increasing interest in multi-computer systems. The system configuration of computer equipment is an important factor in cost-effectiveness.

Even before time-shared systems commanded such a great deal of professional interest, multi- and modular-computer systems were becoming increasingly prevalent and popular. Most of this early interest stemmed from a number of military command and control systems which had important on-line features. Some of these were SAGE, SAC Control System (SACCS), the Air Force Command Post (System 473L) and the Department of Defence Damage Assessment Center (now part of the National Military Command System). A multi-computer philosophy was introduced by the military initially for reliability, but it has important by-products in flexibility, efficiency and economy.

Computer configuration aspects

The multi-computer system has become a generic name for one which is modular in concept and design. It allows the interconnection of various modules such as processors, input/output channel handlers, high-speed memory devices and peripheral units in ways which allow the computer to be re-configured both on a millisecond basis and, in the case of adding or deleting modules, on much longer time-scales such as weeks or months.

Although there are a number of economic advantages to modular computer systems used in time-shared systems, two salient characteristics are reliability and expandability. It has often been noted that equipment or software failure in a time-shared system can have serious effects on hundreds of people, while a batch system usually has enough buffering and elasticity to admit short-length down time. At the very least, since the users are conditioned to lengthy turnaround times, small extensions cause relatively little grief.

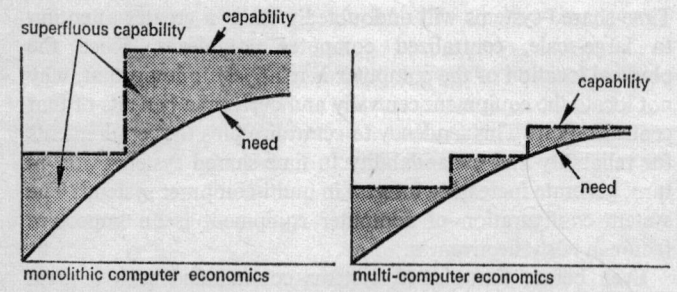

Figure 1 (a) Monolithic computer economics; (b) multi-computer system economics

A significant amount of reliability can be achieved in a multi-computer system with only a modest cost for equipment redundancy. Equipment redundancy in the neighborhood of 20 to 30 per cent can buy the same reliability that 100 per cent equipment redundancy buys in the non-modular systems. If an on-line system is designed for a hundred users, and is currently being used at 75 per cent capacity, one of the four processors could be lost without degrading system performance. Alternatively, if it were being used to capacity, and one processor went down, only the lowest priority (25 per cent) of the work would suffer.

Expandability is probably an even more clear-cut characteristic of some of the advantages in time-shared systems. Figure 1 shows the advantage of a modular system in an expansion situation in minimizing costs of excess capacity capability. Processors, more high-speed memory and more input/output channels can be added to accommodate the growing numbers of on-line users. It is true that this imposes some additional design requirements on the software. The executive, for example, must be written in a way that it need not be altered greatly with the addition of the extra modules. However, this should not be an inordinately costly software factor.

It is likely that many time-shared systems will be designed with a separate input/output computer which interfaces between the basic processor system and the consoles as well as between these two types of equipment and the auxiliary memories (see Figure 2).

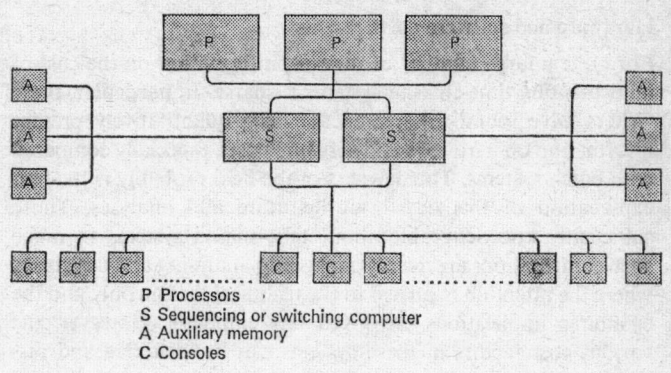

P Processors
S Sequencing or switching computer
A Auxiliary memory
C Consoles

Figure 2

This concept is the one currently employed for SDC's TSS and MIT's Project MAC, and it is also being utilized in the development of modern message-switching systems. The input/output computer is frequently called a 'sequencing' computer or 'concentrator'. It handles the bits and pieces of communication between the end-use devices and the main computer. It can, for example, accept the character by character input, check for format, syntax and the like, make certain initial decisions on priority of the message and, at the appropriate time, transmit the composite message to the main processor. It is economically advantageous in that a simple computer can be used for this task. Also, simple software can be designed since the executive of the sequencing computer need not interact in detail with that of the main processor, and the main processor can be utilized with greater efficiency since it will be interrupted with less frequency.

The concept of the sequencing computer described above is frequently used on communications systems and is referred to as the 'local loop' concept. The basic principle here is to use a simple loop for the local traffic, low bandwidth activities, and allow for multiplexing the information to provide high bandwidth transmission to the main processor. It is interesting to observe that the modern computers being developed expressly for time-sharing operations utilize modularity to a very great extent. Examples of this are the GE-645 and the IBM 360/Model 67.

Hardware and software costs

For quite a large number of reasons, information on the cost of implementing time-sharing systems is sparse. In particular, these writers have found no references which quantitatively present information on hardware and software costs, especially compared with batch systems. The newness of the field probably is the best explanation of this dearth of literature and analyses. Those sufficiently knowledgeable about time-shared systems to make such contributions are deeply engaged in analysing and designing, where the attention is turned to the technical factors only and the economic implications are given less emphasis. However, the various cost factors in these systems can be identified and discussed, and it is constructive to do so.

Hardware costs. Certainly the hardware costs for a system capable of efficient time-shared operation will exceed those of batch processing hardware. Some of the reasons for this increase in cost are:

1. Additional working storage features.
2. Multi-access to and independent operation of working storage.
3. Large internal high-speed memory.
4. Increased storage capacity of auxiliary memories.
5. Hardware speed degradation.

The working storage features necessary for on-line systems result from the needs of the executive to determine the instantaneous status of the computer system when attention is being turned very rapidly from one user to the next. Perhaps the most important feature here is the dynamic relocatability hardware. This is hardware which allows part of a program (frequently referred to as a 'segment' or 'page') to be read in from auxiliary memory into any portion of the physical working storage. That part of working storage may not be the location from which the program operated before, and since there is a requirement that the programmer (user) need not be concerned with the location of his program each time it is to be executed, the modification of the addresses for relocation must be handled automatically. Therefore, in the interpretation of an address, a table look-up is accomplished by the hardware to determine in which portion of the memory the address is to be found, and then the proper modification to the address is made to determine the effective address. Essentially, therefore, there is an associate process which is carried out – the address of the program must be associated or correlated with the portion of the actual memory in which it is contained; a small associative memory is actually included in the machine which has the automatic dynamic relocation capability.

Other working memory features are also deemed desirable. Although it is becoming quite common to have memory protection on computers, some of these features have been extended in the case of time-sharing hardware. For instance, it is common to have a memory protect feature which prohibits writing into any unauthorized memory space. This feature has been extended to the prohibition of *reading* from any unauthorized space as well. This affords an extra degree of assurance that the hardware/software combination is doing what it is supposed to do, and also provides extra assurance of privacy.

Still another feature being added to time-sharing systems is one which indicates whether the portion of memory of a portion of the program has been used or whether it has been referred to or changed. Two bits are added to a memory block; one which would indicate whether the block has been referred to, and one which would indicate whether the information in the block has been changed. The uses of this feature are manifold. For example, one could conceivably design an executive which would shift out a portion of the memory if it has not been referred to or changed for a given period of time. The assumption is made that this is not an 'active' portion of the program.

In order to reduce the non-productive period when the main processor is awaiting new portions of the program which must be transferred from some auxiliary memory ('swap time'), considerable changes must be made in hardware over conventional systems. In conventional systems, memory accesses for input/output transfer are interleaved with those of the main processor, thereby degrading the performance of the processor. Various memory-sharing schemes have been devised to minimize such degradation. However, in time-sharing systems, it is desirable to provide a sufficient independence of action between the memory devices and the auxiliary memory and input/output devices to allow a large amount of transfer to take place independent of the main frame. This requirement arises because of the much greater amount of swapping between auxiliary memory and working storage in a time-sharing system.

Some systems have used interleaved core banks (odd addresses in one bank, even in the other) to increase program efficiency. Since instructions occupy consecutive cells, one can be fetched while the previous one is being executed. In a time-sharing system, however, the input/output transfers between auxiliary memory and main memory predominate. Memory should be organized into integral banks of consecutive locations, then, so that the program and data for one user can be entered into one bank from auxiliary memory (discs or drums) while another user is executing from another bank. It is clear that the main memory should consist of several banks, rather than only two, each of which can communicate with other devices if it is not connected to the main processor. Choosing the number of such banks and the size of each is a highly complex problem in system design, involving trade-offs among circuit cost and operating efficiency, decisions as to optimum sizes of program modules and the cost of executive program software. It is clear with only a little reflection that four 8000-word, independently operating core memory units will operate better (but be more costly) in a time-shared system than a 32,000-word memory organized as two 16,000-word units.

Larger high-speed memories are required for a number of reasons. The most obvious reason is that a complex executive resides in working storage and cannot, because of the high frequency of its usage, be kept even part in auxiliary store. The SDC executive for their TSS is 16,000 words in length and does not represent a complex executive as compared with ones currently being planned. In the General Electric 600 series, 8000 words of high-speed memory are added to the basic core specifically for the resident executive. Still another reason for large amounts of high-speed memory is to increase the probability that the part of the program or data that is required next is on hand in high-speed storage. Ideally, it is desirable to have in the memory all possible parts of all programs that could potentially be activated next; the larger the high-speed core is, the more likely it is that the program part is ready for execution.

The high cost of core

A significant observation about high-speed storage is that it represents the most costly part of the machine. Frequently, storage costs more than the processor. Another significant point is that in comparing batch and time-shared hardware-system costs, one must realize that an additional amount of high-speed memory – probably as much as 50 per cent more – is needed; therefore, it is a significant increment in cost.

Those programs which are active but not in core must still be ready on short order to be transferred to high-speed memory and used. There are probably at least three levels in the auxiliary-memory hierarchy. First of all, there is the magnetic drum which stores program data that can be transferred in at high rates to main memory. These are programs that are currently active – probably programs of users currently at the console. There should probably be as much as 16,000 words of storage for each console station, which implies on the order of 1,000,000 words of drum storage for a fifty-console station system.[1] The next level in the auxiliary-memory hierarchy are those programs and data which have been active during the day or week which are likely to be brought to action. They may also represent portions of a program which overflows allotted drum space. Those programs can be stored on random access disc devices. The third level of hierarchy

1. These figures apply especially to a large-scale, general-purpose, time-shared system.

is now frequently considered archival in nature – magnetic tapes. Magnetic tapes will be used as a general backup for providing an additional reservoir of active programs. Disc packs and data bank devices (CRAM, RACE, IBM Data Cell, etc.) fall in an intermediate category between on-line and archival, having characteristics of both.

The last item mentioned above on hardware costs refers to lowering efficiency of the hardware system rather than an increase in the basic cost of the hardware. In the process of interpreting addresses when programs are relocated (that is, in the action of the relocatability hardware), extra time is required beyond the normal operation of the main frame and the memory. The process of associating the address of each executed instruction with one of the various portions of the program, and then modifying its effective address, requires an additional 15 to 20 per cent of computer time.[2] In other words, the basic memory cycle is slowed down by this amount. This is not incurred by poor programming, but is part of the wired-in characteristics of the computer. Any additional overhead or inefficiency in the machine starts from this point, and is in addition to it. This is a subtle point, frequently not fully appreciated by time-sharing advocates. It is, for all practical purposes, like adding 15 to 20 per cent rental to a machine and, again, comes in addition to any other total system inefficiencies.

Communications and console costs are likewise important in time-sharing systems. Communications costs are almost always a factor in time-sharing systems. While some consoles may be within cable-connection distance of the computer, this is probably impractical for all but the smallest and simplest systems. Communications costs and usage is a far-ranging subject which will not be touched upon here.

The main cost item in peripheral equipment is the user station itself. This may vary from a teletypewriter station costing in the neighborhood of $1000 to an elaborate console costing in the neighborhood of £150,000. A low-cost terminal is one of the

2. Some computers are not degraded by these processes. For example, it is probable that no degradation would be incurred in the case of a processor-limited (as opposed to a memory-limited) computer. However, most computers are memory-limited.

pressing needs of time-sharing technology. Paradoxically, it is increasingly evident that the terminal must have more than simple typewriter capability. The minimum user station is a teletypewriter, but most applications now demand graphic capability (i.e. cathode ray tubes) for a page of information or the equivalent in displays. Thus, attempts to get by with the limited capabilities of the Touch-Tone telephone as a terminal device have not met with success. Note also that cost of buffering the terminal and communicating between it and the central processor are extra.

Software costs

The general factor which leads to increased programming and analysis costs in time-shared systems is that of increased system complexity. Some of the factors, in turn, involved with the increased complexity of the system are:

1. The programmer must make allowances for 'simultaneous' occurrences. Part of this is a design problem and part is a programming execution problem. It involves building the proper networks to react to the various random occurrences in the computer system which result from human inputs which, in turn, provide a multitude of interrupts to the system operation.

2. There is a basic problem of working storage overlay in such a system since there is a very large amount of programming-data swapping between working storage and auxiliary storage. The systems must be properly developed to enable this swapping with a maximum of user efficiency or program execution productivity while, at the same time, giving all users a sufficient number of time slices within a given period of time to allow the system to be responsive. In more recent systems, there are hardware features ('relocatability hardware') which facilitate memory overlay operations. However, the executive must be properly designed to make good use of such hardware features.

3. The memory-management problem becomes far more complex since there will be many levels of data storage depending upon the frequency of usage. There will also be communication among the various storage levels and a logic of describing the data which

is consistent from the point of view of the many users and consistent from the point of view of the many storage levels.

4. The design of a scheduler which takes into account the various conflicting objectives of the system and its users is a continuing factor. To insure a near-optimum system requires considerable paper analyses and system simulation. Unfortunately, the large number of parameters and the environmental anomalies make a unique solution to the scheduling problem a near impossibility.

5. The development of conversational-mode languages and debugging aids is also complicated. These languages break down into two general classes: conversational compilers which are essentially adaptations of existing or off-line compilers; and new utility languages for man-machine communication and command.

Despite all of these apparent increases in software costs, a number of highly respected systems people with experience in both batch and time-shared systems insist that a time-shared system is no more complicated than a sophisticated batch system and, therefore, no more costly. This opinion may or may not hold up under scrutiny; a great deal depends on the system definitions. Certainly IBM will spend more on development of OS/360 than on TSS/360. However, this comparison may not be meaningful for obvious reasons. A time-sharing system designed for restricted usage may well be less costly to implement than a highly general sophisticated batch processor. It seems apparent, however, that time-shared systems are always more complex than batch processors at the same level of generality.

However, the added complexity and costs do not augur ill for the future of time-shared systems. Remember that much of the design and programming being done for time-shared systems today is new. The professionals are greatly increasing their efficiency to produce systems of this kind.

Costing and pricing

Early sections of this report dealt with questions of the relative merits of batch and time-shared systems from economic standpoints. They have dealt also with the relationship of technical features to economic ones. The previous section dealt with costs of hardware and software. This aspect of the economics of time-sharing systems – costing and pricing – is more closely related to business aspects. Costing and pricing refer to how one should account for costs and how charges should be made to customers – these are important aspects to any time-shared system whether it be for commercial usage or to implement in-house capabilities or requirements.

Anyone familiar in detail with the accounting and pricing procedures for large-scale batch systems will have no difficulty with developing accounting and charge policies for time-shared systems. Administrative procedures for the batch systems are relatively straightforward, at least as they have usually been applied. The system equipment-costs are well known for the first shift rental and for marginal additional rental on second and third shifts. Usually each job uses the entire system or, at least for simplicity, it is assumed the entire system is used. One simply keeps accounts of the amount of time the job runs on the computer, and charges the person appropriately.

Time-shared systems will be more complex. Though there are differences, the philosophy of accounting and pricing is not radically different for a time-shared system, or shouldn't be. The time-shared system user will use a very powerful computer for shorter periods of time; perhaps accumulations of time slices ranging from fifty to two-hundred milliseconds. There will be the introduction of the concept of 'overhead computing', where the computer system is performing computations – perhaps extensive – in support of all users. Certain sophistications may be introduced in pricing such as charging the customer according to the priority he has been given in servicing the problems in the queues.

As with any kind of accounting procedure, there are two types of cost: overhead and direct. The former are those that are not attributable to the given user, but benefit all users. The latter are those that are directly attributable to the user. Examples of overhead items are: operation of the executive, swapping between auxiliary and working memories, and idle time. Examples of costs that are (or are more likely to be) direct are: productive main frame computation, console time used, and auxiliary or working memory space used.

Although most of the identifiable costs clearly fit into one category or the other, there are a number that could fit in either category, depending upon the accounting philosophy. As with all accounting systems, the question is whether keeping account of small costs and attributing them to specific users is worth the extra cost of the required monitoring and handling. On one hand, it is desirable to give the customer a complete accounting of just what system capability he used, and thereby reduce overhead costs to an absolute minimum. However, cost accounting can be excessive if carried to a very low level of data processing functions.

A third type of cost can be regarded as a 'one-time' cost. Examples of this are the system design and systems programming costs that are done either initially with a system or at periodic intervals as the system is being modified or upgraded. These costs are not usually regarded as overhead and, of course, they are not direct charges to the customer. In general, they are amortized over a given period of time, and the prices charged for the services must, of course, take these amortization rates into account.

Customer charges – profit and loss

Normally the basis for charges to the customer is the direct costs described above, appropriately burdened. In the simplest case, the customer is charged according to processor time used, which includes an allowance for a normal amount of overhead costs, such as those described in the previous section. Some specialized systems allow a charge per transaction. Some charge procedures will involve keeping track of time to the nearest millisecond for the main frame and for the peripheral devices, and will charge different rates depending upon which of a half dozen or so priority levels are used.

Some clues are now available as to order-of-magnitude costs of time-shared systems from the user's viewpoint, however. Table 1 lists cost data for ten time-sharing systems commercially available. It is interesting to note that there is a factor of six spread in the per-terminal-hour charge for these systems (from $5 to $30), and even more interesting to note that there are two different pricing philosophies. One involves a per-terminal-hour use fee, usually on a sliding scale according to the number of hours used per month. The other provides a fixed fee per month per terminal which in some cases amounts actually to a minimum charge. In one case not represented in the table (Keydata Corporation) pricing is totally dependent upon facilities used.

The variance in prices and pricing techniques would appear to

Table 1 Commercial Time-Sharing Systems

Organization	Computer	Number of users	Fixed fee per month per terminal	Average cost per terminal hour	Additional charge per hour per CPU
Allen-Babcock Computing, Inc.	IBM 360/50	60	$250	None	$240–$480
Applied Logic Corporation	DEC PDP-6	20	None	$5	$360
Bolt, Beranek & Newman, Inc.	DEC PDP-1	16	None	$12·5	None
CEIR, Inc.	GE 235	30	None	$5	None
COM-SHARE, Inc.	SDS 940	32	None	$10	None
General Electric Company (New York)	GE 235	40	$350[1]	$10	$180
General Electric Company (Penn)	GE 235		None	$20–$30	None
Munitype, Inc.	GE 225	50	$150–$350	None	None
IBM-Quiktran[2]	IBM 7044	40	None	$12	None
Tymshare Association	SDS 940	60	None	$13	None

Source: adaptation from data published by Computer Research Corporation, Newton, Massachusetts.

1. Includes twenty-five hours of terminal time and twenty-four hours of CPU time.
2. Systems located in New York City and Los Angeles.

indicate that more experience is required before cost factors in time-shared systems are well understood.

The unsophisticated buyer shoud be wary of any costs which relate only to console time. In the first place, he may be deluded into some belief that console time equals processor time. Even if he has no such delusions, he should realize that the amount of processor time he gets for a given period of console time may vary greatly, depending upon a host of conditions such as number of other users, types of other problems in the system, and the like.

The computation of the price for service will, in principle, not vary from the price of any other service or product which, just as in manufacturing, is based on a certain expected usage or sales rate. If, for example, the charges were based on main processor time only, the price would be based on a certain number of hours of usage per day – say, six hours of billable or chargeable main-processor usage. All overhead costs would be added in such a way as to make the six hours of billable time a break-even point in the system. If the usage goes below the six-hour level, the overhead rate goes up and the system 'loses money'. If the system is utilized more than six hours per day, the system 'makes a profit'.

Once the break-even point is passed in a time-shared system, the operation can, of course, be very profitable. If the break-even point is sufficiently low to allow usage beyond that point without adding equipment, then the profit leverage can be great. However, the profit leverage can be good even if certain peripheral equipments or high-speed memory units have to be added to keep the system from downgrading in the quality of the service as the service amounts are increased. As the quality of the service deteriorates, that is as response times get intolerably large, a processor can be added. The system should be of the multi-computer nature to allow for the efficient addition of such extra capability. Also, the programming system should allow the addition of an extra processor, and if it were designed correctly in the first place, it will be. It is clear that many one-time costs are independent of the number of users. Among these are likely to be physical space, programming system, and most of the computing system. Therefore, as the amount of usage rises, and it can rise almost indefinitely in a well designed centralized system, the profit leverage gets extremely attractive to the entrepreneur or to the organization implementing a system for service in a large company or agency.

15 K. E. Knight

Changes in Computer Performance

K. E. Knight, 'Changes in computer performance', *Datamation*,
vol. 12, 1966, pp. 40–54.

The first twenty years of the computer industry have been hectic ones. Great strides have been taken to provide reliable and inexpensive computation capability. To obtain a clearer picture we will explore our past to see where we have been and how fast we have had to move to get to where we are today. From our analysis of the first twenty years of the computing industry, we have arrived at four fascinating observations that we will discuss in this paper.

1. We generate a performance description for 225 general-purpose computer systems. The performance description estimates the overall capabilities of each computer system based upon its hardware features and basic elementary operations. We obtain estimates of the performance capabilities for both scientific and commercial computation for 225 different computer systems introduced between 1944 and 1963.

2. Using the performance descriptions for the computers introduced in any one year, we generate a technology curve for that year. The technology curve describes the theoretical performance that can be purchased for different monthly rental expenditures.

3. Grosch's law is upheld. For any one year we find the relation between computing power and system cost to be approximately as follows: Computing power = $(C \times \text{system cost})^2$; $C = \text{constant}$.

4. Improvement in number of operations per dollar between 1950 and 1962 has been at an average rate of 81 per cent per year for scientific computation and 87 per cent per year for commercial computation.

Functional description of gp computers

The capability of each system to perform its computing tasks represents the functional description (or evaluation) of that system. For our purposes we will only look at two aspects of computer performance:

1. Computing power, indicated by the number of standard operations performed per second, P.

2. Cost of the computing equipment, which equals the number of seconds of system operations per dollar of equipment cost, C.

Computing power P evaluates the rate at which the system performs information-processing, the number of operations performed per second. Two machines solved a specific problem with different internal operations because of their individual equipment features. P will, therefore, describe operations of equivalent problem solving value to provide the desired measure of a computer's performance. We will estimate P from structure. In order to do this, we first must understand which structural factors influence computing capability. Then we determine the manner in which the structural factors interact to develop the functional model through the use of detailed study of the operation of computing equipment and the problems performed. P consists of three main components:

1. The internal calculating speed of the computer's central processor, t_c.

2. The time the central processor is idle and waiting for information input or output $t_{I/O}$.

3. The memory capacity of the computer, M.

These factors are the important performance measures needed to determine P. We define t_c as the time (in microseconds) needed to perform one million operations, and $t_{I/O}$ as the non-overlapped intput/output time (microseconds) necessary for these one million operations. Therefore, the computer performs $10^{12}/t_c + t_{I/O}$ operations per second. The computer's memory has a strong influence on P. We found that the memory factor interacts with internal operating time to determine computing power as follows:[1]

$$M \times \frac{10^{12}}{t_c + t_{I/O}} = P.$$

The internal speed of the central processor, t_c, is the time taken by the computer to perform its information-processing tasks. The speed equals the internal operation times of each computer, multiplied by the frequency with which each operation is used. To determine the internal speed, therefore, it is necessary to measure the frequency with which the various operations are performed in a typical problem. For scientific computation we considered approximately 15,000,000 operations of an IBM 704 and an IBM 7090, from a mix of over a hundred problems. In the analysis of the operations used in this 'problem mix' the instructions were grouped into five categories:

1. Fixed add (and subtract) and compare instructions performed.
2. Floating add (and subtract) instructions required.
3. Multiply instructions.
4. Divide instructions.
5. Other manipulation and logic instructions – this category combines a large number of branch, shift, logic and load-register instructions.

The relative frequency with which each of the five types were used in the scientific programs we traced is presented in Table 1.

To determine the frequency with which the different operations were used in commercial computation, nine programs were analysed in detail (two inventory control, three general accounting, one billing, one payroll and two production planning). All nine problems were run on an IBM 705, representing over one million operations. We analysed the nine programs using the same five instruction categories selected for scientific computation. The relative frequency with which each of the five types of instructions were used in commercial computation is presented

1. A more detailed description of the development of the functional model is presented in Knight (1963).

Table 1 Functional Model-Algorithm to Calculate *P* for any Computer System

$$P = \frac{10^{12}}{t_c + t_{I/O}} \times \frac{(L-7)T(WF)}{32{,}000(36-7)}$$

$$t_c = 10^4[C_1 A_{FI} + C_2 A_{FL} + C_3 M + C_4 D + C_5 L]$$

$$t_{I/O} = P \times OL_1[10^6(W_{11} \times B \times 1/K_{11}) + (W_{01} \times B \times 1/K_{01}) + \\ + N(S_1 + H_1)]R_1 + (1-P)OL_2[10^6(W_{12} \times B \times 1/K_{12}) + \\ + (W_{02} \times B \times 1/K_{02}) + N/S_2 + H_2)]$$

Variables – Attributes of each computing system

P = the computing power of the *n*th computing system
L = the word lengths in bits
T = the total number of words in memory
t_c = the time for the central processing unit to perform one million operations
$t_{I/O}$ = the time the central processing unit stands idle waiting for I/O to take place
A_{FI} = the time for the central processing unit to perform one fixed point addition
A_{FL} = the time for the central processing unit to perform one floating point addition
M = the time for the central processing unit to perform one multiply
D = the time for the central processing unit to perform one divide
L = the time for the central processing unit to perform one logic operation
B = the number of characters of I/O in each word
K_{11} = the input transfer rate (characters per second) of the primary I/O system
K_{01} = the output transfer rate (characters per second) of the primary I/O system
K_{12} = the input transfer rate (characters per second) of the secondary I/O system
K_{02} = the output transfer rate (characters per second) of the secondary I/O system
S_1 = the start time of the primary I/O system not overlapped with compute
H_1 = the stop time of the primary I/O system not overlapped with compute
S_2 = the start time of the secondary I/O system not overlapped with compute
H_2 = the stop time of the secondary I/O system not overlapped with compute
R_1 = 1 + the fraction of the useful primary I/O time that is required for non-overlap rewind time

Table 1—continued

Symbol	Semi-constant factors — Description	Values — Scientific computation	Commercial computation
WF	the word factor		
	a. fixed word-length memory	1	1
	b. variable word-length memory	2	2
C_1	weighting factor representing the percentage of the fixed add operations		
	a. computers without index registers or indirect addressing	10	25
	b. computers with index registers or indirect addressing	25	45
C_2	weighting factor that indicates the percentage of floating additions	10	0
C_3	weighting factor that indicates the percentage of multiply operations	6	1
C_4	weighting factor that indicates the percentage of divide operations	2	0
C_5	weighting factor that indicates the percentage of logic operations	72	74
P	percentage of the I/O that uses the primary I/O system		
	a. systems with only a primary I/O system	1·0	1·0
	b. systems with a primary and secondary I/O system	variable	variable
W_{11}	number of input words per million internal operations using the primary I/O system		
	a. magnetic tape I/O system	20,000	100,000
	b. other I/O systems	2000	10,000

Table 1–continued

Symbol	Semi-constant factors Description	Values Scientific computation	Commercial computation
W_{01}	number of output words per million internal operations using the primary I/O system	the values are the same as those given above for W_{11}	
W_{12}/W_{02}	number of input/output words per million internal operations using the secondary I/O system	the values are the same as those given above for W_{11}	
N	number of times separate data is read into or out of the computer per million operations	4	20
OL_1	overlap factor 1 – the fraction of the primary I/O system's time not overlapped with compute		
	a. no overlap – no buffer	1	1
	b. read or write with compute – single buffer	0·85	0·85
	c. read, write and compute – single buffer	0·7	0·7
	d. multiple read, write and compute – several buffers	0·60	0·60
	e. multiple read, write and compute with program interrupt – several buffers	0·55	0·55
OL_2	overlap factor 2 – the fraction of the secondary I/O system's time not overlapped with compute	values are the same as those given above for OL_1, (a) through (e)	
	the exponential memory weighting factor	0·5	0·333

in Table 1. The time the central processor stands idle waiting for information input or output, $t_{I/O}$ is a function of the amount of information that must be taken into the computer, the amount of information that must be sent out of the computer, the rate at which information is transferred in and out of the computer, and the degree to which input and/or output can take place while the central processor is operating.

When we studied the input/output requirements we were unable to count the actual number of pieces (or number of words) read or written. Instead, the time the computer's central processing unit operated alone, operated concurrently with I/O, and idled, waiting for information input/output to take place, was measured. From the actual input/output times, and published input/output rates, it was possible to estimate the number of words read and written. The following computing systems were studied to estimate $t_{I/O}$: IBM 704, 705, 650, 7070, 7090 and 1401; Philco 211 and Bendix G15. The figures for the 7090 were accurately obtained, using the system's clock for single channel I/O, double channel I/O and double channel I/O with program interrupt. The other figures were obtained by less precise counting methods. The results obtained from the precise 7090 measures, and from the other systems, were very similar and are presented in Table 1.

The memory capacity M of a computing system greatly influences its computing ability. Increased memory markedly improves the processing of very large problems which would otherwise be split into sub-problems. There are also advantages to larger memories when performing smaller problems because they allow the use of compiling routines, sub-routines, etc. Recently, with the advent of multiple input/output capability, and multiple program operation with executive and interrupt routines, larger memories provide additional advantages for all sizes and types of problems.

We were unable to find a feasible means to measure analytically the influence which memory has upon a computer's performance capability. Our best alternative was to obtain the opinions of the individuals who were most familiar with computers. A total of forty-three engineers, programmers and other knowledgeable people were contacted and asked to evaluate the influence of computing memory upon performance. While their opinions varied, their answers were analogous enough to construct the functional model that estimates the effect memory has upon computer performance. The results of our inquiry are presented in Table 1.

Machines covered

The two characteristics of the functional description for each computer which this study considers are calculated for the general purpose computers (up to the 1963 cut-off date) in the United States known to the author. The list of computers introduced between 1944 and 1963 was obtained through a detailed search of the computing literature. All the systems that did not have structural elements to satisfy the functional model (specifically P), the special purpose computers, were deleted from the list. Computers which are not in the class of functionally similar products defined by the functional model are those that were built and used to perform a set of specialized information processing tasks. As a result these systems contained limited and specialized input/output equipment or limited internal arithmetic capabilities and are not included in our sample.

Most of the recent general purpose computers have been manufactured in quantities from tens to thousands. With quantity production the manufacturers have offered a large number of alternative system configurations. For these computers one functional description does not fully describe the computer. Many of the computers offer over eight memory sizes, three input/output systems, four input/output channel configurations and four arithmetic and control extras. This represents over $(8 \times 3 \times 4 \times 4)$ 384 different computing systems. Although only a few configurations eventually are produced, the modern systems potentially consist of several hundred alternatives. It would be impossible to calculate P for even a few alternatives of each system. We must therefore settle on one configuration for each computer.

There appears to be a good method for selecting the configurations, and that is to consider the most typical configuration of the computer. Where structural changes have been made, we have used the equipment which was available when the system was first introduced. In a few cases where important modifications have been introduced at a later date, these modifications are considered as separate computers, and are treated as such in the study. The calculations of P and C for both scientific and commercial computation for the 225 computers we consider are presented in Table 2.

Table 2 also contains date of introduction for each of the 225 computers we consider. For our study we define the date of introduction as the delivery date of an operating system to the first user. Where the computer is manufactured and used by the same organization, the date of introduction is defined as that when the completed computer passes a minimal acceptance test.

Technology curves

Since the functional descriptions consist of two attributes, we can display them on a two-dimensional graph. Figure 1 contains points obtained when operations/second P is plotted against seconds/dollar C for computers performing scientific computation. Because of the tremendous range of P and C, Figure 1 is drawn on log-log graph paper. The number next to each point identifies the corresponding computer as listed in Table 2.

From an initial glance at Figure 1, it is apparent that the early systems generally fall on the lower left portion of the graph, and the newer ones in the upper right. The graph shows how much computing power is obtained at different costs; there are high-cost systems (few seconds per dollar) and low-cost ones (many seconds per dollar). In any year, an expensive computer has greater computing power (higher number of operations per second) than a less expensive one. It is also apparent from Figure 1 that for a constant C we obtain greater P over time.

A curve that connects the functional descriptions of the computers in a single year describes the computing technology for that year. Improved performance consists of a continual shift over time, enabling an increased number of operations per second to be performed for a given cost.

We now wish to use our data to develop the technology curves. Unfortunately, the points for a particular year in Figure 1 do not form smooth parallel curves. For any one year considerable scattering occurs because (a) not all systems are equally tech-

Table 2 Computing Systems

Computer			Scientific computation		Commercial computation	
No.	Name	Date introduced	P ops/s	C s/$	P ops/s	C s/$
1	Harvard Mark I	1944	0·0379	50·94	0·406	50·94
2	Bell Lab Computer Model IV	Mar. 1945	0·0068	509·4	0·035	509·4
3	Eniac	1946	7·448	31·81	44·65	31·81
4	Bell Computer Model V	Late 1947	0·0674	84·83	0·296	84·83
5	Harvard Mark II	Sept. 1948	0·1712	50·94	0·774	50·94
6	Binac	Aug. 1949	21·75	127·2	11·7	127·2
7	IBM CPC	1949	2·126	207·8	14·37	207·8
8	Bell Computer Model III	1949	0·0674	102·2	0·296	102·2
9	SEAC	May 1950	102·8	50·94	253·8	50·94
10	Whirlwind I	Dec. 1950	110·7	31·81	45·57	31·18
11	Univac 1101 Era 1101	Dec. 1950	682·5	50·94	301·8	50·94
12	IBM 607	1950	5·666	479·6	34·06	479·6
13	Avdiac	1950	108·5	84·83	51·2	84·83
14	Adec	Jan. 1951	54·26	42·42	57·16	42·42
15	Burroughs Lab Calculator	Jan. 1951	5·605	254·5	7·718	254·5
16	SWAC	Mar. 1951	632·2	50·94	324·7	50·94
17	Univac I	Mar. 1951	140·1	24·94	271·4	24·94
18	ONR Relay Computer	May 1951	0·2937	127·2	1·05	127·2
19	Fairchild Computer	June 1951	2	127·2	4·539	127·2
20	National 102	Jan. 1952	1·26	848·3	2·998	848·3
21	IAS	Mar. 1952	467	84·83	305	84·83
22	Maniac I	Mar. 1952	302·7	101·9	163·4	101·9
23	Ordvac	Mar. 1952	268·8	72·76	127·8	72·76
24	Edvac	April 1952	31·56	54·22	14·86	54·22
25	Teleregister Special Purpose Digital Data Handling	June 1952	12·16	78·93	26·43	78·93
26	Illiac	Sept. 1952	123·1	72·76	50·43	72·76
27	Elcom 100	Dec. 1952	1·278	424·2	3·241	424·2

Table 2–continued

Computer		Scientific computation		Commercial computation	
No. Name	Date introduced	P ops/s	C s/$	P ops/s	C s/$
28 Harvard Mark IV	1952	63·99	42·42	64·95	42·42
29 Alwac II	Feb. 1953	10·17	509·4	12·08	509·4
30 Logistics Era	Mar. 1953	52·85	72	39·01	72
31 Oarac	April 1953	24·38	141·4	35·71	141·4
32 ABC	May 1953	29·88	212·1	11·66	212·1
33 Raydac	July 1953	171·3	8·483	244·6	8·483
34 Whirlwind II	July 1953	233·4	21·21	95·96	21·21
35 National 102A	Summer 1953	4·089	116·5	8·4	116·5
36 Consolidated Eng. Corp. Model 36-101	Summer 1953	38·31	181·8	21·07	181·8
37 Jaincomp C	Aug. 1953	4·745	103·9	3·375	103·9
38 Flac	Sept. 1953	61·55	50·94	107·9	50·94
39 Oracle	Sept. 1953	1002	31·81	563·4	31·81
40 Univac 1103	Sept. 1953	749	28·34	666·2	28·34
41 Univac 1102	Dec. 1953	460·3	50·94	240	50·94
42 Udec I	Dec. 1953	16·38	72·67	21·93	72·67
43 NCR 107	1953	16·99	254·5	34·44	254·5
44 Miniac	Dec. 1953	10·91	267·6	9·545	267·6
45 IBM 701	1953	992·7	18·34	615·7	18·34
46 IBM 604	1953	2·766	974·2	20·19	974·2
47 AN/UJQ-2(YA-1)	1953	21·48	84·83	56·16	84·83
48 Johnniac	Mar. 1954	319·2	84·83	284·9	84·83
49 Dyseac	April 1954	72·18	50·9	172·4	50·9
50 Elcom 120	May 1954	5·471	261·9	6·456	262
51 Circle	June 1954	14·04	318·1	10·59	318·1
52 Burroughs 204 & 205	July 1954	80·84	77·94	187·3	77·94
53 Modac 5014	July 1954	6·238	299·8	10·09	299·8
54 Ordfiac	July 1954	2·607	92·51	6·011	92·51
55 Datatron	Aug. 1954	113·7	113·2	243·1	113·2
56 Modac 404	Sept. 1954	7·116	254·5	15·29	254·5
57 Lincoln Memory Test	Dec. 1954	1925	9·285	768·7	9·285
58 TIM II	Dec. 1954	7·414	848·3	7·439	848·3

Table 2–continued

Computer		Scientific computation		Commercial computation	
No. Name	Date introduced	P ops/s	C s/$	P ops/s	C s/$
59 Caldic	1954	23·99	203·8	41·34	203·8
60 Univac 60 & 120	Nov. 1954	0·0924	356·3	1·473	356·3
61 IBM 650	Nov. 1954	110·8	155·9	291·1	155·9
62 WISC	1954	7·736	145·7	6·413	145·7
63 NCR 303	1954	3·491	117·6	8·281	117·6
64 Mellon Inst. Digital Computer	1954	14·23	169·9	10·55	169·9
65 IBM 610	1954	0·1408	519·6	0·437	519·6
66 Alwac III	1954	44·8	302·7	91·42	302·7
67 IBM 702	Feb. 1955	394·4	20·78	1063	20·78
68 Monrobot III	Feb. 1955	0·3743	299·8	1·188	299·8
69 Norc	Feb. 1955	545·8	10·17	268·2	10·17
70 Miniac II	Mar. 1955	11·76	267·6	17·44	267·6
71 Monrobot V	Mar. 1955	0·4678	295·5	1·607	295·5
72 Udec II	Oct. 1955	7·244	84·83	10·65	84·83
73 RCA BIZMAC I & II	Nov. 1955	285·6	5·668	967·9	5·668
74 Pennstac	Nov. 1955	26·75	212·1	22·98	212·1
75 Technitral 180	1955	110	46·19	190·1	46·19
76 National 102D	1955	7·317	112·3	14·2	112·3
77 Monrobot VI	1955	0·3293	222·7	0·966	222·7
78 Modac 410	1955	24·18	203·8	51·84	169·9
79 Midac	1955	101·6	169·9	29	169·9
80 Elcom 125	1955	31·24	164·1	29·01	164·1
81 Burroughs E 101	1955	0·6898	580	2·319	580
82 Bendix G15	Aug. 1955	57·34	419·9	30·25	419·9
83 Alwac III E	Nov. 1955	41·5	249·4	90·15	249·4
84 Readix	Feb. 1956	80·63	194·9	87·99	194·9
85 IBM 705, I, II	Mar. 1956	734	13·27	2087	13·27
86 Univac 1103 A	Mar. 1956	2295	19·49	1460	19·49
87 AF CRC	April 1956	81·66	31·81	28·97	31·81
88 Guidance Function	April 1956	5·246	461·9	7·744	461·9
89 IBM 704	April 1956	10,670	13·18	3785	13·18
90 IBM 701 (CORE)	1956	2378	17·81	1807	17·81
91 Narec	July 1956	444·8	25·45	190·6	25·45

Table 2–continued

Computer		Scientific computation		Commercial computation	
No. Name	Date introduced	P ops/s	C s/$	P ops/s	C s/$
92 LGP 30	Sept. 1956	41·94	479·6	32·75	479·6
93 Modac 414	Oct. 1956	28·26	169·9	42·94	169·9
94 Elecom 50	1956	0·599	139·2	1·776	1039
95 Udec III	Mar. 1957	25·11	72·76	20·85	72·76
96 George I	Sept. 1957	1538	50·94	571·9	50·94
97 Univac File O	Sept. 1957	35·2	41·02	73·17	41·02
98 Lincoln TXO	Fall 1957	1471	10·19	359·6	10·19
99 Univac II	Nov. 1957	1155	22·27	2363	22·27
100 IBM 705 III	Late 1957	2379	13·27	7473	13·27
101 Teleregister Telefile	Late 1957	286	65·98	935·9	65·98
102 Recomp I	Late 1957	25·76	363·8	16·14	363·8
103 IBM 608	1957	15·21	389·7	60·69	389·7
104 Mistic	1957	64·28	101·9	24·5	101·9
105 Maniac II	1957	1491	72·84	1421	72·84
106 IBM 609	1957	18·19	530·7	75·21	530·7
107 IBM 305	Dec. 1957	94·47	163	96·47	163
108 Corbin	1957	1794	50·9	2407	50·9
109 Burroughs E 103	1957	0·6736	551·8	2·286	551·8
110 AN/FSQ 7 & 8	1957	36,730	2·834	15,560	2·834
111 Alwac 880	1957	2198	50·9	959·7	50·9
112 Univac File I	Jan. 1958	42·49	41·05	92·04	41·05
113 Lincoln CG24	May 1958	6394	21·21	5933	21·21
114 IBM 709	Aug. 1958	1869	8·882	10,230	8·882
115 Univac 1105	Sept. 1958	4433	14·5	5527	14·5
116 Lincoln TX2	Fall 1958	82,050	8·483	34,000	8·483
117 Philco 2000-210	Nov. 1958	29,970	17·81	28,740	17·81
118 Recomp II	Dec. 1958	41·36	249·4	28·03	249·4
119 Burroughs 220	Dec. 1958	810·2	79·94	1616	79·94
120 Mobidic	1958–1960	8741	10·19	12,250	10·19
121 Philco CXPO	1958	2622	15·91	1576	15·91
122 Monrobot IX	1958	0·4598	2545	1·334	2545
123 GE 210	June 1959	1884	44·54	5085	44·54
124 Cyclone	July 1959	234·6	215	119·6	215
125 IBM 1620	Oct. 1959	94·79	331·7	47·2	331·7
126 NCR 304	Nov. 1959	1136	40·23	2445	40·23

Table 2–continued

Computer			Scientific computation		Commercial computation	
No. Name	Date introduced	P ops/s	C s/$	P ops/s	C s/$
127 IBM 7090	Nov. 1959	97,350	9·742	45,470	9·742
128 RCA 501	Nov. 1959	638·7	38·97	1877	38·97
129 RW 300	Nov. 1959	218·6	45·58	534·3	45·78
130 RPC 9000	1959	14·5	138·6	9521	138·6
131 Librascope Air Traffic	1959	3043	16·94	6130	16·94
132 Jukebox	1959	16·56	338·9	18·66	338·9
133 Datamatic 1000	1959	480·8	13·44	1455	13·44
134 CCC Real Time	1959	393·8	77·17	280·3	77·17
135 Burroughs E 102	1959	0·667	580	1·847	580
136 Burroughs D 204	1959	2354	68	1183	68
137 AN/TYK 6V BASICPAC	1959	1365	50·9	493	50·9
138 CDC 1604	Jan. 1960	58,290	18·34	20,390	18·34
139 Librascope 3000	Jan. 1960	5177	12·47	25,320	12·47
140 Univac Solid State 80/90 I	Jan. 1960	329·1	124·7	489·6	124·7
141 Philco 2000-211	Mar. 1960	105,844	14·845	55,740	14·85
142 Univac Larc	May 1960	142,600	4·619	40,450	4·619
143 Libratrol 500	May 1960	21·07	286	20·38	286
144 Monrobot XI	May 1960	4·839	890·7	10·3	890·7
145 IBM 7070	June 1960	2813	23·98	5139	23·98
146 CDC 160	July 1960	119·3	354·3	49·63	354·2
147 IBM 1401 (Mag. Tape)	Sept. 1960	496·7	83·14	1626	83·14
148 AN/FSQ 31 & 32	Sept. 1960	172,200	6·235	48,360	6·28
149 Merlin	Sept. 1960	8306	42·42	2925	42·42
150 IBM 1401 (Card)	Sept. 1960	340·9	215	967·8	215
151 Mobidic B	Fall 1960	5251	12·72	8630	12·72
152 RPC 4000	Nov. 1960	89·81	249·4	54·11	249·4
153 PDP-1 (MT)	Nov. 1960	4455	41·57	2173·3	41·6
154 PDP-1 (PT)	Nov. 1960	166·6	215	57·16	215
155 Packard Bell 250 (PT)	Dec. 1960	62·23	506·9	22·21	506·9
156 Honeywell 800	Dec. 1960	28,790	14·85	23,760	14·85

Table 2–continued

Computer		Scientific computation		Commercial computation	
No. Name	Date introduced	P ops/s	C s/$	P ops/s	C s/$
157 General Mills AD/ECW-57	Dec. 1960	143·9	141·7	44·03	141·7
158 Philco 3000	Late 1960	102·2	155·9	66·13	155·8
159 Maniac III	Late 1960	11,140	25·45	4723	25·45
160 Sylvania S9400	Late 1960	62,510	9·306	49,550	9·306
161 Target Intercept	Late 1960	16,800	33·89	16,070	33·89
162 Westinghouse Airbourne	1960	10,950	12·47	4806	12·47
163 RCA 300	1960	1466	25·98	687·7	25·98
164 Mobidic CD & 7A AN/MYK	1960	12,410	10·39	15,430	10·39
165 Litton C7000	1960	18,200	11·34	5323	11·34
166 Libratrol 1000	1960	84·16	254·5	50·85	254·5
167 GE 312	1960	122	299·8	47·12	299·8
168 Diana	1960	102·1	127·2	48·85	127·2
169 DE 60	Feb. 1960	0·6382	1155	1·855	1155
170 Burroughs D107	1960	311·8	63·62	73·95	63·62
171 AN/USQ 20	1960	22,390	20·78	23,670	20·78
172 AN/TYK 4V Compac	1960	1610	41·57	616·1	41·57
173 General Mills Apsac	Jan. 1961	16·22	424·2	7·084	424·2
174 Univac Solid State 80/90 II	Jan. 1961	3199	69·28	3044	69·28
175 Bendix G20 & 21	Feb. 1961	37,260	33·17	17,060	33·17
176 RCA 301	Feb. 1961	323	113·4	1055	113·4
177 BRLESC	Mar. 1961	47,240	12·72	28,550	12·72
178 GE 225	Mar. 1961	6566	77·94	7131	77·94
179 CCC-DDP 19 (Card)	May 1961	5159	138·6	3027	138·6
180 CCC-DDP 19 (MT)	May 1961	7908	59·38	8073	59·38
181 IBM Stretch (7030)	May 1961	371,700	2·078	631,200	2·078
182 NCR 390	May 1961	2·034	328·2	10·43	328·2
183 Honeywell 290	June 1961	354·3	207·8	182·8	207·8
184 Recomp III	June 1961	48·28	311·8	35·76	311·8

Table 2—continued

Computer			Scientific computation		Commercial computation	
No.	Name	Date introduced	P ops/s	C s/$	P ops/s	C s/$
185	CDC 160A	July 1961	1015	138·6	1780	138·6
186	IBM 7080	Aug. 1961	27,090	11·34	30,860	11·34
187	RW 530	Aug. 1961	13,460	59·38	5086	59·38
188	IBM 7074	Nov. 1961	41,990	19·49	31,650	19·49
189	IBM 1410	Nov. 1961	1673	62·35	4638	62·35
190	Honeywell 400	Dec. 1961	1354	71·67	2752	71·67
191	Rice Univ.	Dec. 1961	7295	50·9	2378	50·9
192	Univac 490	Dec. 1961	17,770	24·94	15,050	24·94
193	AN/TYK 7V	1961	4713	41·57	9077	41·57
194	Univac 1206	1961	20,990	42·42	17,700	42·42
195	Univac 1000 & 1020	1961	3861	66·33	3292	66·33
196	ITT Bank Loan Process	1961	492·6	34·64	1916	34·64
197	George II	1961	298	31·81	675·1	31·81
198	Oklahoma Univ.	Early 1962	7723	50·9	2616	50·9
199	NCR 315	Jan. 1962	3408	65·63	11,460	65·63
200	NCR 315 CRAM	Jan. 1962	3364	73·36	9896	73·36
201	Univac File II	Jan. 1962	33·46	38·97	94·49	38·97
202	HRB-Singer Sema	Jan. 1962	129·2	890·7	56·94	890·7
203	Univac 1004	Feb. 1962	1·789	479·6	25·29	479·6
204	ASI 210	April 1962	8868	135·5	4114	135·5
205	Univac III	June 1962	22,720	27·11	22,790	27·11
206	Burroughs B200 Series-B270 & 280	July 1962	163·3	95·93	615·3	95·93
207	SDS 910	Aug. 1962	4841	249·4	2355	249·4
208	SDS 920	Sept. 1962	9244	65·63	4964	65·63
209	PDP-4	Sept. 1962	220·2	479·6	75·97	479·6
210	Univac 1107	Oct. 1962	138,700	12·47	76,050	12·47
211	IBM 7094	Nov. 1962	175,900	8·782	95,900	8·781
212	IBM 7072	Nov. 1963	22,710	34·64	8694	34·64
213	IBM 1620 MOD III	Dec. 1962	214·8	259·8	56·89	259·8
214	Burroughs B5000	Dec. 1962	43,000	32·82	15,910	32·82
215	ASI 420	Dec. 1962	27,790	44·54	11,090	44·54
216	Burroughs B200 Series – Card Sys	Dec. 1962	114·3	160·1	437·2	164·1

Table 2–continued

Computer			Scientific computation		Commercial computation	
No.	Name	Date introduced	P ops/s	C s/$	P ops/s	C s/$
217	RW 400 (AN/FSQ 27)	1962	7437	12·47	11,240	12·47
218	CDC 3600	June 1963	315,900	11·34	74,900	11·34
219	IBM 7040	April 1963	21,420	44·54	90·79	44·54
220	IBM 7044	July 1963	67,660	23·98	23,420	23·98
221	RCA 601	Jan. 1963	68,690	13·86	58,880	13·86
222	Honeywell 1800	Nov. 1963	110,600	17·81	57,750	17·81
223	Philco 1000 Transac S1000	June 1963	6811	65·63	10,440	65·63
224	Philco 2000-212	Feb. 1963	369,800	9·169	84,230	9·169
225	Librascope L 3055	Dec. 1963	114,000	10·39	30,620	10·39

nically advanced, and (b) there are errors in the estimates of P and C.

The first reason for the scatter of points needs little explanation. In the computing industry, there have been many systems introduced, and these have resulted in a wide range of performance from improved to poorer. Some systems will make significant improvements and fall far to the right of the other points. Alternatively, many systems will not match the capabilities of existing computers and will lie in the range of the industry's previous know-how.

The second reason for the scatter is the expected variance in the estimates of the functional descriptions. P was obtained by means of the functional model, which estimated each system's actual performance. There are differences both in the pricing policies of the manufacturers and in our ability to determine what equipment constitutes each particular system that creates a variance in C. In the calculations we performed, many small errors could have crept into the estimates of P and C to produce random error, even if all the systems came from an identical level of technological knowledge.

Recognizing that variance exists, it is necessary to use a curve-fitting technique to estimate the desired technology lines. For this study we have used least square regression analysis. From a visual analysis of Figure 1 it appears that the technology curves for the different years are approximately the same in shape, with a shift

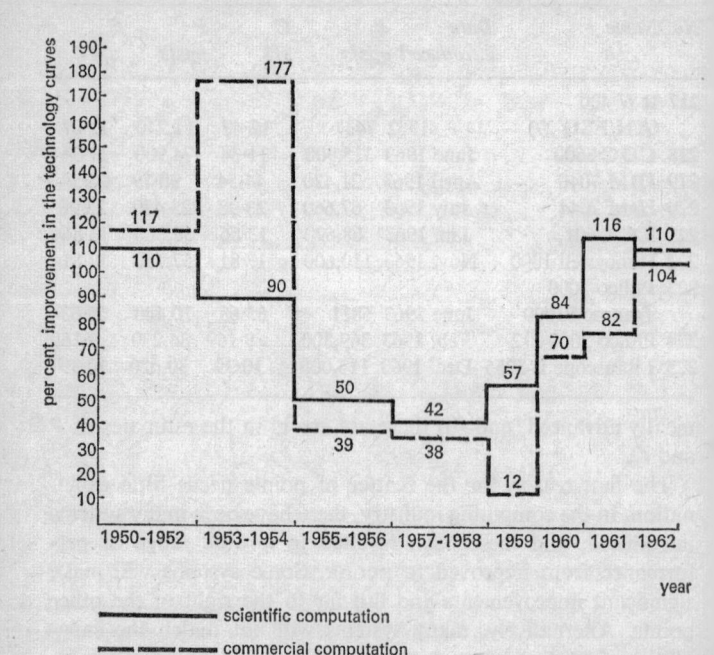

Figure 1 Average yearly shift of the technology curves

to the right over time. Thus, the data were fitted to the following equation:

$$\ln C = a_0 + a_1 \ln P + a_2 (\ln P)^2 + \beta_1 S_1 + \beta_2 S_2 + \ldots + \beta_7 S_7. \qquad 1$$

The as and βs represent the regression coefficients to be determined by the least squares analysis. The $S_1,\ldots,S_7$ represent dummy variables (or shift parameters) for the different years considered. To fit the curve, the data were grouped into eight time-periods (i.e. 1962, 1961, 1960, 1959, 1957–58, 1955–56, 1953–54 and 1950–51–52). The earlier years were combined because of the small number of systems introduced in each of these years. The dummy variables were used in the following manner: for 1962, $S_1,...,S_2$ were all set equal to 0; for 1961, $S_1 = 1$ and $S_2 = S_3 = ... = S_7 = 0$; for 1960, $S_2 = 1$ and $S_1 = S_3 = ... = S_7 = 0$; ... and finally for 1950–51–52, $S_7 = 1$ and $S_1-S_2 = ... = S_6 = 0$. P and $(\ln P)^2$ were both initially included in the equation since a visual analysis of the lines made them appear curved.

After the initial regression estimate, all points that were more than half a standard deviation below and to the left of the curve for their year were omitted. Eliminating points in this manner provides a distinct procedure for determining which points we will include in the final determination of technology curves, and forces the technology curves to the right to provide a more accurate picture of the performance limits.

The regression analysis, using the data for computer performance in scientific computation with **1**, showed that $(\ln P)^2$ term was not significant. The least squares technique was then used to fit **2** to the data.

$$\ln C = a_0 + a_1 \ln P + \beta_1 S_1 + \beta_2 S_2 + ... + \beta_7 S_7. \qquad 2$$

For the linear equation, all the terms were significant and the correlation coefficient was $r = +0.9569$. Since the correlation coefficient equalled only $+0.9596$ with **1**, it appeared most reasonable to use the simpler linear equation to plot the technology curves. In the calculation of both the polynomial and the linear equations, over one hundred-and-twenty observations were used so that the sample sizes would be adequate. The equation for the scientific computation technology curves is as follows:

$$\begin{aligned}\ln C = \; & 8.9704 - 0.51934 \,(\ln P) \\ & -0.3650 \;(1961) \qquad -1.6639 \;(1955\text{--}56) \\ & -0.7874 \;(1960) \qquad -1.9859 \;(1953\text{--}54) \\ & -1.0724 \;(1959) \qquad -2.5013 \;(1950\text{--}51\text{--}52) \\ & -1.3028 \;(1957\text{--}58) \end{aligned} \qquad 3$$

We now perform a similar analysis for commercial computation. The results of the calculation of the technology curves for systems performing commercial computation are shown in **4**.

$$\ln C = 8 \cdot 1672 - 0 \cdot 459 \, (\ln P) \qquad \qquad 4$$
$$\begin{aligned}
&-0\cdot3643 \; (1961) && -1\cdot187 \; (1955\text{--}56)\\
&-0\cdot6294 \; (1960) && -1\cdot454 \; (1953\text{--}54)\\
&-0\cdot8561 \; (1959) && -2\cdot164 \; (1950\text{--}51\text{--}52)\\
&-0\cdot9011 \; (1957\text{--}58)
\end{aligned}$$

Grosch's Law upheld

We analyse the meaning of the technology curves by first restating the general equation for the curves:

$$C = (a_0)Pa^1 \cdot e^{\beta 1} e^{\beta 2} \ldots e^{\beta 7} \qquad \qquad 5$$

where $\ln a_0 = a_0$

and $a_0, a_1, \beta^1, \beta^2, \ldots, \beta_7$ are the values calculated with the least square regression analysis.

From **5** we obtain the following:

$$\text{seconds/dollar} = k \begin{pmatrix} \text{Shift parameter to} \\ \text{adjust for year} \end{pmatrix}$$

(operations/s) $a1$ **6**

For any particular year we can combine the constant, k, and the shift parameter into a new constant C [(k)]×(shift parameter) = C. If we, therefore, set $a_1 = -a_1$, **6** now becomes:

$$\text{dollars/second} = \frac{1}{C} \, (\text{operations/s})a1. \qquad \qquad 7$$

For scientific computation the value for $a1 = -0\cdot519$ so that a_1 equals $0\cdot519$. For commercial computation $a_1 = -0\cdot459$ so that a_1 equals $0\cdot459$. We can therefore assume that a_1 is approximately equal to $0\cdot5$ and rewrite **7** as follows:

$$\text{System cost} = \frac{1}{C} \sqrt[2]{\text{Computing power}} \qquad \qquad 8$$

This represents a very interesting result because it indicates that within the limits of the computing technology one can construct four times as powerful a computer at only twice the cost.

$$\text{Computing power} = (C \times \text{system cost})^2 \qquad \qquad 9$$

That computing power increases as the square of cost was proposed in the late 1940s by Herb Grosch. Since that time the relationship expressed in **9** has been referred to as Grosch's Law. We have seen the industry develop a sense of humor over its twenty-year life with frequent jokes being made in reference to Grosch's Law. In a recent article by Adams (1962), the author proposes to 'replace the square (Grosch's Law) by the square root'. Grosch's Law has received much attention because of its implications about economies of scale, yet has never been supported with adequate quantitative data. We still need to question whether the Law (Computing power = Constant (Cost)^2) is true, or if it is the artifact of the computer companies' pricing policy. The popularity of the Law and the difficulty in setting prices leads us to suspect the possibility of some bias in our data.

We must express another word of caution before we attach too much significance to Grosch's Law. In calculating the technology curves we were able to use the systems actually built. The equations derived are, therefore, applicable within the limited range of computers studied. Special consideration has to be given to the fact that there are definite limits to the maximum computing power that can be obtained at any one time. As the bounds of technological knowledge are reached, additional computing power is purchased at a very high price. For high value of P the technology curve will not remain a straight line but will curve downward to show an ever increasing negative slope. The reason that this did not show up in the regression analysis is that only a few computers came close to the maximum limits of computing power. Three noticeable ones are the AN/FSQ 7 and 8 (the Stage computers), the Univac Larc and the IBM Stretch. These computers each obtained a new high evaluation for absolute computing power, but at considerably lower number of operations/dollar. Grosch's Law did not hold for these three machines because the increases in power were obtained at less than the squared, or even a one to one, relationship with Cost – the slope of the curve, or a^1, is less than minus one. We cannot build larger and larger computers at reasonable costs since at any point in time there are absolute limits to the size and speed obtainable. This fact needs to be kept in mind when talking about **8**. The most powerful computing systems we could possibly build today or tomorrow would not be the most economical.

In order to estimate where the turning point occurs we use the computers that have had, at one time, the maximum absolute efficiency. For scientific computation there are eight systems, and for commercial computation ten. The point where the line crosses the technology curves for each year provides an estimate of where the technology curves start to slope downward to yield diminishing marginal returns for systems with greater computing power.

Performance improvements from 1950 to 1962

The continual stream of performance improvements appears to result from the dynamic nature of the industry itself. Most people in the computing field search conscientiously for faster and more economical machines. However, most of these individuals have a limited idea of what has happened over the past twenty years. For instance, they greatly underestimate the number of innovative systems produced and the amount of performance improvement which actually has taken place. The shift in the technology curves illustrates the performance advances. From 1950 through 1962 the technology curves have an average improvement of 81 per cent per year for scientific computation and 87 per cent per year for commercial computation. There has been some variance in yearly per cent improvement. The improvements in both scientific and commercial computation have been fairly similar, with the first five years, 1950–4, and the last three years, 1950–62, showing greater improvement than the years 1955–9. The large commercial computation improvement in 1953–4 that we mentioned earlier as being significantly above the mean, can be explained by the great increase in speed and the number of machines using magnetic tape units. Since commercial computation relies more upon input/output capability than does scientific computation, the improvements and increased utilization of magnetic tapes aided this category more than they did the other.

As a result of tremendous improvement from year to year, a computer has been marketable for from three to six years. With the great rate of improvement, by the time most users get around to purchasing a system it is greatly inferior to the newer ones being introduced. This illustrates the tremendous obsolescence problem the industry must face if the present rate of improvement continues. The problem will become especially acute if purchasers try to order machines now being designed for delivery one or two years away, rather than take an existing machine. Most computers already in production require from six months to two years for delivery.

References

ADAMS, C. W. (1962), 'Grosch's Law repealed', *Datamation*.
KNIGHT, K. E. (1963), 'A study of technological innovation: the evolution of digital computers', unpublished Ph.D. thesis.

Part Six
Other Aspects of Management Information Systems

Information systems are so ubiquitous and so much has been written about them that it is not easy to decide what areas to exclude. In this final section I have included the results of some interesting research which is being currently carried out on information systems.

Reading 16 describes the impact of introducing a computer into a human system, and suggests how the problems inherent in change might be ameliorated.

Reading 17 presents the results of an investigation into the flow of information within several research laboratories. How do research scientists search for information? The results of the study are intriguing and point the way to similar studies in the management field.

Reading 18 discusses the important problem of controlling the accuracy of computer output. The author argues that top management, and not just the company accountant, should be aware of the new control and auditing concepts.

16 E. Mumford

Planning for Computers

E. Mumford, 'Planning for computers', *Management Decision*, vol. 2, 1968, pp. 98–102.

In his masterly book *Planning and Control Systems: A Framework for Analysis* (1965) Anthony attempts to clear up some of the confusion which seems to befog both the theory and practice of planning. He distinguishes between two aspects of planning which he sees as fundamentally different – namely, *strategic planning* and what he calls *management planning and control*. He defines strategic planning as policy formulation and goal setting for the organization as a whole; a process which involves deciding on company objectives, choosing the resources to be used to achieve these objectives and the policies which are to govern the acquisition, use and disposition of the resources. Stated in these terms strategic planning is very much a staff and top management process. Management planning and control he defines as a type of planning concerned with the administration of the enterprise – for example, bringing new systems of work into operation and formulating personnel practices to meet departmental needs. He sees these localized planning functions as line activities.[1]

Anthony believes that a failure to distinguish between these two types of planning activity leads to practical difficulties and imprecise thinking. One unfortunate consequence of seeing planning as a unified process is the tendency to assume that a single group of people should be responsible for it. This leads, within companies, to staff groups undertaking both strategic planning

1. Anthony includes planning *and* control in his definition because he believes that these are interdependent processes, carried out by the same people and used for the same purpose. In his book he shortens the term to *management control*. However, as this article focuses attention on planning rather than control, I will use the abbreviation *management planning*.

and management planning – whereas the latter is more appropriately a line management responsibility. A second danger is that individuals will make generalizations about planning without recognizing the fundamental differences within the planning function. For example, a managing director may tell his executives 'this company expects creativity at every level of management' whereas, in reality, while creativity is essential at the strategic planning level in his company, it may be much less important at the management planning level. A third danger is that too much attention will be given to one aspect of planning and not enough to the other.

Who should plan what?

Separating the planning process into two distinct parts – each with its own frame of reference, objectives and set of experts – is very useful when considering the introduction of computers. If this kind of technical change is related to the strategic planning/ management planning concept it becomes apparent that current practice does not distinguish between the two and this may be a reason why the implementation of computer systems has not always proved a painless process. Observation of computer introduction shows that strategic planning (to set electronic data processing objectives, assess and create resources, and evaluate alternative means of achieving the objectives through computer assisted solutions to problems) and management planning for implementing new EDP systems tend to be undertaken by the same people, namely the computer technologists. It is unusual for this group to confine its recommendations to the strategic planning areas, leaving line management a major say on the most appropriate system to meet its needs and with complete authority over how and when the new system shall be introduced into its departments.

This assumption of responsibility for both strategic and management planning leads to Anthony's second pitfall, the emergence of invalid generalizations. With computers the danger arises from the computer experts' belief that, because strategic planning is directed at a rational evaluation of company objectives and improved ways of attaining these through utilizing electronic data processing systems, a rational-technical approach also serves best at the management planning stage when implementation policies and tactics are being considered. This belief ignores an important difference between the two types of planning for, whereas strategic planning has as its source discipline economics, management planning has its basis in sociology and psychology. Strategic planning is an analytical, creative activity, while management planning depends more on persuasion, good human relations, assessing subordinate needs and efficient administration. In the author's experience great emphasis, time and attention is given by both computer specialists and top management to the strategic planning area. Much less attention is given to the management planning area, chiefly because computer people regard it as of secondary importance.

Personnel must be considered

Because many computer specialists assume control of both strategic and management planning this leads to the rational-technical approach appropriate for strategic planning also being used in planning for implementation. Few recognize the advantages of involving the management in the latter activity or the importance of paying attention to the sociological and psychological variables which are likely to influence staff attitudes to the new work procedures. Anthony points out that management planning must always be people orientated. Unhappily, for the reasons set out above, with computers it is usually systems orientated in the technical sense of the term. Too often consideration of people appears to be left out of the planning process altogether or is the part which is least well thought out. This means that what is often a company's scarcest and most expensive resource is treated as something that is not amenable to planning. Yet there does not seem to be any empirical evidence to support statements of the 'you cannot plan for people' variety.

If the primary task of the line manager is to produce an environment in which the total resources of his department can be deployed in the most effective way for attaining organizational objectives, then line managers must be heavily involved in the management planning aspects of introducing computers and must be aware of the conditions which have to be met both in order to persuade employees to accept new work methods, and to ensure that these are designed in such a way that human potential and development is not stunted (see Miles, 1965). The evidence of research findings suggests that managerial resistance to computers is often greater than subordinate resistance. Removing management planning responsibility from line management may be an important reason for this. No line manager is likely to be enthusiastic about a system which is planned, designed and introduced by a group over which he has no jurisdiction and little influence.

Conflicting attitudes

Walker has recently provided some reasons why computer experts make better strategic planners than management planners, while the reverse is true of line management (1968). He suggests that the former group sees the company as a technical system designed to achieve technical and economic objectives and that they regard human beings as necessary but unpredictable elements in this system. In principle their aim is to replace these inefficient human links with machine links. In other words, they have an engineering concept of the company (see Mumford, 1966). In contrast, line management tends to view the company as essentially a social system. It thinks of the company and its department as being set up to meet production or marketing demands and of its own role as being that of directing and coordinating the activities of subordinates so that goods or services are produced and targets are reached. With this approach machines are seen as an extension of human beings, helping them to carry out their tasks. Unlike the computer expert, the line manager is concerned with such things as motivation, leadership style, cooperation and good relations; matters of great importance for successful management planning.

Both of these approaches have limitations for, as Walker points out, all companies are what sociologists call socio-technical systems – that is environments in which men and machines interact together to accomplish the primary objectives of the enterprise. One of the aims of system design should be to take advantage of the potential of both men and machines and bring the two together in a way which increases efficiency and produces a satisfying and stimulating work environment.

If the engineering concept of the company is allowed to develop without modification, then there is the danger of computers producing tight control systems in which people are subordinated to the demands of technology. This kind of system is not necessarily efficient because tight control usually means rigidity and difficulty in responding to change. As rapid technical change is now an industrial fact of life, it would seem that a degree of organizational slack which allows a company to respond readily to change is highly desirable. Computer systems need to be designed to provide this and a recognition and development of man-machine interaction in systems design would seem to be one way of achieving it.

Although the line manager will always be concerned with the motivation, morale and development of his subordinates, he can no longer avoid taking account of the impact of computers on the organization of work. By 1975 it is estimated that there will be 10,000 computers in operation in this country and few offices will escape contact with EDP systems. Therefore, line managers can no longer think of their departments as people interacting with each other, they must accept that interaction is more likely to be with a computer terminal than with the man at the next desk or machine.

Three-phase planning

Let us now return to our consideration of Anthony's planning model and see if we can modify this so as to throw greater light on the planning requirements for successfully introducing computers. The strategic planning/management division is helpful in suggesting reasons for defects in EDP planning, but it does not exactly fit what needs to take place. A more appropriate approach is to divide the planning process up into three parts, calling these strategic planning, socio-technical systems planning and tactical planning. Strategic planning, as Anthony suggests, will be carried out by the computer specialists and top management, while socio-technical systems planning will be a cooperative exercise carried out jointly by the computer experts and the management of the user department where the new system is to be introduced. Tactical planning will be the responsibility of user-department management alone, although it will have available the advice of staff specialists such as the personnel department.

Strategic planning for computers

Strategic planning will cover the determination of electronic data processing objectives for the company as a whole, the nature and extent of these objectives being influenced by the factors set out in Table 1. Few objectives will remain unchanged for long periods: most will need to be reformulated as conditions alter within the company and in its external environment. Therefore, it is essential to have established procedures which will enable top management to quickly identify new or changed conditions so that it can restructure objectives in the light of them.

Once top management has determined the EDP objectives, it must set out alternative courses of action likely to assist in achieving these objectives and attempt to forecast the consequences of each one of these in terms of financial or efficiency pay off, short- and long-term plans, ease of introduction, impact on the structure and organization of the company and effect on staff. At this stage management must also assess the availability and cost of the resources required by particular alternatives – for example, knowledge, expertise and software.

Observation of EDP planning practice shows that computer technologists and top management tend to focus on the financial/efficiency pay-off and on hardware, while ignoring or giving scant attention to the other variables set out above. This can lead to serious difficulties, for plans which are economically and technically sound often fail for political or social reasons which could have been anticipated and avoided. Constraints limiting particular kinds of computer development must also be taken into account – these may be financial, technical or in the field of human relations.

Because this kind of forecasting must consider the consequences of a particular course of action for profits, technology, the structure of the company and for staff, it is essential for top management collaborating with computer specialists in strategic planning to be multi-disciplinary in interests. The strategic planning group should include financial, organizational and personnel experts. If top management considers only the economic or tech-

Table 1 Factors Influencing the Nature of EDP Objectives

	Factors providing a stimulus to EDP planning	*Factors inhibiting EDP planning*
Educational and Social	Influential innovating group	Poorly accepted innovating group
	Likelihood of minimum resistance from 'user'	Anticipated resistance
	Knowledge of top management	Poorly educated top management
Economic	Fast return on capital	Slow return on capital envisaged
	New benefits – information, efficiency	New benefits not desired
	Market pressures	Few market pressures
	Poor labour supply	Plentiful labour supply
	Risk capital available	Tight money situation
Technical	Proved nature of equipment	Doubts about equipment
	Good result from feasibility study	Poor feasibility study
	Backing-up services	No technical expertise
	Own technical expertise	Existing system effective
Ideological Projective	Pro-change ideology	Conservative attitudes
	Favourable projection of consequences of computerization	Unfavourable projection of consequences
	Poor evaluation of other course of action	Other course of action suitable and preferable

nical aspects of computers it is likely to be taken by surprise when computer developments throw up unexpected organizational or personnel problems. Fast, crisis planning has then to take place and this can lead to stress, anxiety and a loss of control over events.

Finally, once the planning group has considered the consequences of alternative courses of action it must decide on which course of action is most appropriate, given objectives, resources and constraints. Figure 1 sets out these steps in the strategic planning process.

In practice the strategic planning process is not quite as nicely sequential as the diagram suggests. The author has found that

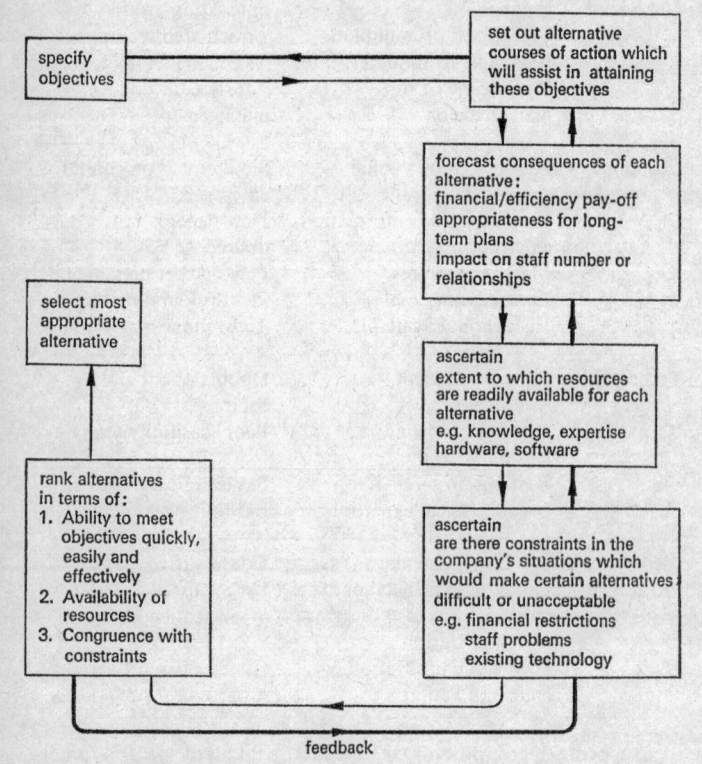

```
┌──────────────┐         ┌──────────────────────────┐
│  specify     │────────▶│ set out alternative      │
│  objectives  │◀────────│ courses of action which  │
└──────────────┘         │ will assist in attaining │
                         │ these objectives         │
                         └──────────────────────────┘
                                     │
                                     ▼
                         ┌──────────────────────────┐
                         │ forecast consequences of │
                         │ each alternative:        │
                         │ financial/efficiency     │
                         │ pay-off                  │
                         │ appropriateness for long-│
                         │ term plans               │
                         │ impact on staff number   │
                         │ or relationships         │
                         └──────────────────────────┘
                                     │
┌──────────────┐                     ▼
│ select most  │         ┌──────────────────────────┐
│ appropriate  │         │ ascertain                │
│ alternative  │         │ extent to which resources│
└──────────────┘         │ are readily available for│
       ▲                 │ each alternative         │
       │                 │ e.g. knowledge, expertise│
┌──────────────┐         │ hardware, software       │
│ rank         │         └──────────────────────────┘
│ alternatives │                     │
│ in terms of: │                     ▼
│ 1. Ability to│         ┌──────────────────────────┐
│ meet         │         │ ascertain                │
│ objectives   │         │ are there constraints in │
│ quickly,     │         │ the company's situations │
│ easily and   │         │ which would make certain │
│ effectively  │◀────────│ alternatives difficult or│
│ 2. Availabil-│         │ unacceptable             │
│ ity of       │         │ e.g. financial           │
│ resources    │         │      restrictions        │
│ 3. Congruence│         │      staff problems      │
│ with         │         │      existing technology │
│ constraints  │         └──────────────────────────┘
└──────────────┘
                       feedback
```

Figure 1 The strategic planning process

the process of evaluating alternative courses of action causes many companies to rethink their objectives. A continual feedback process operates throughout the decision stages. Often a company's final decision on how to proceed is related to a set of objectives which are quite different from those it started with.

Socio-technical systems planning

Once management has decided to embark on a particular course of action this has to be translated into operational terms. For example, if management decides to start computer developments by computerizing stock control, plans have to be made for changing the procedures of the existing stock-control department. This planning area can best be handled by departmental management and computer specialists getting together and jointly designing an appropriate new work system. The computer man will be able to say what is technically possible and desirable, while the line manager says what is viable in terms of his objectives, particularly his desire to run an efficient department which, at the same time, provides a stimulating and satisfying work environment. This brings both technical and social goals together in the planning process. The approach set out in Figure 1 would still be appropriate at this level of planning.

In offices an unchecked technical approach has led to work becoming routinized and de-personalized. In a bank, for example, work at the bottom of the clerical ladder became tedious and boring after computerization, and clerks complained bitterly about it. The avoidance of this kind of situation is of great importance to the line manager interested in effectively utilizing his staff. His aim should be to arrange the computer technology of his department so that jobs retain their interest or even increase in interest, even though the numbers of people required to do them may be considerably reduced. Job enlargement has been a successful way of preventing the de-skilling of shop-floor work. This is equally possible with computer technology. Ideally, a company's personnel manager ought to be able to give advice in this area, as knowledge of the sociological and psychological aspects of job design should be part of his expertise.

Questions which need answering during this systems planning phase include: What is the computer's impact going to be on numbers of staff employed, on job security, on job skill and content and, most important, on job relationships? Before management approves any new work system, it should always ask: How will this affect the way we hope employees will work together?

Computers should not be turned into conveyor belts which

shift data about 'untouched by human hand'; the shop floor has for too long suffered from this kind of production system. A more desirable objective is to increase man's efficiency and further develop his talents by giving him access to up-to-date information immediately he needs it (on-line, real time EDP), thus greatly increasing his planning and decision taking skills. The man and the machine should be complementary to each other, not in a master/servant relationship with the machine in the dominant role.

Socio-technical systems planning of the kind described here requires two things if it is to work. First of all both top management and the computer specialists must recognize that systems design at user-departmental level must be a joint activity between computer personnel and line managers, with neither party assuming a dominant role. This is already the case in many British companies which are experienced and successful in their computer developments. But in too many companies computer technologists appear to impose what *they* see as a suitable system upon line management. Education is, of course, an important factor here; because where line managers know nothing of computers or their use they will tend to lean heavily upon the computer experts. It is extremely important that all managers should, from now on, have a reasonably good knowledge of computer usage and potential, although they do not need to be hardware or software experts. Secondly, line managers must have a very clear idea of the personnel responsibilities of their job, the kind of conditions which their staff require in order to give of their best and develop their skill and knowledge potential. This suggests that the line manager of the future will have to be as much a specialist in sociology and psychology as in work processes.

As automation spreads throughout offices and across the shop floor, the design of effective socio-technical systems is likely to be a major challenge to tomorrow's managers. It is clear that if we do not control technical devices like the computer then they are likely to control us.

Tactical planning

Designing policies and systems for EDP developments is extremely important, but both of these exercises are useless unless policies are carried out and systems implemented. Tactical planning for getting new systems in and enthusiastically accepted by the staff who have to operate them is therefore an essential aspect of planning. As D. W. Ewing points out in the *Harvard Business Review* (1967), this problem is hardly ever discussed when planning experts meet. Most of the emphasis is on the role of computers, reporting methods, criteria for evaluating progress, and so on. Ewing says:

Late in 1966 the National Industrial Conference Board, surveying a cross section of US manufacturing companies, made an inquiry into the activities of their long-range planning units. The respondents indicated that planning departments collected and analysed information, disseminated information, proposed goals.... But none of them reportedly paid regular attention to the human element.

The reason for this absence of concern for people in the planning process appears to be a product of the kinds of experts we employ in this function. In the EDP field we have already indicated how computer technologists have an engineering concept of the company and, as yet, few computer or management-service departments employ sociologists or psychologists who could draw attention to behavioural variables in planning situations. Similarly, although it can be strongly argued that personnel managers should be involved in planning for technical change, few are at other than a manpower requirements level.

However, at the tactical planning level, it is impossible to ignore staff reaction to systems change. A new system, no matter how well designed, will not run effectively unless staff are convinced that it has benefits both for the company and for themselves. This conviction will only arise if management implements computer developments skilfully and reassuringly. Here there can be little doubt that the person most likely to gain staff confidence and who should be most competent to assess the impact of a new work system on individual and group behaviour, is the manager of the user department. Tactical planning *must* be entirely his responsibility although here again, if he has access to a progressive personnel department, he may wish to secure its assistance and advice. Tactical planning, to be successful, must be preceded by a detailed analysis of likely problem areas. Here the manager should take account of the following:

Do staff have any specific doubts or fears about computers? What are these and how can they best be resolved? These fears may be of redundancy, of a reduction in promotion opportunities, or of the changed nature of work.

How can good relationships be maintained throughout the change-over period between department staff and computer experts? The latter will be continually in the user department.

How can stress and conflict be avoided during the change-over period? Change of this kind is usually accompanied by overwork and anxiety.

Consideration of these problem areas raises questions of joint consultation, communication, education and compensation: unfortunately, there is not space to discuss them here. It also raises the question of timing and phasing the change-over, often of crucial importance from a morale point of view. In some situations staff faced with a new computer system have to drag their feet for many months and then are given extremely short notice of the change-over date; in others the new system is brought in at a speed which makes acceptance and adjustment very difficult.

As well as being an important element in successful strategic planning, feedback is also important at the tactical planning level. The line manager must always be prepared to revise his plans in the light of changed events or unexpected reactions from staff. Planning has little virtue unless it influences and responds to what people think and do. Figure 2 shows one approach to this problem.

Conclusion

This article has attempted to set out some of the current defects in planning for EDP systems. A common source of difficulty is the tendency to regard planning as one activity, to be performed by a single group of people. It is suggested that planning for computers is a three-phase activity, incorporating strategic planning, socio-technical systems planning and tactical planning. Each of these planning aspects requires particular knowledge, skills and perspectives and is best handled by different groups of people – strategic planning by top management and computer specialists, socio-technical systems planning jointly by computer specialists

```
┌─────────────────────────────┐     ┌──────────────────────────────────────────┐
│ specify objectives          │     │ specify likely obstacles to achieving    │
│                             │     │ objectives                               │
│ time span of change         │     │                                          │
│ maintenance of morale       │──┐  │ anxious and hostile attitudes            │
│ minimization of stress      │  │  │ non-cooperation or                       │
│ and conflict                │  │  │ unwilling cooperation                    │
│                             │  │  │ poor understanding of EDP                │
│                             │  │  │ consequences                             │
└─────────────────────────────┘  │  └──────────────────────────────────────────┘
                                 │                        │
                                 │                        ▼
┌─────────────────────────────┐  │  ┌──────────────────────────────────────────┐
│ answer the following        │  │  │ specify mechanisms for overcoming        │
│ questions                   │  │  │ obstacles and achieving objectives       │
│                             │  │  │                                          │
│ what feedback               │  │  │ staff involvement in tactical            │
│ mechanisms are required to  │  │  │ planning process                         │
│ check tactical planning     │  │  │ consultation                             │
│ success?                    │  │  │ communication                            │
│                             │  │  │ negociation                              │
│ what policy issues are      │  │  │ compensation                             │
│ involved and must           │  │  │ education                                │
│ be decided in advance,      │  │  │                                          │
│ e.g. redundancy?            │  │  └──────────────────────────────────────────┘
│                             │  │                        │
│ what criteria of tactical   │──┤                        ▼
│ planning success            │  │  ┌──────────────────────────────────────────┐
│ are to be used?             │  │  │ set out plan                             │
└─────────────────────────────┘  └─▶│ including                                │
                                    │ a general plan for groups known          │
                                    │ to be neutral or approving of the change │
                                    │                                          │
                                    │ sub-plans for groups or                  │
                                    │ individuals needing special treatment    │
                                    │                                          │
                                    │ alternative plans to meet                │
                                    │ uncertain predictions                    │
                                    │                                          │
                                    │ detail timing and phasing of plan        │
                                    └──────────────────────────────────────────┘
```

Figure 2

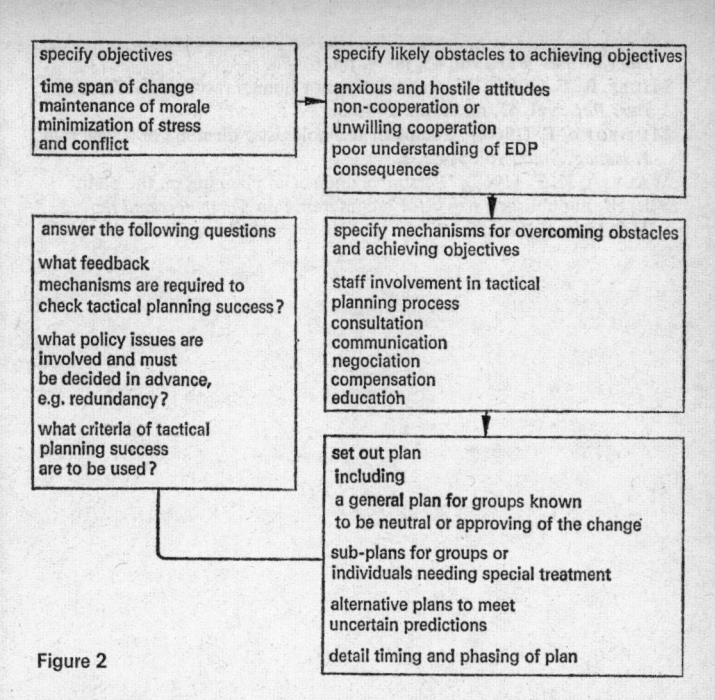

and line management and tactical planning by line management alone.

This approach should lead to an avoidance of the second major planning defect, that of planning for technology, but not for people. If computers are to be a major benefit to industry, and the men and women who work there, then computer systems must be designed so that the computers and human beings enhance the abilities of each other. At present there is a danger that the machine will control and debase the man. Most of us do not want computers which compete with human beings, perhaps because we are not sure who would win.

References

ANTHONY, R. N. (1965), *Planning and Control Systems*, Harvard University Press.

EWING, D. W. (1967), 'Corporate planning at a crossroads', *Harvard Bus. Rev.*, vol. 45, no. 4, pp. 67–76.

MILES, R. E. (1965), 'Human relations or human resources', *Harvard Bus. Rev.*, vol. 43, no. 4, pp. 148–63.

MUMFORD, E. (1966), 'Computer technologists: dilemma of a new role', *J. manag. Stud.*, vol. 3, no. 3.

WALKER, K. F. (1968), 'Personnel and social planning on the plant level', unpublished paper for a conference on *Computers and the Non-Manual Worker*.

17 T. J. Allen and S. I. Cohen

Information Flow in Research and Development Laboratories

T. J. Allen and S. I. Cohen, 'Information flow in research and development laboratories', *Administrative Science Quarterly*, vol. 14, 1969, pp. 12–19.

No research and development laboratory can be completely self-sustaining. To keep abreast of scientific and technological developments, every laboratory must necessarily import information from outside. There are two obvious ways of doing this. The literature can be used by each member of the laboratory staff to keep informed about recent developments in his field; or knowledgeable people outside the laboratory can be consulted for this purpose.

Several recent studies have shown, however, that the average engineer makes little or no use of the scientific and professional engineering literature (Berul *et al.*, 1965; Allen, 1966) and, furthermore, that there is a consistent inverse relation between the performance of industrial and governmental engineers and scientists and the extent to which they use people outside of their organization as sources of information (Allen, 1964 and 1966; Schilling and Bernard, 1964). There is equally consistent evidence, however, of a strong direct relation between intraorganizational communication and performance (Allen, 1964; Allen, Gerstenfeld, and Gerstberger, 1968; Schilling and Bernard, 1964).

It is probably safe to say that poor performance is not due directly to any negative contribution from the information source itself. Rather, it is lack of information, which prompts the use of an information source and which is the underlying cause of poor performance when information is not supplied by the source. Consultants within the laboratory appear to be better able than external consultants to fulfill this need for information.

Hagstrom (1965) found a strong positive relation between performance and extraorganizational communication. In his study, however, the organization (an academic department) occupied a subsidiary position to a more inclusive social system, the 'invisible college' or academic discipline. Although the communication process was external to the academic department it was *internal to the academic discipline*.

The concept of a shared coding scheme (Katz and Kahn, 1966) offers a rather simple explanation for the differences between industrial and academic situations. Scientists in academic institutions do not have schemes for perceiving and ordering the world that are peculiar to their academic institutions. They feel aligned with scientists who share their particular research interests regardless of their organizational affiliation, and these invisible colleges mediate their coding schemes. In industrial and governmental laboratories, however, the organization is of primary importance to its members. The organization demands a degree of loyalty and affiliation far outweighing that required by academic departments; and mutual experience and schemes of ordering the world that are bureaucratically imposed are characteristic of the organization and can be quite different from the schemes of members of their particular discipline in other organizations.

The existence of different coding schemes in different organizations introduces the possibility of mismatch and attendant difficulties in communication between organizations. The mismatch problem is compounded when incompatibilities between two coding schemes go unrecognized. Allen (1966) suggested mismatching as the explanation for the observed inverse relation between extraorganizational communication and performance. It is possible that this mismatch can be reduced by key individuals who are capable of translating between two coding schemes either through personal contact or knowledge of the literature, and who can act as bridges linking the organization to other organizations and workers in the field. Such individuals are possible sources for the transmission of information.

The present paper is concerned with the flow of technological and scientific information both into and within the research and development laboratory. The contrast in the performance of internal and external consultants led to hypothesizing the existence of special routes through which technical information most effectively enters the laboratory. Based on studies of mass communications (Lazarsfeld, Berelson and Gaudet, 1948; Katz and

Lazarsfeld, 1955; Katz, 1960; Coleman, Katz and Menzel, 1966), the existence of a two-step process was hypothesized, through which the average engineer was connected by an intermediary to information sources outside of his laboratory. If special routes exist, it would be important to know what determines their structure; therefore an investigation was made of factors that might influence the structure of each of three forms of technical communication networks.

Hypotheses

Two major hypotheses were generated, based upon the findings of earlier studies in mass communication and upon other research on information flow.

1. *Influence of organization structure.* The structure of the technical communication network of the laboratory will be significantly influenced by two factors:

(a) The structure of the formal organization; that is, the pattern of formal organizational relationships in the laboratory.

(b) The structure of the informal organization; that is, the pattern of friendships and social relations among members of the laboratory.

2. *Technological gatekeepers.* Individuals who occupy key positions in the communication network of the laboratory; that is, those to whom others in the laboratory most frequently turn for technical advice and consultation, will show more contact with technical activity outside of the laboratory:

(a) They themselves will be better acquainted than others in the laboratory with such formal media as the scientific and technological literature.

(b) They will maintain a greater degree of informal contact with members of the scientific and technological community outside of their own laboratory.

Research methods

This study was conducted in two research and development organizations: Laboratory A, a department with forty-eight employees in a medium-sized (approximately five thousand employees) aerospace firm. Thirty of the forty-eight members of this department returned questionnaires. This is an extremely poor response for a sociometric study, and the data would not be reported, except that they add an interesting supplement to the findings in the second organization.

Laboratory B was relatively small and self-contained, and actively engaged in work on new materials and devices in the fields of direct energy conversion and solid-state electronics, for both military and industrial applications. The data were collected from twenty-eight of the thirty-four professional members of the laboratory by means of written questionnaires followed by brief personal interviews.[1]

Sociometric relations

Four questions were asked of each respondent. One of these dealt with the social relations within the laboratory; the other three provided indications of the routing of technical information through the organization. In laboratory B, additional questions dealt with individual information-gathering behavior, including questions on technical reading habits, amounts of technical discussion, and contact with members of other organizations.

Figures 1 and 2 illustrate the pattern of two sets of relationships among the members of laboratory B. In Figure 1, the arrows indicate the direction of choices in social contact; Figure 2 shows the pattern of choices for technical discussion. Figure 1, showing the choices between Ph.D.s and non-Ph.D.s shows only three social contacts directed toward the non-Ph.D.s (Figure 1b), whereas five of a total of nine choices are directed toward the Ph.D. group (Figure 1a); but in only two cases, subjects 24 and 28, is the choice reciprocated.

Sociograms were compared for two or more types of choice (e.g. technical discussion and socialization), by comparing the

1. Examination of résumés for the six non-respondents revealed no striking differences between these and the other laboratory members. One of the six held a Ph.D. Two had been just recently employed by the laboratory, and explained that they were not well enough acquainted with other members to complete the questionnaire in a meaningful manner. Of the remaining four non-respondents, one was out of town at the time and the other three had an aversion to questionnaires.

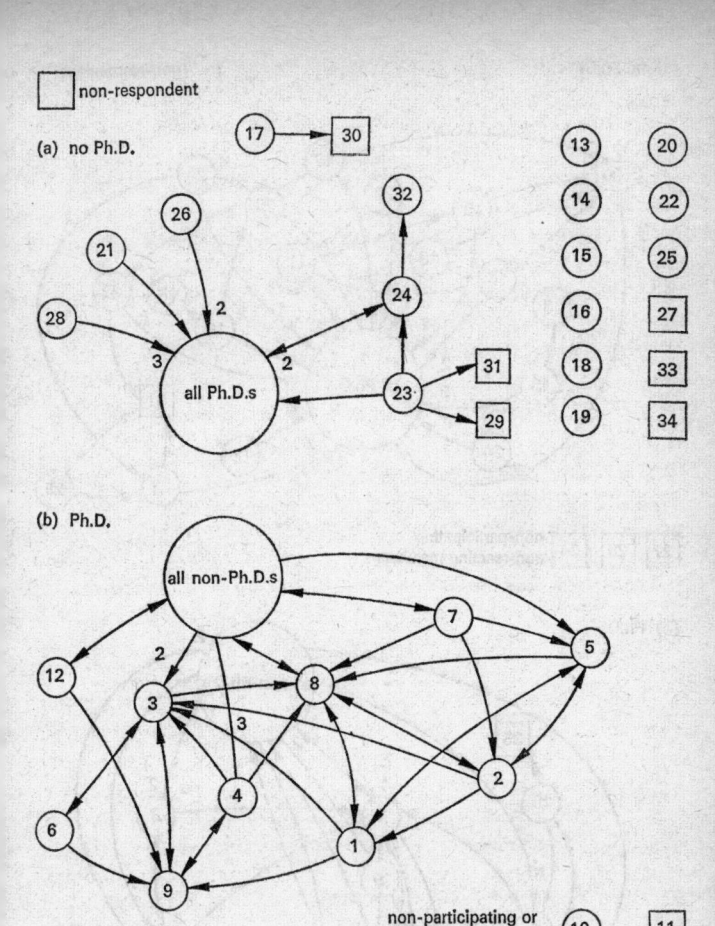

Figure 1 Choices for social contact in laboratory B. Numbers 1 and 2 in circles represent the research directors: numbers at arrowheads indicate numbers of connections where more than one

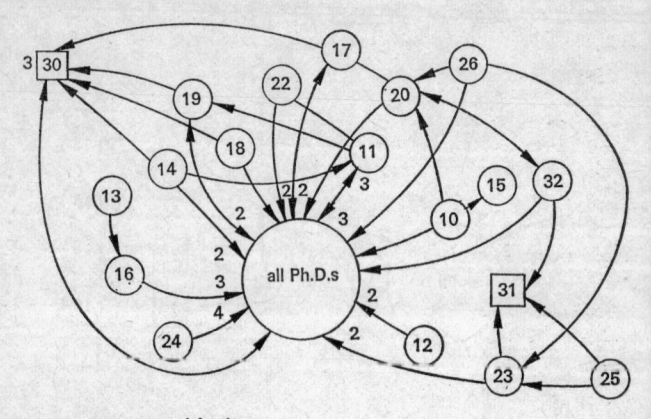

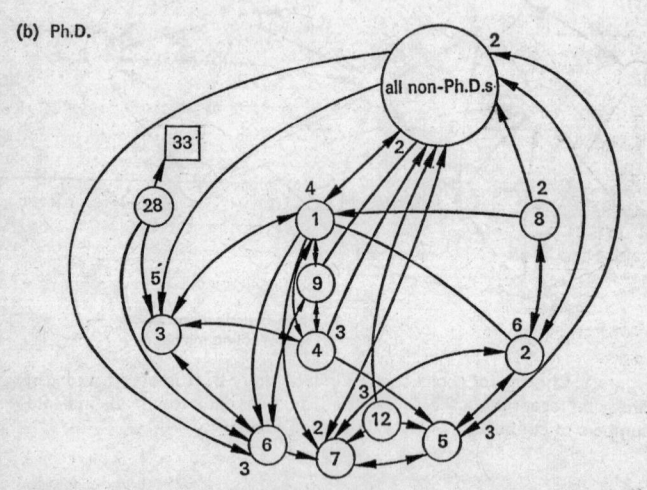

Figure 2 Choices for technical discussion in laboratory B. Numbers 1 and 2 in circles represent research directors: numbers at arrowheads indicate number of connections where more than one.

degree of overlap between the two actual networks with the amount of overlap that would be expected under chance conditions. The number of overlapping choices expected by chance will vary as a function of the number of sociometric choices made by each individual. For example, if every individual in the laboratory chose five others for socialization and five for technical discussion, there would be expected, by chance, a greater number of overlapping connections in the two networks than would be expected if each person had chosen only four others. The expected number of overlaps was computed for each person who returned a questionnaire. This expected number was based on a binomial probability model in which the probabilities of overlap and non-overlap are a function of the number of actual choices made by each individual respondent. The problem is directly analogous to the classical birthday problem (Feller, 1950, pp. 31–2), except that each individual is allowed to have several 'birthdays' (e.g. four), and the number of days in the year is set equal to the size of the organization (thirty-four) from which the choices are made. The probabilities of overlaps expected at random for a respondent choosing four other persons for socialization and five for technical discussion are:

Number of choices common to both relations	0	1	2	3	4	5
Probability of occurrence	0.02	0.24	0.48	0.24	0.02	0

Expected values for the total sample are obtained by summing all of the individual values. The observed distribution of overlaps is then compared with this expected distribution by means of a one-sample Kolmogorov-Smirnov test. In Figure 3, the bar graphs show the observed number of overlapping choices and the number predicted by the random model.

Results and discussion

Relationship among choices

Figure 3 compares three communication-oriented choices with the socialization choice. There is strong relationship in the selection of individuals for socialization and the selections of those for technical discussion in both laboratories. In laboratory B, this is due only partially to the rather tight clique found among the Ph.D.s in the laboratory. As a matter of fact, among the Ph.D.s alone, the amount of overlap is not significantly above chance. The networks for critical-incident information and for new research ideas show a decidedly weaker relation to the

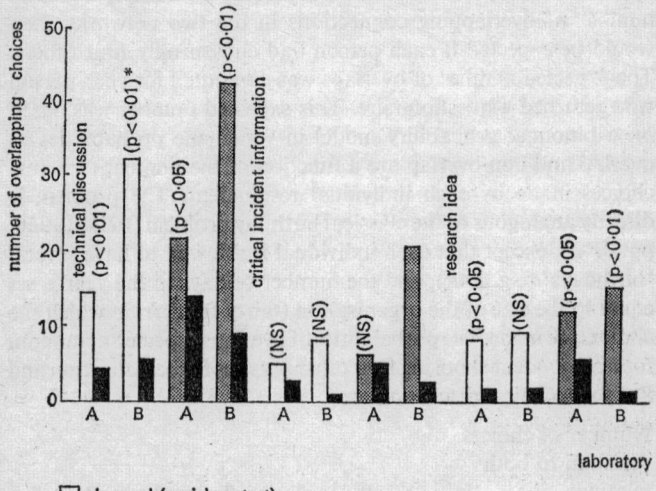

Figure 3 Number of overlapping choices between the social contact and work group structure and three networks of technical information flow in research and development laboratories A and B. *Determined by Kolmogorov one-sample test: NS: difference not statistically different

socialization network in the laboratory. Only in the communication of new research ideas in laboratory A is the observed amount of overlap significantly above chance expectation. The informal organization is then strongly related to the technical discussion network, but is far less influential in determining the flow of critical ideas, or of ideas for new work. Its relation to communication is limited to the general information flow that occurs during technical discussions. Nevertheless, technical discussions among colleagues are certainly an important general device for transferring technical information. Although it is impossible from such data as these to determine the direction of the causal link; that is, does socialization bring about transfer of technical information, or do people socialize more with those with whom they like to discuss technical problems, it appears that the informal organization of the laboratory occupies an important position in the transfer of information.

The question now remains of the impact of formal organizational structure upon communication. In laboratory A, organizational relationships were taken directly from the departmental organization chart. The work group was considered to consist of a first-line supervisor and those reporting to him. In laboratory B, no organization chart existed. Since its organization was quite flexible and revolved around a number of long-term and short-term projects under the direction of two research directors, consideration of formal structure was restricted to *ad hoc* project groups. The respondents in laboratory B were asked to name 'The people whom you consider to be members of your present work group.' In both laboratories, the amount of observed overlap between the social-contact network and the formal organizational structure was far from being statistically significant; therefore they appear somewhat independent and should exert independent influences on information flow.

The relation between formal organization and technical communication is much stronger (Figure 3) than was evident in the case of informal organization. Work-group structure influences not only technical discussion but the flow of new ideas, and in laboratory B critical ideas as well. Here there is no doubt about the direction of causality. If two people are closely related organizationally, they will be more likely to discuss technical problems and possibly even more likely to provide each other with critical research information. In the case of transmitting new research ideas, it is obvious that an individual with an idea for a new research project will first express that idea to his immediate supervisor.

Controlling for the effects of the formal organization, by comparing only those social and technical discussion links external to each individual's work group produces a somewhat weaker, but still significant, relationship than that found when work-group members were included. The formal organization is therefore the more important, but not the sole determinant of the structure of the technical-communication network of the laboratory.

Influence of status on communication

Several studies (Hurwitz, Zander and Hymovitch, 1960; Newcombe, 1961) have shown that the presence of prestige or status hierarchies in a social system will affect the flow of information. Individuals of high status will tend to like one another and to communicate frequently; individuals of low status will neither like one another as much nor communicate as much. Furthermore, lower-status members of the social system will direct most of their communication toward the higher-status members, without complete reciprocation.

The communications and social-contact networks in laboratory B provide almost perfect examples of these relationships. Figures 1 and 2 show the influence of a status differential (in this case exemplified by possession of the doctorate degree) on the communication network in the laboratory.[2] The Ph.D.s apparently communicate quite freely among themselves, but they seldom socialize or discuss technical problems with the non-Ph.D.s. This could, of course, impede organizational performance, but an even more serious effect is evident. The non-Ph.D.s in the laboratory scarcely ever socialize with one another and they discuss technical problems among themselves far less than their Ph.D. colleagues. Furthermore, the non-Ph.D.s direct most of their socialization (64 per cent) and technical discussion (60 per cent) to Ph.D.s. The Ph.D.s, in contrast, direct only 6 per cent of their socialization and 24 per cent of their technical discussion to non-Ph.D.s.

The tendency of the lower-status members of a dichotomous hierarchy to direct their communications upward has been explained by Kelley (1951) as a form of substitute upward locomotion. 'Communication serves as a substitute for real upward locomotion in the case of low-status persons who have little or no possibility of real locomotion.' Kelley points out, however, that

2. Since there were only two Ph.D.s in laboratory A, the relationship was not apparent there.

this statement holds true only for those low-status persons who show some desire to move upward. Cohen (1958) has replicated these results with another experimental group, and finds further that one form of upward communication (conjectures about the nature of the higher-status job) increases both when locomotion is desired but not possible and where it is possible but not desired.

In laboratory B, upward mobility is highly desired but, in the short run, impossible. It is therefore not surprising that the non-Ph.D.s should attempt to enhance their own status through association with the higher-status members of the laboratory. In an organization in which both Ph.D.s and non-Ph.D.s work together on the same tasks, the most rewarding experiences, publication, recognition, etc. tend to be restricted to those holding the advanced degree. The non-Ph.D.s are therefore resigned to gaining reflected glory as satellites of the higher-status group, and tend to avoid association with their lower-status colleagues.

Information habits and communication choices

Figure 2 shows very clearly that some individuals are much more frequently chosen than others for technical discussion. These frequently chosen individuals, or sociometric 'stars', were cited as sources of critical incident information. (This analysis was performed in laboratory B only, because although there were stars in laboratory A, nothing is known of their information-gathering behavior. It was not possible to obtain data on the information-gathering behavior of leaders and a matched sample of non-stars.) They may well be key links between the internal-information network of the laboratory and the scientific and technological communities outside of the laboratory. To examine this possibility, the 'stars' in two sociometrically-determined information networks were compared with their colleagues to determine whether they showed any systematic differences in their information-gathering behavior. Specifically, it is hypothesized that the stars will make greater use of such sources as literature and professional friends outside the organization; in other words, that they will act as 'technological gatekeepers'.

The eight respondents most frequently chosen for technical discussion (the number of times that is at least one standard deviation above the mean for the laboratory; that is, six or more) have more exposure both to the literature and to oral sources outside of the laboratory than the average professional in the laboratory (Table 1).

Table 1 Communication Behavior of Individuals at Key Positions of Technical-Communication Network.*

Communication characteristics of personnel	Number of technical discussion choices		Source of critical incident information	
	Six or more ($N = 8$)	Four or fewer ($N = 20$)	Yes ($N = 7$)	No ($N = 21$)
Use of personal friends outside the laboratory as sources of information	64	25†	67	30†
Use of technical specialists within the laboratory as sources of information	50	40	57	40
Number of technical periodicals read	88	40‡	100	45‡
Number of professional and scientific periodicals read	75	35§	86	35§

* Numbers in table represent percentage above the median.
† $p < 0.10$
‡ $p < 0.05$
§ $p < 0.001$ Mann–Whitney U-test

This contrast is especially pronounced in the case of scientific and professional literature; that is, journals published under sponsorship of scientific and engineering societies.[3]

Both research directors are included among the eight 'stars'. This was at first surprising, since the question asked was directed at the discussion of purely technical questions and should have excluded administrative and organizational standing. Both were

3. The names of all technical periodicals to which each respondent subscribed or read regularly was obtained, and those sponsored by engineering and scientific societies were separated out in the analysis.

apparently very competent technically, however, and were included among the seven individuals who were cited as sources of critical incident information, and were between them responsible for all of what the respondents almost unanimously agreed were the four best technical ideas that anyone in the laboratory had had in the previous years. Eliminating the two research directors from the analysis in Table 1, does not significantly change the results (for professional friends outside the laboratory, $p = 0.11$; for the reading of professional and scientific periodicals, $p = 0.0001$).

When requested to indicate the source of any information which influenced the course of their most recently completed research projects, twelve respondents cited seven other individuals within their own laboratory as the source of such information. In Table 1, these seven people are compared in terms of their own information-gathering behavior in the same manner as were the technical discussion stars. Again there is the pattern of greater contact with experts outside of the organization and more exposure to the literature.

There were therefore two classes of individuals in laboratory B. The majority had few information contacts beyond the boundaries of the organization. A small minority had rather extensive outside contacts and served as sources of information for their colleagues. There is then evidence of a two-step flow of information, in which about six individuals act as technological gatekeepers for the rest of the laboratory.

The gatekeepers themselves showed some variation in the type of information sources they used. Some relied more upon the literature while others relied more on oral sources. A comparison of relative exposure to technically oriented friends outside of the organization and to the scientific and professional literature shows a slight positive correlation (Kendall, tau $= 0.27$), but the relation does not approach statistical significance ($p = 0.21$).

Discussion

Individual gatekeepers use different sources of information: some transmit late information from the literature, others, from oral sources.

They may also differ in how their information is applied, but this possibility cannot be tested with the present data. In mass-communication research (Katz and Lazarsfeld, 1955), opinion leaders were found to be differentiated by topic; those who were influential in public affairs were not necessarily influential in determining fashion patterns. Moreover, the area of influence was related to media exposure; public-affairs leaders read more news magazines and fashion leaders more fashion magazines. Thus, the content of the messages processed by the various gatekeepers in research and development laboratories should be examined in more detail. The selection of literature or oral sources by gatekeepers may be based upon the kind of information in which the gatekeeper specializes; and the sources may vary in their ability to provide different types of information. For example, there is evidence to suggest that the literature provides general information about the status of a technological field, while oral sources provide more detailed information about particular techniques (Menzel, 1966; Scott, 1959; Goodman, Hodges and Allen, 1966). Gatekeepers who specialize in the state-of-the-art should tend to read, while those specializing in particular techniques should tend to talk to external sources.

There does not appear, as yet, to be a way to identify gatekeepers on an *a priori* basis. It is quite clear, however, that they are important contributors to the efforts of the laboratory. In both laboratories, the gatekeepers held significantly more patents, had published significantly more papers than their colleagues, and tended to be first-line supervisors (two-thirds of the gatekeepers are first-line supervisors in laboratory A, and the two research directors in laboratory B). Gatekeepers were more frequently Ph.D.s in laboratory B, and one of the two Ph.D.s in laboratory A was a gatekeeper.

Does an individual become a gatekeeper because he occupies a managerial position, or does his promotion to management result, in part, from his contribution as a gatekeeper? Holding a managerial position certainly provides an individual with easier access to people outside his organization, but it is hardly likely to stimulate his technical reading. If promotion to a supervisory position is a reward for technical communication, it may be self-defeating strategy. It places the man in a position in which his next promotion will be to block his effectiveness as a transmitter of technical information. The second promotion will probably remove him too far from the technical work to allow him to remain current in technical information, and will impose an administrative separation between himself and the average engineer. This can be seen in laboratory A, where the department head was two organizational levels above the engineers and was not considered a gatekeeper.

There are two further implications for management. First, the factors which influence the flow of technical information should be understood, since some of them are under management's control and can be used to improve the communication system. Second, the value of gatekeepers should be recognized. Research management often fails to make effective use of these individuals. One obvious first step is to ease their access to outside sources through such devices as paid attendance at professional meetings and liberal travel-budgets. In addition, they should be allowed easier access to the literature. To minimize cost in providing access to search and retrieval systems, such access should be given first (and perhaps solely) to the technological gatekeeper. Making adequate use of them may allow a drastic reduction in the number of entry points required to any automated literature-retrieval system.

Furthermore, recognition and reward for performance as transmitters of information will ensure that gatekeepers continue in that capacity. Management presently appears either to discourage this activity by failing to reward it, or to reward the gatekeeper by promotion and thereby make it impossible for him to continue as a transmitter of information.

References

ALLEN, T. J. (1964), 'The use of information channels in research and development proposed preparation', working paper, MIT, Sloan School of Management, paper 97–64.

ALLEN, T. J. (1966), 'Performance of communication channels in the transfer of technology', *Industrial Manag. Rev.*, vol. 8, no. 1, pp. 87–98.

ALLEN, T. J., GERSTENFELD, A., and GERSTBERGER, P. G. (1968), 'The problem of internal consulting in research and development organization', working paper, MIT, Sloan School of Management, paper 319–68.

Berul, L. H., Elling, M. E., Karson, A., Shafrity, A. B., and Sieber, H. (1965), 'Department of Defense user-needs study', Auerbach Corporation.

Cohen, A. R. (1958), 'Upward communication in experimentally created hierarchies', *Human Relations*, vol. 11, pp. 41–53.

Coleman, J. S., Katz, E., and Menzel, H. (1966), *Medical Innovation: A Diffusion Process*, Bobbs-Merrill.

Feller, W. (1950), *An Introduction to Probability Theory and Its Applications*, Wiley.

Goodman, A. F., Hodges, J. D., and Allen F. G. (1966), 'Final report: DOD user-needs study. Phase 2: flow of scientific and technical information in the defense industry', North American Aviation Inc.

Hogstrom, W. O. (1965), *The Scientific Community*, Basic Books.

Hurwitz, J., Zander, A., and Hymovitch, B. (1960), 'Some effects of power on the relations among group members', in D. Cartwright and A. Zander (eds.), *Group Dynamics*, 2nd edn, Harper & Row.

Katz, D., and Kahn, R. L. (1966), *The Social Psychology of Organizations*, Wiley.

Katz, E. (1960), 'The two-step flow of communication', in W. Schramm (ed.), *Mass Communications*, 2nd edn, University of Illinois Press.

Katz, E., and Lazarsfeld, P. F. (1955), *Personal Influence*, Free Press.

Kelley, H. H. (1951), 'Communication in experimentally-created hierarchies', *Human Relations*, vol. 4, pp. 39–56

Lazarsfeld, P. F., Berelson, B., and Gardet, H. (1948), *The People's Choice*, Duell, Sloan & Pierce.

Menzel, H. (1966), 'Scientific communication: five times from social-science research', *Amer. Psychol.*, vol. 21, pp. 999–1004.

Newcombe, T. M. (1961), *The Acquaintance Process*, Holt, Rinehart & Winston.

Scott, C. (1959), 'The use of technical literature by industrial technologists', Proceedings of the International Conference on Scientific Information.

Schilling, C. W., and Bernard, J. (1964), 'Informal communication among bio-scientists', Biological Sciences Communication Project Report no. 16A-1964.

18 J. J. Wasserman

Plugging the Leaks in Computer Security

J. J. Wasserman, 'Plugging the leaks in computer security',
Harvard Business Review, vol. 47, 1969, pp. 119–29.

Many companies are working to develop new business applications for electronic data-processing (EDP). All too often this effort is not accompanied by a proportional effort to develop computer control systems which will protect the company's assets from misuse or error. Yet the importance of effective computer control is increasing, for a number of reasons:

1. The growing size and complexity of EDP systems, which make errors more costly and more difficult to detect.

2. The sophistication of third-generation hardware, where original documents may exist only in the form of magnetic records within the computer, placed there directly from remote terminals. (This development presents many new problems, such as security of data, and it increases the number of sources where incorrect inputs can be generated.)

3. The growing reliance of management on information generated by computer systems, not only for financial data but also in such areas as marketing, production, engineering and forecasting.

4. A continuing shortage of skilled computer personnel, which leads to rapid turnover and the hiring of marginal workers.

When management does think of computer control systems, it tends to focus mainly on fraud, and there have been some widely publicized cases of this. But the real problem for most companies is not fraud but ordinary human error, which can cost a company millions of dollars without criminal intent on anyone's part. Computer security thus involves a review of every possible

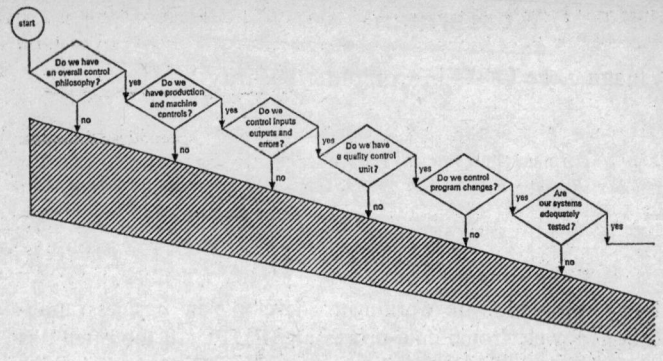

Figure 1 Steps toward a secure computer system

source of control breakdown – a highly demanding, but not impossible, job.

New control concepts

One factor that has made the job more difficult is lack of awareness by many executives of new control concepts required for computer systems. EDP systems are so new that few top executives have had much first-hand experience with them. While computer manufacturers do attempt to give executives an understanding of computer capabilities, the introduction is often quite general and the need for controls is not sufficiently emphasized.

Because of this basic misunderstanding about EDP systems, many companies have eliminated traditional controls for checking human calculations – 'the computer doesn't make mistakes'. But computers are programmed and operated by humans, who still do make mistakes. Therefore, traditional control-techniques still can be important and should be evaluated in terms of their usefulness to EDP systems. In addition, new control concepts must be devised to use the powerful capabilities of the computer. Although top management has the primary task of formulating a basic control policy, *all* employees connected with an EDP system have a responsibility to ensure that data processing is adequately controlled.

One slowly developing trend that fosters this approach is the strategic placement of a qualified top-level executive whose primary responsibility is to direct the corporate computer efforts. With this technical know-how available on the executive level, the company has taken a positive step toward establishing an up-to-data control philosophy. The company can then establish meaningful procedures to protect computer programs and data against error, malice, fraud, disaster or system breakdowns.

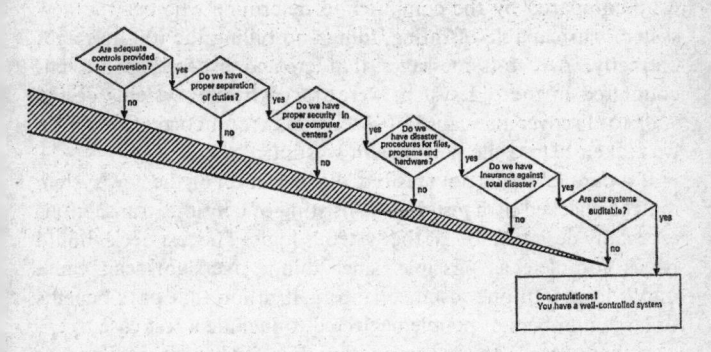

In this article, we will analyse these potential problem areas and show how a combination of good judgement and machine capabilities can control them. Figure 1 summarizes the problems and the primary elements in an adequate control system.

Getting off to a good start

Testing is vital to the success of a system and, therefore, is worth careful scrutiny. In particular, the last test phase, where all elements of a new installation are tested as a unit, indicates whether the system is reliable. Here the best method is to run the new and old systems in parallel, comparing results where possible.

For example, parallel testing was successfully applied to a telephone company operation involving rating and billing of toll messages. When the new system was considered ready for use, the design staff extracted 300,000 toll messages that were prepared for processing by the old system. The 300,000 messages were adjusted so they could be entered as inputs to the new system.

The results of processing these messages through both systems were compared by the computer to determine whether the new system was capable of rating, filing and billing the toll messages correctly. Any toll messages that created exceptions not encountered in the old system were traced by the systems design staff to discover the cause of discrepancy, and corrective action was taken before the new system was introduced.

If a parallel test is not feasible, the operation of the new system may be checked by a test deck consisting of fictitious transactions especially designed to test the system's logic. The test deck should be as complete as possible, since minor oversights can cause major losses. In one instance, an organization that pays benefits to large numbers of people neglected to include a test case to ensure that a check on the termination data for benefits was part of the computer program. As a result, many millions of dollars were paid out to persons whose benefit periods had expired.

Canvassing of data

Finally, during the changeover to the new system, a careful check should be made to ensure that all data are converted as required. This may sound elementary, but it is very important. For instance, one major corporation, when making a changeover, failed to convert all the data from its old system, and this failure cost the company nearly three million dollars.

The controls also should ensure that data are converted only once, or a company may find itself duplicating asset-records or billing its customers several times for the same item.

A final check should be made to ensure that the data going into the new system have been verified and are as complete and error-free as is economically feasible. Control totals of items such as dollars and units based on the old system should be checked as the records are converted. One way of doing this is to write, *prior to conversion*, computer programs that will edit individual records for missing data and invalid codes; this step amounts to 'scrubbing' (i.e. cleaning) the data in the old system. For example, prior to converting to a new payroll system, the employee records from the old system should be checked to ensure that significant data, such as tax codes and social security numbers, are present and valid. The problems of converting to a new system are great enough without adding the burden of erroneous data.

Quality control

As part of a plan for monitoring an EDP system, a quality control unit should be established to sample the accuracy of data both before and after computer processing (see Figure 2). Such quality control-units were common in the pre-computer era, when it was possible to follow the flow of data by checking documents as they were processed manually. The era of large-volume computer input and output makes quality control even more important.

The degree of training needed for the quality control unit depends on the sophistication of the system. The unit's major function is to spot data that are obviously unrealistic. For example, if the number of errors is increasing, the quality of incoming data should be scrutinized more carefully at its source to determine the cause(s) of error. This type of control and analysis will detect minor problems before they become major and will indicate where the system needs to be reinforced through additional training or improved controls.

Input, output and errors

As part of the control unit, an input section (see Figure 2) should maintain positive controls over all transactions it receives and, wherever possible, should identify them by type, source, and date. Once such controls are established, they should be part of an interlocking system of control totals which serve to assure that data accounted for as input are not subsequently lost or distorted.

As for controlling the accuracy of a system's output, care must be taken to ensure that machine controls cannot be overridden because of human error. For example, although it possessed an apparently foolproof system, one company came close to a disastrous loss of records stored on a master computer tape because

1 systems design staff
2 computer center
3 input/output sections
4 control unit
5 quality control unit
6 internal auditing

▓ processing unit

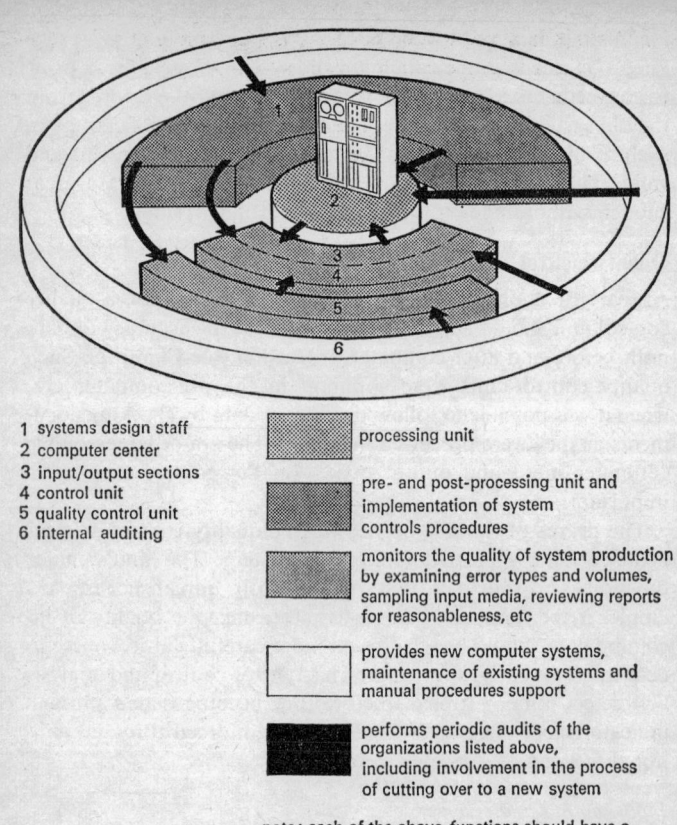

▓ pre- and post-processing unit and implementation of system controls procedures

▓ monitors the quality of system production by examining error types and volumes, sampling input media, reviewing reports for reasonableness, etc

☐ provides new computer systems, maintenance of existing systems and manual procedures support

■ performs periodic audits of the organizations listed above, including involvement in the process of cutting over to a new system

note: each of the above functions should have a person(s) designated responsible for organizational control standards and coordination of standards with other organizations

Figure 2 Relationships among control groups

of an operator's mistake. The tape was updated daily by adding the latest day's results to the master file. A computer operator once mistakenly used the previous day's master tape, which was kept as a backup. The computer program recognized that the wrong tape had been mounted and printed out a message saying so, but the operator ignored the message and pushed the restart

352 Other Aspects of Management Information Systems

button. The fact that one day's results were missing from the master file was not discovered until twenty days later, and reconstructing the master file was extremely costly.

When the serious consequences of such an error were recognized, the internal auditors requested the systems-design staff to change the program so that the master file could be processed only if the proper tape were mounted.

Output controls over receipt and distribution of data will ensure reasonableness, timeliness and completeness of computerized results. Output data should be balanced against machine-generated control totals when practical.

While some errors in an EDP system are inevitable, the manner in which they are corrected and re-entered may determine the success or failure of the system. Even when the fact that errors are being made is noted, system designers often neglect manual and machine methods of correcting the mistakes. A good control-system should provide a built-in method of error analysis, including information on the type, quantity, value and age of errors, so that the source can be determined and corrective action taken.

In the case of systems that process large volumes of data and, as a consequence, are subject to a significant number of mistakes, management should consider maintaining a master file of detected errors that provides a positive control of errors, records their magnitude, quantity, source and age. Statistics from this file will provide management with a computerized indication of error trends, which can then be countered by appropriate controls.

Other checks and safeguards

There should be written instructions for all machine operations. These instructions should be kept complete, current and understandable; and computer-room managers should ensure that their operations personnel are following the procedures outlined. The best control system is no better than the performance of the people who run the computer operation, so records of the performance of both men and machines should be kept. Supervisors should also periodically review operator interventions, machine halts and other occurrences indicating unusual conditions.

Records of machine performance, preventive maintenance periods and schedules of operation should, of course, be kept current. All this falls in the category of what are often called 'production and machine controls'.

The EDP library deserves more attention than it usually gets. Many companies fail to realize the size of their investment in programs and data files for an EDP system. The loss of a production or program tape can be very costly, so careful controls should be established to ensure that tapes are removed from the library only when needed, that only authorized personnel have access to the library, that all tapes are clearly labelled, and that records of tape use are kept.

Library controls should also include maintenance of backup tapes (usually referred to as 'grandfather', 'father' and 'son', depending on how far back they go). Such backup data can restore current data files in case the latest tapes are damaged or destroyed.

The problem of maintaining backup files is more complicated for the newer random-access computer systems, in which outdated information is erased as new data are processed. However, magnetic tape can duplicate the various files contained on storage devices (such as discs, drums and data cells) so that the system can be restored to its most current status in case of hardware or program failure.

Program changes

In view of the possibility of major losses resulting from minor program changes, management should limit the number of people who are authorized to change operating programs or internally stored program data. The slightest change can have extraordinary effects. For instance, at Cape Kennedy a space launching failed recently because, during a program change, a computer symbol equivalent to a comma was inadvertently omitted from the program. The omission sent the rocket so far off course that it had to be destroyed.

In company operations, the possibility of fraud through unauthorized program changes is obvious. For example, in one bank, a programmer altered a savings account program to transfer the 'round-off' fractions of cents in the interest calculation to an account he maintained under a fictitious name; he was able to withdraw large sums of money before his scheme was detected.

Yet as far as internal security is concerned losses from fraud are dwarfed by losses from honest mistakes resulting from unauthorized program changes. The likelihood of loss from mistakes can be substantially reduced if programs are changed only by those persons having the proper authority.

An adequate security system should make clear the type of information to be made available to each employee. Classified information, such as data relating to customer credit, shareholders, payroll, marketing and manufacturing processes, must be categorized by appropriate security levels.

Today, setting up a security program is complicated by the growing use of remote terminals. It is not uncommon for a company to have its computer in one center, data transmission points in several different cities or states, and assembly of final reports in still another location. When employees hundreds of miles away are in direct contact with the computer files, there must be controls to ensure that the files are not changed from remote locations without authorization, and that classified or sensitive data are available only to authorized personnel in those locations. For instance:

1. The number of remote terminals through which computer files can be changed should be limited.

2. Identification codes for each terminal and authorization codes should be used for the limited number of employees who are authorized to operate remote equipment. The computer should be programmed to check the validity of the codes before it accepts or gives information. Since personnel turnover is high, identification codes should be changed frequently.

3. The adequacy of controls themselves should be checked. One way is to have supervisors try to gain access to a remote terminal without authorization. If they can use the terminal without being challenged, so can others.

External security

While fraud tends to be overpublicized as a problem of internal security, just the opposite seems to be the case in matters of security against outsiders. Yet knowledge about computer systems is widespread enough that numerous persons outside the company may use a system's weaknesses for their own profit. A striking illustration of how this calls for controls occurred when banks introduced computerized accounting systems.

In these systems each customer had his account number preprinted in magnetic ink on his deposit slips and checks. A supply of the preprinted deposit slips was sent to all bank customers, and blank deposit slips were made available at the bank. Several cases of fraud came to light in which customers defrauded the bank by interspersing their magnetically coded deposit slips with the blank deposit slips provided at the bank. An unsuspecting customer using the defrauder's deposit slip would have his deposit credited to the defrauder's account, because the computer would apply the deposit to the account number that was magnetically inscribed on the deposit slip. After calling the bank to find out the balance in his account, the defrauder would withdraw his supposed funds. Many thousands of dollars were stolen until a system of controls was developed.

This simple but ingenious fraud is typical of the new challenges to security systems that EDP advances create. Even the concentration of vital records, programs and equipment in a single location – an obvious security problem produced by having a centralized EDP operation – often goes unnoticed by management.

Guarding the system

There is every reason to keep unauthorized personnel and visitors out of the computer room. Yet many companies view their computer installations as showplaces, welcoming visitors with relatively little supervision and failing to provide even minimum security precautions. These companies apparently have not considered the possible losses from damaged files or lost programs and the consequences of having equipment out of service.

Protection from disaster

The EDP system control plans should include protection against disruptions ranging up to major disasters.

One of the most obvious protective measures – and hence one that is often overlooked – is simple observance of fire prevention rules. There should be well-established and frequently practised procedures for protecting files, programs and hardware against fire hazards. As far as is possible, duplicates of all vital files, programs and related documentation should be maintained in another location. Provision should be made for emergency use of backup equipment and even temporary manual processing of critical data.

Most companies are aware of the risks inherent in fire, flood or natural disaster, but other potential hazards may not be so obvious. To illustrate, lack of a complete set of backup files caused a serious problem for one company. An employee, who was cleaning the interior of a magnetic drum cabinet, attached his magnetic flashlight to the frame of the unit. The magnet destroyed a portion of the data on the drum, a portion which the company did not ordinarily duplicate. The company lost six days of computer time reconstructing the lost data. In addition to the need for backup files and programs, this situation points out the need for proper training of personnel who maintain computer equipment.

Equipment or program failure is a continual problem. With high-speed EDP systems, the possibility of losing, duplicating, or misprocessing transactions because of these failures is great. 'Recovery/restart' is the term applied to the programs and procedures used by a computer system to isolate and correct failures and to continue processing after a failure has occurred. These procedures may range from a simple re-run of the job being processed to a very elaborate and complex system involving programs designed specifically for this function.

Adequate insurance

Increasing investments in program development, computer hardware (if owned) and stored data make it important for management to evaluate a company's insurance coverage. Is there enough insurance to avert substantial *financial* loss in the event of an EDP system disaster from causes such as fire, natural disaster and vandalism? Recent unrest on college campuses has accounted for three serious situations involving computer centers:

1. In Montreal, Canada, at Sir George Williams University, students set fire to the computer center, causing an estimated one million dollars damage to computer equipment.

2, 3. At Brandeis and Northwestern Universities, militant students occupied the computer centers. In both of the latter situations the students held the computer as a hostage, so to speak, and were not destructive.

A number of insurance companies offer EDP policies. In calculating the amount of coverage needed, the insurance and data processing managers should determine the cost of reconstructing files (both revenue producing and administrative data) in case they are destroyed, and of carrying on normal business while this is done (Neville, 1969). The added cost of using backup equipment should also be taken into account.

Control of/by people

In data processing, one employee can perform functions that were previously assigned to several business units. Unless there are proper controls, such as those mentioned, knowledgeable but unscrupulous employees can manipulate programs for their own benefit, and incompetent employees can cause lasting damage by making errors. If duties are properly separated, the possibility of such damage is minimized, since each employee will have only a limited role in the entire system's operation.

However, management has tended to overlook separation of duties because of the rapid growth in computer use and the general shortage of personnel. Separation of duties may also be overlooked when a reduction in EDP staff or a combining of functions is carried out as a means of cost saving with the new system. These factors often make management dependent on a handful of experienced EDP people who 'grew up with the system' and have a monopoly on operating know-how. This increases the vulnerability of records and makes it difficult to assess individual performance and pinpoint weak spots in the EDP system.

Only one person or operating group should be responsible for an operation at any one time. Ideally, this means drawing lines between the employees who authorize a transaction and produce the input, those who process the data and those who use the output for reports or for other management purposes. The same controls should cover scheduling, manual and machine operations, maintenance of programs and related functions. For example, programmers should not have access to the entire library of programs, if only to guard against the possibility of malicious damage.

An equally important control measure is rotation of employees within the EDP group. This has a twofold value:

1. It prevents an employee or group of employees from so dominating one area of operations that losses from fraud or error are not detected.

2. The high rate of turnover among computer personnel makes it prudent to avoid relying on any individual. Every employee should be replaceable by someone with a working knowledge of the position.

New role for auditors

The advent of computers caught the audit world unprepared. Most executives still envisioned the auditor doing the traditional finance-oriented audit; a few managements had their auditors take a look at the new computer world, but the auditors lacked the knowledge and know-how they needed to master it. Thus there was a scarcity of auditors grounded in computer system principles and equipped to effectively deal with computerized operations.

In the Bell System, an executive decision was made in 1959 to utilize the internal auditing staff as an important new influence on the development of future computer-control systems. Bell realized that computer processing imposed new control requirements, new areas of audit interest, and the elimination of some traditional audit concerns. In order to establish an effective EDP audit function, management selected a staff of EDP auditors who had a good grasp of auditing principles and sufficient aptitude and knowledge of the EDP field, and it gave them the following objectives:

1. Develop new computerized audit techniques and have them built into the system wherever possible.

2. Develop control requirements and techniques, and emphasize to the systems design staff the need for an adequate control system.

3. Evaluate the effectiveness of the control system while it is still in the design process.

4. Evaluate all other areas, such as system testing and conversion, where controls are essential.

In general, the EDP auditor was not to assume responsibility for the development of a control system but was to evaluate the procedures and facilities being designed. This was an important point, for management saw that if the auditor did design control systems, he would lose his objectivity and, in effect, end up auditing himself. Similarly, he was not to be responsible for enforcing control procedures, but only for evaluating the effectiveness of these controls. The EDP auditor thus became a 'devil's advocate' on behalf of top management.

The new approach to EDP auditing was called 'preconversion auditing'. It provided management with an independent control appraisal of future computer systems.

In an approach like the preconversion audit, management is called on to mediate between the systems design and auditing viewpoints. If there is a difference of opinion on a control question, it is up to management to listen to both points of view and make a decision by weighing the cost of controls against the degree of risk involved.

Making the system auditable

It is the auditor's responsibility to ensure that computer systems are auditable when they become operational. He should be continually on the alert for possible effects that the proposed new system will have on internal controls, and should develop audit requirements accordingly. It has become increasingly difficult to audit using conventional techniques, because hard-copy printouts are being substantially curtailed and very often source documents are not in a readily usable sequence. More often than not, information required by the auditor is no longer readily available without additional costly computer runs, and computer time is becoming more and more difficult to obtain. For these reasons, it is essential for him to make his audit requirements known to the systems people at the earliest possible time.

It seems clear that the EDP auditor should attempt to make optimum use of computer technology as an audit tool. He should attempt to have audit techniques and routines built into the computer system, where it is feasible and economical to do so. In this manner, much of the auditing work can be performed as a byproduct of the regular operation at little or no extra cost.

The mini-company test

As indicated earlier, the test deck is one useful method of checking a new computer system. The method is popular among auditors. A refined and more sophisticated method is what I call the 'mini-company' test. A mini-company can be defined as a means of passing fictitious test transactions through a computer system simultaneously with live data, without adversely affecting the live files or outputs. In other words, it is a small sub-system of the regular system. A separate set of outputs, including statistics and reports, are produced for the mini-company. This not only ensures that the test material does not interfere with any outputs concerning the real company, but also enables the auditor to check that statistics and reports are being prepared correctly (see Figure 3).

Let us see how the mini-company concept might be applied to a hypothetical payroll system:

1. Suppose the computerized payroll system of the hypothetical company has a master-tape file that contains a record for each employee in the company. Each pay period, a payroll computation program is run which has as its input the current master file and transactions consisting of employee time-allocation (hours worked, absence, vacation days and so forth) during the pay period. The program produces three output tape files: (a) an updated master-file, (b) a payroll register and check file and (c) a reports file.

To define the mini-company, a fictitious department 9999 is established. It, of course, consists of fictitious employees. Records must be established for the employees on the live master-file. Once the master records are established, fictitious transactions will be prepared to be applied to these records. The fictitious master-records and associated transactions constitute the mini-company base and must be designed to test as much of the payroll system's program logic as possible. Mini-company transactions are entered into the payroll computation and run right along with live transactions.

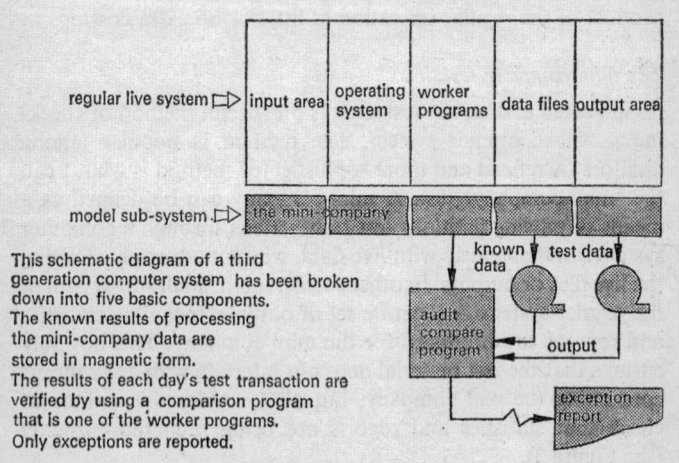

This schematic diagram of a third generation computer system has been broken down into five basic components. The known results of processing the mini-company data are stored in magnetic form. The results of each day's test transaction are verified by using a comparison program that is one of the worker programs. Only exceptions are reported.

Figure 3 Testing the main system with a mini-company

The mini-company data are separated from the live data in a subsequent computer run. Then the live data or 'output files', as they are called, are processed in the normal manner, with checks printed and scheduled reports made. Similarly the mini-company data are processed to produce a payroll register, checks and reports. The results produced by computer processing of the mini-company's input are compared with results previously calculated outside the computer to determine if any irregularities in controls or processing have occurred.

This concept is particularly advantageous because it permits continuous testing of the system on a live basis. Auditors will utilize the mini-company for periodic system-reviews, and a quality-control group can use the continuous-testing capabilities to great advantage in meeting its daily responsibilities for monitoring the quality of system production.

Other auditing techniques

In addition to the mini-company, other special audit programs can be developed. Briefly, here are some special programs which can be used by the auditor on either an off-line or on-line basis:

Comparison. Matches two duplicate files contained on magnetic tape, cards or discs; determines if they are identical; and identifies any unmatched records. (This type of program has been used in the Bell System to verify rating tables for toll messages. In one instance tape files containing tables of approximately thirty-five thousand rating points were compared in approximately ten minutes using second-generation computer hardware. The advantages of the comparison program are its ability to perform 100 per cent verification and identify for the auditor any exceptions for more detailed review.)

Sampling. Samples records in a file on a random basis.

Extraction. Extracts specific records from the file.

Compilation. Checks mathematical computations made by the computer, such as adding or subtracting related fields of data or multiplying a data field by a constant. (This type of program is particularly useful in verifying the proper application of formulas in computer runs. For example, if employee group-insurance deductions are developed in a payroll system by multiplying annual salary by a fixed rate, the compilation program can make these calculations independent of the regular programs. The comparison program just outlined can then be used to determine if the results of the compilation program and the regular payroll runs are in agreement.)

Systems that are auditable also should meet the requirements of public accountants and various government agencies. For example:

1. Certified public accountants need the ability to audit computerized records of assets, liabilities, expenses and income for yearly financial statements.

2. Internal Revenue Service auditors want to check on how transactions are handled, whether expenses are correct and whether all income is stated properly.

3. Department of Defense contract auditors want to check that expenses are properly allocated to government contracts.

Conclusion

The establishment of a well-controlled and auditable computer system no longer should be the impossible dream of the executive.

The attack arrows have as their objective destruction of the 'well-protected system'. If the system is properly controlled, each of the factors represented by an arrow will be interrupted and negated by applicable control elements as it attempts to penetrate the control maze.

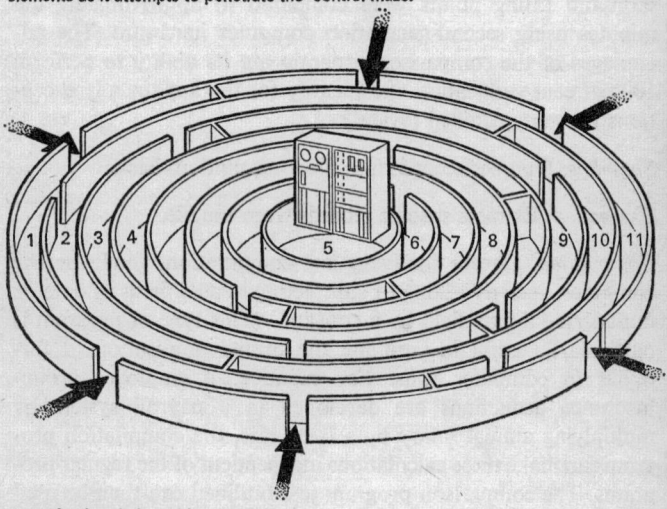

 1 production and machine controls
 2 separation of duties
 3 quality control
 4 computer room security
 5 well-protected system
 6 disaster insurance
 7 conversion controls
 8 internal auditing
 9 testing controls
10 control program changes
11 program controls

Figure 4 The control maze

364 Other Aspects of Management Information Systems

Management might picture a computer control system as a control maze (see Figure 4). Each control function should complement another function, so that a breakdown in one area is corrected by controls in another area. Most losses through error or fraud can be prevented by such interlocking controls.

No one group should bear complete responsibility for protecting the computer system. The need for controls should be instilled in the entire organization, starting with top management and extending to all personnel.

Reference

NEVILLE, H. G. (1969), letter to the editor re 'Danger ahead! Safeguard your computer', *Harvard Bus. Rev.*, vol. 47, no. 3, p. 40.

Further Reading

The nature of management information

F. R. Koppel, 'The information revolution', *Columbia J. World Bus.*, vol. 1, 1966, pp. 37–42.

R. N. McMurry, 'Clear communications for chief executives', *Harvard Bus. Rev.*, vol. 43, 1965, pp. 131–47.

D. Rapaport, 'What is information?', *Synthèse*, vol. 9, 1953, p. 157.

A. K. Wickesberg, 'Communications network in the business organization structure', *Acad. Manag. J.*, 1968, p. 253.

The design of management information systems

H. I. Ansoff, 'The firm of the future', *Harvard Bus. Rev.*, vol. 43, 1965, pp. 162–78.

P. Drucker, 'Managing the computer', *Manag. Today*, 1967, pp. 46–9, 94.

L. R. Fiock, 'Seven deadly dangers of EDP', *Harvard Bus. Rev.*, vol. 40, 1962, pp. 88–96.

R. J. Mockler, 'Developing a new information and control system', *Michigan Bus. Rev.*, vol. 20, 1968, pp. 13–19.

P. H. Thurston, 'Who should control management information systems?', *Harvard Bus. Rev.*, vol. 40, 1962, p. 135.

Management information in real time

W. R. McCreight, 'Real-time revolution in medicine', *Computer Bull.*, vol. 12, 1968, pp. 8–10.

R. E. Sprague, 'On real-time systems', *Manag. Services*, vol. 1, 1964, p. 40.

R. Winsburg, 'The hard road to real time', *Manag. Today*, 1967, pp. 90–95, 152, 162.

R. K. Zimmer, 'On real-time systems for customer-service organizations', *Manag. Services*, vol. 4, 1967, p. 25.

Scanning the business environment

Anonymous, 'Information retrieved for management', *Data Systems*, 1967, p. 34.

C. T. Meadow, *The Analysis of Information Systems*, Wiley, 1967.

Evaluation of management information systems

J. Dearden, 'Time span in management control', *Finan. Exec.*, vol. 36, 1968, pp. 23–30.

J. Diebold Associates, 'Information: its cost and value', *Data and Control Systems*, 1967, p. 34.

A. B. Frielink (ed.), *Economics of ADP*, North-Holland Publishing Co.

J. T. Garrity, 'The payout on computers', *McKinsey Q.*, 1965, p. 20.

L. R. Huesmann and R. P. Goldberg, 'Evaluating computer systems through simulation', *Computer J.*, vol. 10, 1967, pp. 150–56.

Other aspects of management information systems

D. F. Cox and R. E. Good, 'How to build a marketing-information system', *Harvard Bus. Rev.*, vol. 45, 1967, pp. 145–54.

W. J. Pedicord, 'Advanced data systems for personnel planning and placement', *Computers and Automation*, 1966, p. 20.

E. H. Porter, 'The parable of the spindle', *Harvard Bus. Rev.*, vol. 40, 1962, pp. 58–66.

M. E. Shaw, J. C. Gilchrist and L. C. Walker, 'Some effects of unequal distribution of information on wheel-group structure', *J. abnorm. soc. Psychol.*, vol. 59, 1954, pp. 554–6.

D. A. Wren, 'Interfare and interorganizational coordination', *Acad. Manag. J.*, 1967, p. 69.

Acknowledgements

Permission to reproduce the Readings in this volume is
acknowledged from the following sources:

1. Martin Secker & Warburg Ltd
2. John Wiley & Sons Inc.
3. *Harvard Business Review*
4. American Management Association Inc.
5. McKinsey & Company Inc.
6. *Harvard Business Review*
7. Fortune
8. P. M. R. Hermon
9. *Harvard Business Review*
10. The Macmillan Company, New York
11. *Abacus*
12. CCM Professional Magazines Inc.
13. International Business Machines Corporation
14. F. D. Thompson Publications Inc.
15. F. D. Thompson Publications Inc.
16. *Management Decision*
17. *Administrative Science Quarterly*, T. J. Allen and S. I. Cohen
18. *Harvard Business Review*

Author Index

Aguiler, F. J., 12
Allen, T., 12, 331
Ansoff, H. I., 194
Anthony, R. N., 317
Arthur, H. B., 67
Axsmith, D. J., 283

Bedford, N. D., 220
Bernard, J., 331
Bevis, H. W., 206
Brady, R. H., 225
Brenner, S. R., 218
Bright, J., 129
Bruner, J., 203
Burck, G., 170
Burnham, D., 151
Burnett, M., 36

Callahan, J. R., 218
Cherry, C., 19, 29
Clee, G. H., 61
Cohen, A. R., 341
Coleman, J. J., 333
Cordiner, R., 75
Culliton, J. W., 131

Demets, J., 147, 153
Devons, E., 190
De Scipio, A., 61
Dill, W. R., 42
Dubin, R., 40

Emery, F. E., 12
Ewing, D. W., 194, 327

Feller, W., 337
Field, J. W., 124
Forrester, J. W., 247

Garrity, J. T., 128, 221
Gerstberger, P. G., 331
Gill, W. A., 218
Goodman, A. F., 344

Grosch, H., 310
Grosz, M., 147
Guetzkow, H., 40, 42

Hagstrom, W. O., 331
Hertz, D., 152
Hooper, D. W., 11, 222

Jaques, E., 225

Kahn, R. L., 332
Katz, D., 47, 332
Klein, H. E., 124

Lanzetta, J. T., 197
Lave, L. B., 222
Lazarsfeld, P., 47, 332
Leavitt, H. J., 12, 40, 41, 77, 154
Leontief, W., 208
Likert, R., 228

Mann, F. C., 228
Martin, J., 170
McGarrah, R. E., 178
Meadow, C. T., 14
Menzel, H., 332, 344
Merret, A. J., 214
Meredith-Smith, J., 219
Miles, R. E., 320
Mumford, E., 228, 320

Nelson, R., 222
Neville, H. G., 358
Newcombe, T. M., 340

Onsi, M., 220

Prest, A. R., 218
Poppel, S. D., 11, 215, 222

Ream, N., 149
Roby, T. B., 197

Root, L. E., 74
Ruggles, R. L., 197

Schilling, C. W., 331
Scott, C., 344
Simon, H. A., 40, 145, 156, 203
Sloan, A. P., 145
Smalter, D. J., 197
Steiner, G. A., 74
Stigler, J., 222

Teele, S. F., 75

Teitsworth, C. S., 67
Thurston, P. H., 128
Turvey, R., 218
Tuthill, D. W., 228

Walter, G., 21
Ward, T., 228
Whisler, T. L., 77, 149, 151
Williams, L., 228
Winter, S. G., 222

Young, J. Z., 17

Subject Index

Accountant and information, 220
Accounting systems, 63, 70, 86, 96, 102, 136, 155, 176, 250, 259, 264
Airline reservations, 158, 163
Applications packages, 117
Appraisal of scanning efforts, 198
Attitudes and information, 30
Asset utilization, 223
Audit of
 computers, 359
 compilation, 363
 preconversion, 360
 sampling, 363
 technique with computer, 359, 361, 363

Batch processing systems, 286
BOAC, 158
BOADICEA, 161
 applications, 165
 budget, 166
 returns on, 167
Boredom and computers, 325
Business environment, 189
 scanning the, 189

Central information and display point, 197
Centralization, 145
Channels of information, 279
Coal industry, communication problems, 31
Command structure, 228
Communication, 18, 28, 158
 among peers, 48, 49
 and performance, 332
 as regulator, 35
 authoritarian, 49
 circuit, size of, 48
 closed, 51
 direction of, 38
 downward, 43
 down-the-line, 43, 46
 external, 54
 horizontal, 48
 nets, 40
 preconditions of, 24
 problems of, 29
 upward, 50, 340
Communications research centre, 24, 31, 37
Competitive information, 64, 67
Complexity and information, 196
Computer
 as a super clerk, 97
 benefits of, 240
 budget, 160
 cost control system, 242
 digital, 10, 76
 economics of, 103, 214
 expenditure, 94, 98, 99, 101, 213
 evaluation of, 214, 216
 policy, 160
 power, 292, 310
 profit orientated control method, 242
 reporting by, 180
 results from, 106
 security, 347
 technologists, 318
 time allocation, 11, 216
Computing system, attributes of, 294
Computers, historical list of 1944–63, 300–307
Confidence and communication, 26
Console, cost of, 285
Consultants
 management, 11
 R and D, 331

Subject Index 377

Control groups, 191
  information, 74, 117, 170, 173
  of computer, 240
  of EDP, 348
  of people, 358
Conversion of data, 350
Coordination of information, 190
  through communication, 194
Core, memory, cost of, 283
Corporative relations, 23, 34
Critical ideas, flow of, 338
Cost-benefit method of
  computer evaluation, 217
  effective method, 217, 221, 277
  hardware, 280
  saving method, 219
  software, 280, 285

Data bank, 14, 114, 135
  conversion, 350
  definition of processing, 126
  query, 164
Decision-making
  centres, 194
  rules, 256
Designing MIS, 90, 129
Digital computer, 10
Disclosure, how much?, 206
Disc packs, 284
Diversified staffing, 121
Down-the-line information systems, 205
Dynamic relocation, 281

EDP, 87
  objectives, 323
  planning, 321
Engineering concept of company, 327
Environmental information, 64, 66, 205, 250

Errors
  input, type of, 351
  file on computer, 353
Evaluating computers, 213
  basic approach, 226
  in long term, 224
  non-output cost-benefit, 227
Evaluating MIS, 246
Exception information, 145, 152, 179
  principle, 179
Executive observation, 134
Exhortation and information, 33

Feasibility,
  economic, 104, 107
  of computer, 104
  operational, 109
  technical, 104, 107
Feedback, 21, 39, 44, 53, 324
File protection, 357
Filter, 13
  input, 14
  output, 14
Financial information, 131
Formalism, 32
Formal organization, 340
Frame of reference, 25, 26, 200
Fraud by computer, 347

Guarding the EDP system, 356
GM computer system, 146
Goals, planned, 60
Government information, 207, 208
Grosch's law, 291, 310

Head of information agency, 57
Heuristic decision-taking, 156
Hierarchy and information, 254
Horizontal
  communication, 48

classification of information
   systems, 125

IDP, 124
Image, 248
Informal groups, 48
Information, 10
  and accounting systems, 63
  benefits of, 219
  changing patterns of, 201
  competitive, 68
Information
  definition of, 215
  departments, 77
  delays, 261
  evaluation of, 222
  environmental, 66
  flow in R and D, 331
  for key managers, 200
  habits, 341
  integration of, 198
  internal, 69
  interest and influence, 201
  model of firm, 251
  processing system, 247
  quantitive, 69
  relevant, 200
  requirements, defining, 63
  sensitivity to, 203
  static, 60
  system, overhauling, 89
  transfer, 339
Initial costs of EDP, 241, 243
Input, 248
Insurance of computers, 358
Intangible benefits, 239, 275
Interface with
  computer, 119
  environment, 256
Interleaved core banks, 282
Interlocking system of control, 351
Internal information, 64, 69, 85

Interrogating MIS, 154
Intraorganizational communication, 331
Inventory control, 152, 163, 171, 233, 257, 274
Invisible college, 332
Invoicing by computer, 237

Job enlargement, 325
Joint products, data and information, 226

Kalmagorov-Smirnov test, 337
Knowledge and information, 10

Live testing of system, 362
Local loop concept, 280
Logistics information, 132, 172, 182
Long-range
  planning, 194
  information, 221
Loop, information, size of, 38, 46

MAC computer project, 279
Managment control, 173, 175, 182
  and logistics, 182
Marketing information, 71, 111, 133, 153
Mass communication research, 344
Memories
  capacity of, 297
  high speed, 282
Message switching, 159, 167
Middle management and computers, 143, 154
Mini-company audit test, 361
MIS, 13, 62, 87, 102, 138
  evolutionary development of, 113

Modular computer system, 278
Modules, 277
Monitoring capacity of computer, 151
Morale and computers, 321, 328
Multi-computer system, 277
Multi-disciplinary teams, 322

National computer centre, 11
Nets
 communication, 160
 two-level, 40
 wheel, 40
Non-output effects of computers, 228

Objectives, decomposition method, 147
Operating manager, 127–8
 reports, 85, 174
Opinion leaders, 47
Organization, 19
 of EDP, 135
Organizational
 policy, 47
 space, 39
 structure, 60, 61, 154, 333
Output from EDP, 250

Parallel testing of system, 350
Payback period on computer, 244
Payoff on computers, 96
People orientated approach, 319
Performance improvement of computers, 1944–62, 312
Personnel data, 131, 174, 178 257
Planning
 control of, 317
 information, 64, 257
 of computers, 318
 strategic, 317
Production and machine controls, 354
Profit on computers, 234, 235
Programme library, 359
Programming, 126, 130
 changes, 354
Psychologists, social, 10

Quantity, control of input, 351
Query to data bank, 164

Real time, 143, 160, 169
 accounting, 176
 characteristics of, 171
 control, 178
 fallacies of, 181
 long-range outlook on, 183
 myth of, 169
 potential applications of, 171
 practicality of, 175
Recentralization, 144
Redundancy, system, 278
Reporting by
 computer, 180
 cycles, 264
R and D, 134
Resistance to computers, 320
Risk analysis, 118

Scanning horizon, 202
 environment, 190
SEAC computer, 32
Sensors of EDP system, 256
Shared coding scheme, 332
Signals in communication, 27
Simulation
 models, 118, 156, 220
 run, 259
Socio-emotional support, 48
Socio-technical systems, 320, 326

Sociometric relations, 334–7
Status and communication, 341
Strategic
  information, 91
  opportunites and MIS, 116
  planning, 173, 177, 322, 324
Swap time, 282
System, 12, 21
  closed, 12
  department, 126
  economic, 20
  information, effectiveness of, 83
  open, 12
  performance, 278
  physical, 247
  total information, 83, 84, 118, 124, 133, 139, 153
Systems
  decentralized, 127
  specification, 127

Tactical
  decisions, 256
  planning, 322, 326
Tapes, control of use, 353

Technological gatekeepers, 333, 341
Technology curve of computers, 291, 299
Terminals, computer, control of, 355
Time-shared systems, 277
  costing of, 287
  pricing of, 288
Time-span of decision, 225
Time lags, 261
Top management
  information, 193
  involvement, 121
Total information system, 83, 84, 118, 124, 133, 139, 153
Training in MIS, 93
Two-step information flow, 47, 343

Vertical classification of EDP systems, 130

Work-group structure and communication, 339
Working capital and computers, 238

Penguin Management Readings

Business Strategy
Edited by H. Igor Ansoff

Collective Bargaining
Edited by Allan Flanders

Consumer Behaviour
Edited by A. S. C. Ehrenberg and F. G. Pyatt

Management and Motivation
Edited by Victor H. Vroom and Edward L. Deci

Management Decision Making
Edited by Lawrence A. Cyert and Richard M. Welsch

Management Information Systems
Edited by T. W. McRae

Management of Production
Edited by M. K. Starr

Marketing Research
Edited by Joseph Seibert and Gordon Wills

Modern Financial Management
Edited by B. V. Carsberg and H. C. Edey

Organizational Growth and Development
Edited by W. H. Starbuck

Personnel Management
Edited by D. E. McFarland

Programming for Optimal Decisions
Edited by P. G. Moore and S. D. Hodges

Systems Thinking
Edited by F. E. Emery